Practicing Ethnography
in a Globalizing World

D1563134

Practicing Ethnography in a Globalizing World

An Anthropological Odyssey

June C. Nash

ALTAMIRA
PRESS

A Division of
ROWMAN & LITTLEFIELD PUBLISHERS, INC.
Lanham • Boulder • New York • Toronto • Plymouth, UK

ALTAMIRA PRESS
A Division of Rowman & Littlefield Publishers, Inc.
A wholly owned subsidiary of The Rowman & Littlefield Publishing Group, Inc.
4501 Forbes Boulevard, Suite 200
Lanham, MD 20706
www.altamirapress.com

Estover Road, Plymouth PL6 7PY, United Kingdom

British Library Cataloguing in Publication Information Available

Library of Congress Cataloging-in-Publication Data

Nash, June C., 1927–
  Practicing ethnography in a globalizing world : an anthropological odyssey /
June C. Nash.
    p. cm.
  Includes bibliographical references and index.
  ISBN-13: 978-0-7591-0880-6 (cloth : alk. paper)
  ISBN-10: 0-7591-0880-3 (cloth : alk. paper)
  ISBN-13: 978-0-7591-0881-3 (pbk. : alk. paper)
  ISBN-10: 0-7591-0881-1 (pbk. : alk. paper)
  1. Ethnology—Research. 2. Ethnology—Field work. 3. Ethnology—
Methodology. 4. Culture and globalization. I. Title.

  GN345.N38 2007
  305.80072—dc22

                                              2006022777

Printed in the United States of America

⊗™ The paper used in this publication meets the minimum requirements of
American National Standard for Information Sciences—Permanence of Paper
for Printed Library Materials, ANSI/NISO Z39.48-1992.

For Frank Reynolds, who shares with me the burden of time, and
For Eric, Laura, and the twins, Lionel and Theodore, who will continue
to bear the future of time.

Contents

Part IV: The Hobbesian World of Terror and Violence

Preface

This book draws upon ethnographic approaches I have used in five decades of fieldwork on three continents. These encounters have taken me from Mayan villages in Guatemala and Mexico resisting European acculturation and now mobilizing regionally for autonomy, to Mandalay rice cultivators engaging spirit animism as they accommodate to national independence, to Bolivian mining communities confronting the International Monetary Fund conditions for remaining in global markets, and to a U.S. industrial city that once served the military-industrial complex producing Polaris and Nikon missiles and is now a recruitment depot for foot soldiers in a preemptive war. I hope this personal odyssey will serve anthropologists preparing to go into the field as a guide for what to do and what not to do.

My interpretations draw upon multiple perspectives related to gender, ethnic, and class orientations. They involve reflective analyses of global changes through studies of ongoing processes in particular places. In developing these interpretations, I have drawn upon paradigms related to structural functionalist, Marxist, feminist, postmodernist, and social activist approaches that stimulate but do not define my own approaches. By engaging a personal perspective in reviewing my encounters with these major paradigms of the past and present, I hope to encourage students and colleagues to cultivate their own critical perceptions. This should help overcome the tendency to take ways of knowing as dogma to be revered or discarded along with the ethnographic accounts from which they sprang. I call for an approach that is pragmatic and dialogical, drawing on ethnographic data and theoretical insights from past and contemporary collaborators as we pursue our own odyssey of discovery.

My own ethnological experience prompts me to embrace a generational perspective on a wide array of problems. The children and grandchildren of Mayan collaborators who were subsistence producers and artisans are now working in cities as taxi drivers, tourist employees, and undocumented migrants in New York or Florida. Protected by isolation and the lack of communication channels until the recent past, people who did not consciously think of themselves as Mayan, or even Tzeltal speakers, but rather identified as "the true people, people who speak the true word," now proudly sell their products as authentic Mayan pottery or textiles. In the Lacandón settlements they rose up as indigenous people to demand a new relation with the state allowing them the autonomy to define their own way of life.

Burma in 1960 was an interlude that gave me perspective on communities of the Western Hemisphere. Peasants in the vicinity of Mandalay had just emerged from British rule a decade before and were beginning to forge a place for themselves in postcolonial Southeast Asia when I arrived with my family. The tolerance I saw then in the countryside villages where spirit animism coexisted with Buddhist and Muslim faith was a lesson in the potential for pluricultural coexistence that the West, and I, had not as yet assimilated. Upon my return to Latin America as a field site with Aymara- and Quechua-speaking miners I was better able to perceive the pluricultural perspective because of my experience with Burmese. Mayan peasants considered themselves to be Catholic even while responding to preconquest cosmic forces related to the eclipse of the moon or the rituals to bring rain, now addressed to Santo Tomas rather than Chac. Quechua- and Aymara-speaking miners, who distanced themselves from their indigenous identity as they identified as a working class, still maintained a spiritual relation with hill and mountain spirits. When the International Monetary Fund (IMF) forced the closure of the mines in 1986, many miners migrated to the Chapare to cultivate coca for the global drug market, or to El Alto outside of La Paz to drive trucks or buses in this burgeoning communication center. Their children embrace their indigenous identity as they organize rural cultivators to assert their rights as the original people and to become political leaders in national office. One member of these migrant Aymara families, Evo Morales, is now president of Bolivia. Scholars who rejected a class analysis now often suspect that ethnic identity will reduce the human condition. This charge undermines the identities forged in social movements aimed at vindicating injustices.

Piqued by the questions that tin miners asked about my own country I returned to my roots in Massachusetts working with General Electric workers in Pittsfield, Massachusetts. It was the most difficult fieldwork I have encountered, since I had to overcome my assumptions to ask about familiar customs in order to understand the many distinct interpretations people of the same culture hold. The work I did in the post-Vietnam era of the 1980s grounded me in my reappraisal of militarization pursued by the Bush administration in the third millennium. I saw all the assumptions predicated on modernity reversed, as many Americans rejected the secularized, rational values that once seemed to epitomize mainstream culture.

This generational view promotes an awareness of social processes that is a corrective to short-term, single-dimensional assessments of progress and prospects. The advantage of a long-term retrospective view on the many field sites comes in the testing out of hypotheses over generations. What is now often called identity politics in new social movements is bringing to the surface implicit assumptions that were never challenged before and forging class movements out of ethnic politics.

It is my hope that the essays I have written en route in this long-term engagement in a variety of geographical settings and cultural spaces will encourage students to expand their own anthropological horizons, and through this arrive at comparative frameworks of analysis for analyzing globalization processes. The comparative nexus will no longer be bounded by particular times or places. The people we now study live in an increasingly global context and are often forced to be highly flexible in their activities. In these new situations, our task as anthropologists is to generate analytic constructs that take the rapidly changing boundaries seriously into account. But as anthropologists it still remains that of approximating the entire range of human variation within a holistic frame of reference in our analytical constructs.

I hope to convince future anthropologists to judge ethnographies in relation to how well they promote understandings of constantly changing problem orientations, not just the particular frame of reference and analytical categories that have informed them. Using this experientially and theoretically oriented approach as background, the reader can ask questions about what motivates our research. How do people of distinct cultures confront the common problems that arise with global integration? How do underlying notions and culturally constituted perspectives frame one's perception of the world? How do we learn to appreciate the everyday norms and values that enable various kinds of communities and societies to function, and how are these norms and values being systematically disrupted and strategically reconfigured?

Introduction

An Anthropological Odyssey
From Structural Functionalism to Activism

In this book I demonstrate how ethnographic approaches capture and analyze global changes through studies of ongoing processes in particular places. It engages a personal perspective on my encounter with major paradigms of the past and present as I utilized them during my lifetime of anthropological research. Critiquing the tendency in recent decades of taking past ways of knowing as dogma to be revered or discarded along with the ethnographic base from which they sprang, I call for a more pragmatic approach. Seeking the insights gained from present and past paradigms, I urge anthropologists to judge ethnographies in relation to how well they promote understandings of constantly changing problem orientations. Since my ethnological experience spans five decades of research in a variety of cultures, I am able to embrace a global perspective on a wide array of problems. These encounters have taken me from Mayan villages resisting European acculturation and now mobilizing regionally for autonomy, to Mandalay rice cultivators engaging spirit animism as they accommodate to national independence, to Bolivian mining communities confronting the International Monetary Fund conditions for remaining in global markets, and to a U.S. industrial city that once served the military-industrial complex producing Polaris and Nikon missiles and is now a recruitment depot for foot soldiers in a preemptive war. I draw interpretations from multiple perspectives related to gender, ethnic, and class orientations. This long-term engagement in a variety of geographical settings and cultural

1

spaces can encourage students to expand their own anthropological horizons, and through this arrive at cross-cultural comparative frameworks of analysis. Using this experientially and theoretically oriented approach as background, the reader can ask questions about what motivates our research. How do people of distinct cultures confront the common problems that arise with global integration? How do underlying notions and culturally constituted perspectives frame one's perception of the world? How do we learn to appreciate the everyday norms and values that enable communities and societies to function, and how are these systematically disrupted?

PART I. PARADIGMS AND POSTURES

The three chapters in part I consider some of the paradigms anthropologists have developed and how they influenced the production of ethnology. I contend that discarded paradigms such as structural functionalism and economic materialism have often generated thoughtful analyses that can continue to elucidate aspects of behavior. What must be cultivated are good ethnographic descriptions that contain enough observations and reflections to allow for alternative explanations and hypotheses as conditions change. The danger of most paradigms occurs when they become ideological postures that undermine careful ethnographic inquiry.

As each new cohort of researchers joins the ranks of anthropology, the field broadens the scope of investigations into human behavior. Following World War II former colonial subjects became important critics of the field, bringing the perspectives of emergent leaders to the fore. The lines between primitive and civilized were challenged as the assumptions that supported categories such as tribal and national were debunked. With the advent of feminine perspectives since the 1970s, attention to the everyday aspects in the maintenance of life promoted a new enlightenment that highlighted a whole new arena of problems and possibilities. I capture the moments in which I began to question existing ways for thinking about political, social, and cultural changes in the world, calling for a continuing critique of racism, sexism, classism, and ethnic bias that would release anthropology from its own biases.

The first chapter provides an autobiographical tour of the paradigms I have tried in research and teaching spanning fifty years. In the second chapter a critical rereading of peasant notions of the limited good notes the positive connotations of an awareness of finite natural resources, contrasting this with current trends fostering consumerism and the plundering of nature in a globalizing world. The final chapter examines a new enlightenment promoted by feminine perspectives.

Chapter 1. When Isms Become Wasms: Paradigms Lost and Regained

Exploring the major paradigms in which ethnographic work was cast from my graduate student days in the 1950s to the present, I assess the ideological intolerance for the discoveries of their predecessors as anthropologists respond to the latest paradigms. Yet these "outmoded" models cultivated insights that are then cast in terms responding to the latest paradigmatic trends. Structural functionalist analyses allowed ethnologists up until the post–World War II independence movements to capture important insights into colonial societies even as they were gaining independence. The historical materialism that followed is still under attack without consideration for the many insights to be gained from a class analysis by those who espouse "postmodernism" in the "anthropological critique" of the 1980s. This critique arrived, not coincidentally at a time when fieldwork became increasingly dangerous and when the Eurocentric and male-dominant perspectives that once dominated the field were being decentered by women and those who once served only as objects of inquiry. It also came at a time of major social and political changes culminating in the end of the Cold War and the ideological formations that supported the two major camps. Researchers analyzing the transformations brought about by regimes of flexible accumulation and the fluid transnational movements of goods and people gained new perspectives from the generation of postmodernist models of alternative identities and the recognition of researchers' own subjectivities. In its turn the involution of the discipline that occurred with the postmodernist focus on reflexivity and discourse analysis was countered by an emergent activist persuasion responding to the urgent crises that peaked in the uprisings of marginalized indigenous people in the 1980s and 1990s. I suggest that activist anthropology overcomes the tendency to question the very reality of social problems prevalent in postmodern persuasions, promoting collaborative relations with those we study—relations that yield new insights that reflect the concerns of those who are transforming the structures of domination both at home and abroad. The danger lies in the complicity that comes with committed long-term participatory research, a hidden persuasion that was forever haunting fieldworkers that becomes more transparent in the work of activists than those who assumed an objective stance in relation to the people they studied.

Chapter 2. The Notion of the Limited Good and the Specter of the Unlimited Good

George Foster shattered the codes of peasant ethnography when he published "Peasant Society and the Image of the Limited Good" in 1965.

Peasants, who had just been discovered as ethnographic subjects, were invulnerable to criticism as oppressed and potentially revolutionary actors in history. By disclosing the assumptions that underlay behaviors that were otherwise explained in terms of traditional imperatives or fatalism, he opened up a debate that still kindles productive controversy. I believe the empirically derived model of the limited good that Foster constructed to explain peasant behavior also cultivates conservation practices that benefit sustained development. I contrast this with development processes that cultivate a notion of the unlimited good. While this opens up horizons that stimulate technological innovations and prolong the life span, it also promotes wasteful practices of profligate credit card consumption, deficit spending, and inflated stock markets. Peasants, who have had to pay for the consequences of the debt crisis of the 1980s and the financial markets crisis of 1997, are now facing elimination in the global markets of third millennium. Now that the real limits of nonrenewable resources can be envisioned, development agencies seeking alternative programs to those of neoliberal market economics draw inspiration from indigenous groups that balance the needs of a population with available land and resources. The holistic perspective gained in balancing collective needs with scarce resources provides an alternative to the specter of impoverishment fostered by unlimited growth benefiting only a few.

Chapter 3. Women in Between: Globalization and the New Enlightenment

I highlight the importance of women's perspectives in a "new enlightenment" that overtakes the earlier age of enlightenment. In the eighteenth-century Cartesian view of nature as something to be controlled and dominated, women were identified with nature and man with culture. Women were relegated to an immanent position in a world of transcendent male philosophers, scientists, and conquerors who defined, categorized, and ruled a society made rational by their civilizing mission. Women's everyday work in reproducing society was invisible until recent decades when feminist scholars and activists began to explore women's contributions to society and the survival of the human species. Women's mediating positions linking families to communities and communities to larger political, economic, and social circuits become crucial to survival where global development processes have undermined social reproduction programs in the community and the nation. Tracing three instances in which women have emerged as a political force, I argue that the multilateral and resilient approach that women often manifest is shared with indigenous populations and others whose marginalization in political, economic, and social life enables them to assess more clearly their personal situation in relation to global issues. Whether their marginality stems from racial/ethnic differences, from gender, or from class, consciousness of the injustices prevalent in societies provides a baseline for understanding global trends in embodied terms. This kind of knowledge, cultivated in the immanent roles assigned to subordinates in the world system, promotes a new enlightenment based on gender-balanced and multicultural understandings. Once collectively mobilized, it could become strategic in confronting domination by globalizing transformations. As yet, the women's movements that have surfaced in case studies described—export-oriented assembly operations on the Mexican-U.S. border and in Nicaragua, and in the indigenous women's autonomy movements of Chiapas, Mexico—have not attained mainstream stature, yet they illustrate the potential women in such movements have shown in transforming society.

PART II. REFLECTIONS IN THE ETHNOGRAPHIC MIRROR

These papers analyzing the processes of change during times of extreme social and economic stress expose some of assumptions and oversights with which I began my research. Learning from the actions and interpretations of collaborators as I became actively engaged in participatory research I show how these biases were dispelled as the need for new strategies in fieldwork became apparent. Drawing on episodes of social trauma explored in postcolonial Burma and during the U.S.-instigated coup in Guatemala, I reflect on the political forces in play that were ignored in the framing of problems in the early encounter and the need for addressing these in fieldwork.

Chapter 4. Multiple Perspectives on Burmese Buddhism and Nat Worship

In this chapter based on research done in Patheingyi Township in Upper Burma in 1960, I record the explanations of conflict and change in terms of traditions relating to *nats*, or animistic spirits, that had figured importantly as protagonists in ancient stories. Drawing on structural functionalist theory of the time, I relate the nat spirits to village and regional social relations, showing how ritual offerings reinforce these ties. The stories provided explanations for what was happening in people's daily lives and a model for appeasing powers beyond their control. When I participated in a lavish *shinbyu*, or feast marking the initiation of novitiates in the Buddhist monastery, I discerned another layer in the complex relations of spirit animism and Buddhism. A village headman was killed for having revealed the deposit station for tribute to guerrillas who were the

remains of a rebellion against the British colonial government. Upon
questioning the participants I became aware that the dead man's widow
and others in the village had dreamed that he had returned as a nat. The
ceremonial offering to the Buddha in the festival ensured that his spirit
would move on to another world. This analysis of the structural transformations achieved through the ritual fulfilled the analytical scope of the
structural functional model then current. In a postscript to the article first
published in 1966, I record impressions from a visit to the field site in 1998
and my brief encounter with the township officer who was active in my
earlier stay. This prompted reflections on the civil war occurring when
peasants were caught between guerrilla troops, whose independence
movement was intercepted by the British decision in 1948 to grant Burma
the independence they had fought for, and the contesting forces of U Nu's
government with the growing military power of Ne Win. The story of the
slain headman and the family's strategy of overcoming the fate of his becoming a nat spirit was an opening to examining peasant relations with
the postcolonial state as they attempted to appease the new power structure. Even while addressing the linked Buddhist and animistic beliefs en-
acted in the shinbyu, the early article failed to assess the wider context of
social disruption occurring in postcolonial reconstruction. Viewed from
the vantage point of critical anthropology a quarter century later, the shinbyu could be seen as a means of resolving conflicts that prevailed in the
postwar setting. The prevalence of nat festivals I witnessed in my 1997 re-
visit to Rangoon and Mandalay confirms my understanding that nat worship still provides a spiritual recourse for the peasantry. Since the junta relies on the Buddhist order to provide legitimacy, the dances, music, and
liquor offered to the major nats may now rekindle the rebellious desires
of the people to overthrow an increasingly unpopular government.

Chapter 5. The Limits of Naïveté in Anthropological Fieldwork: The 1954 U.S.-Instigated Coup in Guatemala

During my student days in the 1950s rebellions, domestic violence, alcoholism, drugs, and corruption in public office were considered peripheral
to the field project; today they have become central to ethnography.
Fledgling anthropologists entered field situations innocent of counterinsurgency plots spawned in the emergent globalization system and were
studiously unconscious of the impact of our presence. Now too much is
known about the undercover plots of secret agents to ignore or deny U.S.
intervention in the field sites we choose. Recalling my experiences in
Guatemala during and after the U.S.-instigated coup in 1954, I assess its
aftermath in the decades of genocidal war that followed. While the coup
has provoked some of the best and some of the worst ethnologies of our

time, its lasting effect has been to force us to see ourselves in the mirror of our work and to force us to relinquish the pose of objective observer divorced from the moral implications of the encounter. The question that Max Gluckman (1964) raised about the limits to naïveté in anthropology in the 1960s becomes ever more relevant as we become more conscious of the role we play in analyzing, ignoring, or denying the political context of our work. Who is going to benefit by what we do or fail to publish, and who might be compromised by our interpretations? What role can we play as activists, both to reveal what we learned about past errors and to try to bring about a change in direction?

PART III. ENGAGEMENT IN SOCIAL MOVEMENTS TODAY

The study of social movements was central to sociological inquiry when anthropology was still mired in ahistorical functionalist modes of inquiry. This changed rapidly when indigenous people became protagonists of their own history in movements throughout the world as miners, oil explorers, and bioprospectors invaded their retreat zones or when investments were made in their traditional territories. Movements based on the mobilization of class interests in industrial mining, or on the mobilization of indigenous claims for land and autonomy, expand the anthropological inquiry into transformative processes as old structures crumble and new cohorts of actors arise. In part III, social movements inspired by the changes brought about in globalization are explored through the lens of social engagement. Anthropologists are developing innovative strategies of engagement in social movements as participant activists who will disclose and influence the processes of resistance and change.

Chapter 6. Social Movements in Global Circuits

Globalization processes related to the expansion and integration of capitalist investments, production, and markets in new areas have generated social movements of people mobilizing to protect their lands, their cultural identities, and their autonomy. At the same time, the improved communication systems and the development of a global civil society acting through grassroots movements, the United Nations, and nongovernmental organizations (NGOs) promote a growing awareness of inequities in the distribution of wealth and of misfortune related to human rights violations. News of political imprisonment and of impoverishment is disseminated in global circuits along with promotions of consumer goods and luxury products.

This chapter focuses on global processes noted in anthropological publications, showing how social movements are engendered in order to oppose what people perceive as threats to central values enunciated above. These processes and the responses they may trigger include (1) the fragmentation and recomposition of society, (2) secularization and fundamentalist reactions, (3) deterritorialization and the politics of space, and (4) privatization and global cosmopolitanism. The assumption that global integration would lead toward a faceless, borderless, and homogenized world that exists only to consume the products that are endlessly reproduced in a global assembly line has not been supported in ethnographic case studies. What careful study reveals is that social movements often subvert or transform the thrust of these processes. These may express visceral desires repressed by global regimes of labor and consumption, or they may channel central values related to human rights, environmental conservation, autonomy, and social justice. These desires and values provide an ever-changing frame of reference that animates social movements and serves to validate the changes they institute.

Chapter 7. Interpreting Social Movements: Bolivian Resistance to Economic Conditions Imposed by the IMF

In the 1980s anthropology tended toward involution, stressing interpretation rather than exploration in anthropological investigations. Reviewing texts produced during the anthropological age of exploration in earlier decades of the century, or reworking vignettes from ever-scantier field experience, anthropologists central to the field made their reputations by cultivating literary tropes rather than discovering exotic customs in distant lands. The authors of *Writing Culture* (Clifford and Marcus 1986), for example, urged ethnographers to focus on texts in order to discover the systems of meaning inherent in the subjects of our discourse. Yet in the ever-more refined analysis of texts, we may lose sight of the larger issues addressed in earlier anthropological discourse. Furthermore, the emphasis on rediscovering meaning in past texts or even in currently produced writing of anthropology often trivializes the discovery of everyday events happening in the world around us.

In this chapter, I extend the interpretive analysis of culture from eye-winks, cockfights, and canonized texts in anthropology and literature to the social movement in which I became involved when over ten thousand members of Bolivian mining communities organized to protest a series of austerity decrees and new economic policies imposed by the newly re-elected president, Victor Paz Estenssoro, in 1985 and 1986. Engagement in crises such as this enabled anthropologists to move from an ostensibly objective and uniform portrayal of cultures to the reflexive and simultaneously multivocalic approach called for in the "critique of anthropology." The focus on the variety of interpretations and reinterpretations that the actors made of the events in which they participated does not, however, end with the analysis of rhetoric. Contrasts among the interpretations of the leaders and followers within the movement, including those of the government, the Catholic Church, and the media, provide the matrix for understanding the shifts in the structuring of power. Learning from co-participants the unstated premises on which they acted enabled the participant anthropologist as activist to assess the process as the movement developed. A second March for Peace in 1990 when indigenous people of the highlands met with their counterparts in the lowlands formed the basis for a national indigenous movement. This brought down two neoliberal governments in the 1990s that failed to respond to their demands for pluricultural relations with the state and sustainable economic policies responding to the needs of indigenous people. This chapter calls for attention to the interpretations of people within the cultures studied as they change in response to transformative social action.

PART IV. THE HOBBESIAN WORLD OF TERROR AND VIOLENCE

The disruption of subsistence economies and the fragmentation of the moral economy without construction of institutional controls on the emerging global economy have led to unprecedented violence manifested in the wars of the twentieth century and genocidal attacks in the undeclared wars of the third millennium. The pessimistic outlook of the seventeenth-century social philosopher Thomas Hobbes who predicted a war of all mankind if restraints by a social contract were not instituted might well be realized. Human rights activists are trying to implement such controls through United Nations covenants, yet the force to back them is sadly lacking.

The essays in this section consider the export of militarization as the United States imposes militarization on subaltern countries through regime change or counternarcotraffic policies and on domestic sites as the military-industrial complex is reinvigorated in the emerging American Empire. Comparing Mayas of Guatemala, where the democratic revolution of 1944–1954 was aborted by the U.S.-instigated coup in 1954, with Mayas of Chiapas, Mexico, where U.S. counternarcotraffic policies reinforce Mexican repression of indigenous rebels, I show in chapter 8 how militarization of these countries overcomes resistance by indigenous peoples to unpopular neoliberal trade policies. Chapter 9 shows the impact of the military-industrial complex during the Cold War in the 1980s, when it reinforced the hegemony of capitalism in the industrial city of Pittsfield,

Massachusetts, by providing secure, high-wage jobs, and currently in the war in Iraq where privatization of the war and outsourcing of military production reduce patriotic commitment. Other cities that have served as sites for military production have, like Pittsfield, become industrial waste sites, or brownfields, but they still serve as recruitment stations for youths who see few alternative opportunities in a deindustrialized America.

Chapter 8. The Export of Militarization: Counterinsurgency Warfare in the Periphery

Ethnography provides a methodology for capturing the culture imposed by war with teams that include forensic anthropologists assessing the evidence analysis of bones along with social anthropologists capturing the memories of survivors. What differentiates the wars of the past three decades in Central America and now Mexico are the extended encounters in which the lines between civilian and military are obliterated as the military pervades the domestic and political spheres. At the same time that counterinsurgent armies pervade the most intimate spaces of the society, they threaten the validation of an armed force as defenders of the civilian population and national security. In addition to the body count of the dead, which number in the hundred thousands, thousands of women are left widowed and hundreds of thousands of children are orphaned. Seen through gendered eyes in predominantly indigenous settings, I raise questions about the military as a defender of national security. When women, the very population armies claim to be defending, increasingly become the victims of armed encounters in internecine wars, it raises questions as to the distinctions between civilian and military, between legal and illegal, and between war and peace. When women protest the presence of the military living within their towns, it undermines the macho culture on which militarism is constructed. When women take up arms in guerrilla movements that oppose military repression, they further threaten the stereotypes of gender in ways that undermine patriarchal power. Viewing the military through indigenous lenses provokes us to question the legitimacy of the military as defenders of national sovereignty or of civil order in the counterinsurgency warfare waged in Latin America. The questions become acute when we address the militarization process that threatens to take over all social and governmental functions in indigenous areas where whole societies are threatened by predatory investors backed by military force. Since most of the two hundred thousand victims of the civil war in Guatemala were Mayas, a comparison with the neighboring Mexican state of Chiapas where Mayas make up a third of the population offers a basis for assessing the changing relations of indigenous people with the state with the onset of militarization.

Chapter 9. At Home with the Military-Industrial Complex

The U.S. launching of a preemptive strike against Iraq has revitalized the military-industrial complex that grew in the Reagan Cold War era, climaxing in the first Gulf War with Iraq. What appears to be a continuing war against terrorism extends U.S. control throughout the world, raising military costs with the ever-spiraling demand for weapons that threatens social programs at home. Returning to my fieldwork site in Pittsfield, Massachusetts, where the General Electric plant was a center for the military-industrial complex put in place during the Reagan regime in the 1980s, I ask questions about what the militarization of society may do. The growing dependence on ordnance production for military orders distorted economic priorities in the 1980s, leaving Pittsfield a brownfield area when General Electric closed the plant at the end of the decade. The incipient critique of imperialist wars by Vietnam veterans was for some silenced as they became incorporated as patriots more than a decade after their return, but others remain bitter about the recourse to war by those who, in the words of one Vietnam veteran, "push the buttons," and send others out to fight. In the transition in the United States from a military-industrial complex that recognized distinct spheres of policy related to government, the military, and business during the Cold War, to a fusion of corporate, Pentagon, and U.S. government command structures in the current war, the line between civilian and military life is erased. Washington may pretend to be the control center of an emerging American empire, but Pittsfield's youth no longer have the well-paid jobs and security that a military-industrial economy once ensured.

I

PARADIGMS
AND POSTURES

1

When Isms Become Wasms

Paradigms Lost and Regained

This chapter is a revision of a paper presented on the seventy-fifth anniversary of the Department of Anthropology at the University of Chicago in 1995. I kept the title, "When Isms Become Wasms," since it evokes the apolitical context of the 1950s when I began my graduate studies. Just a few years before I arrived on campus, the House Un-American Activities Committee had invaded university campuses across the nation, investigating Communist thought. Although Robert Redfield turned the spotlight against the investigators in a brilliant cross-examination—he was an attorney before turning to anthropology—when they arrived at the University of Chicago, anticommunism inhibited the paradigms with which we framed our texts. In this version of the paper, I follow the Marxist and postmodern critiques included in the original paper with the activist paradigm, which has become increasingly important in a globally integrated world. As the people we once pretended to study holistically become headlines in the conflict reports of our daily newspapers, we have been forced to relate in more collaborative ways in our participant observation fieldwork.

Activism does not represent so much a new paradigm as it does a new emphasis in gaining rapport in an increasingly polarized world. It carries a greater cargo of responsibility both to our collaborators in the field and our colleagues in academia. The question of complicity that was always present in long-term intimate relations in fieldwork becomes more difficult to sort out when we share concerns in the same struggle. This dawned on me when I read an account of journalists who had become embedded with U.S. troops in Iraq. They expressed concerns about their own tendencies to reflect the troops' commitment to the U.S. command operations as they shared the daily threat of death in stressful situations. Good anthropologists, just like good reporters, can maintain critical attention to their own complicity. In the pragmatist tradition in which I came of age in the 1940s, the ideologies of Communism, Fascism, and Socialism were treated as distortions of the political process. This was summed up in a *Readers Digest* column called "Quotable Quotes" at a time when it served as a vehicle for disseminating hegemonic U.S. interests: "We are all looking forward to the time when isms become wasms"—meaning Communism, Socialism, and Fascism.

By the time I entered graduate school in the 1950s I learned to appreciate a deeper layer of isms encapsulated in the paradigms with which we confronted field data. I have watched at least four of these paradigmatic isms sink into wasms. When I arrived at the University of Chicago in the 1950s, evolutionism of the kind fostered by Edward Tyler when anthropology was still the "child of imperialism" was already banished because of its tendency to equate superior genes and social progress with Euro-American progress. I took my qualifying exams in the heat of the next great wave of structural functionalism introduced by Radcliffe-Brown and Malinowski. Its superiority to putative histories and Eurocentric assumptions spawned by Tyler's unilineal evolution lay in the heritage of ethnographic studies that inspired practitioners even as the theory was attacked and finally eroded by historical materialism and feminism. Postmodernism has still not been completely defined as its critics line up to demolish it in the new wave of activism. Caught in the cracks of each of these schemata were enough ethnographic crumbs to feed the next wave of shock troops. A good ethnographer, I learned, provides enough evidence for reinterpretations responding to changing interests and conditions that foster them.

This review of some of the isms I have seen reduced to wasms asserts the importance of grounding anthropological paradigms in the practice of ethnography. I shall consider some of the lasting contributions of ethnology that survived the paradigmatic shifts of the past and go on to assess the impact of cultural critique. My major concern is that those who espouse postmodernism as an ideology are promoting an involution of anthropological perspectives that disparages ethnographic sources of insights. Yet while the reflexivity cultivated by the cultural critique may begin by masking in new terms some of the old Eurocentric positions on global processes, it has also cultivated multiple perspectives. This reawakening to meanings contained in ethnographic descriptions from the past may be furthered by the emerging commitment to collaborative research in social activism.

STRUCTURAL FUNCTIONALISM
AND BOASIAN CULTURAL MATERIALISM

I arrived at Chicago on the crest of structuralism and functionalism when these two British imports were written into all proposals. We ventured into the field not simply to find out what was there, like Columbia University's Boasian cultural materialists or California's Kroeberian culturologists, but to do a "structural functionalist" study of whatever we discovered. Radcliffe-Brown had taught at Chicago just a few years before, and Evans-Pritchard was still fresh in the memory of students who had drunk with him in Jimmy's on Fifty-seventh Street. In fashioning our ethnographic inquiries, we were enjoined to read Sir Henry Maine in order to appreciate the transformation from status in simpler societies to contract in more complex societies. It all seemed to fit so well, with Durkheim's organic and mechanical opposition echoing the polarization of Toennies's gemeinschaft/gesellschaft and yielding the folk/urban dichotomy.

But even as we learned the dichotomies in which we were expected to frame our structural functional inquiries, we picked up from our mentors the complexity of simple societies and the contradictions expressed by the folk. Few of Redfield's critics read the ethnographic context in *The Folk Culture of Yucatan* (1941). In exploring the lifeways of newly arrived folk in Dzitas, the bustling center of henequen commercialization in the Yucatán peninsula, he shows how Mayas from the countryside move from ethnic categories into proletarian status on the lowest rung of the labor force. A couple of decades later, Sydney Mintz rediscovered this transition of rural peasants to proletarians in a Marxist (or historical materialist) framework. Positivists of Redfield's era found empirical support for the folk and urban society in a synchronic model with the remote Quintana Roo community representing the past, Dzitas the burgeoning present, and Chan Kom the future of Yucatán—and Mexican—society. Many of these ideal models fell apart when historians later demonstrated that the charmed religious *cofradía* described by Redfield in Itzas was the core of a guerrilla group that, even before Cancún was taken over by Club Med, was staging a war of resistance to the modernization processes represented in henequen-producing centers. Later ethnographers have shown that Chan Kom was not a traditional folk community but the advancing front of indigenous people moving into lands they claimed under the agrarian reform act of 1917. Nonetheless, as Morris Janowitz, a sociological colleague of Redfield at the University of Chicago, maintained in a paper presented at the annual meetings of the American Anthropological Association (AAA) in the 1960s, Redfield's central thesis regarding the movement of ideas, behaviors, and technology from urban centers to periphery in regionally integrated economies held up empirically better than any other thesis in social science of that era.

Redfield encouraged debate in his seminars with his students and with his colleagues. He likened progress in social science to the movements of the fox in Aesop's fable, contradicting, backtracking, leaping over adversaries, while that in the physical sciences was the step-by-step advance of the hedgehog, whose insectivorous habits enjoined a careful scrutiny of the terrain and exhaustive reconnaissance of its resources. An early student of Redfield, Sol Tax, wrote one of his first great papers, "World View and Social Relations in Panajachel" (1937) debunking the folk mystique as he demonstrated the secular, commercial outlook of the penny-pinching Panajacheleños. Sol Tax, who was more the hedgehog than the fox, eschewed most isms (unless you include in this category empiricism); he taught us to appreciate the complex interworkings of Panajachel onion growers who rejected the ox and plow and other colonial innovations based on a rational calculus of the greater returns from intensive cultivation of cash crops rather than fodder for animals on lands whose values had been driven up by tourism. Tax was faulted for calling the petty commercial exchanges of Panajachel *Penny Capitalism* (1950) since they did not result in the accumulation of capital. But he, along with others of his generation, proved the rational allocation of resources by peasants. This characteristic was—in his time—denied to the peasantry whom most developmental specialists saw as mired in traditional patterns. It took another four decades for the "new" developmental critique (Escobar 1995) to reinvent his early insights.

We might have written a postmodernist ethnography from what we learned in socializing with our professors in the Haskell tearoom or working for them as work-study students. Tax was the ultimate empiricist, as I learned from retyping the second and third drafts of *Penny Capitalism* with its endless tables of products and earnings. He once said in a seminar that within a few summers of fieldwork with the Fox Indians he had become such an expert on the kinship and marriage exchanges that they came to ask him advice on who their children could marry without violating incest prohibitions for collaterals. Tax was also a very intuitive person who rarely allowed this characteristic to appear in his text: he once contrasted his own reluctance to pass the grocer on his street corner in Hyde Park while carrying two huge bags of groceries from the supermarket to the equanimity of the Panajacheleño buying corn from a producer who sold it a penny a kilo cheaper than his brother within view of each other in the local market.

Even as we were cultivating the role of "Concept Destroyers," the title of a skit we presented to the faculty that caricatured our role as anthropological critics, we absorbed the subliminal advice of our professors that there was a world worth discovering out there. The subscript was that we could best realize this by leaving our preconceptions behind and finding out what people were thinking, saying, and doing in the field. Sherwood Washburn expressed this in his advice to students going into the field for the first time: they should never be in a hurry, that they had to gain the right to ask knowledgeable questions. Following McQuown's advice just to listen, and especially with a tape recorder, I carried a huge tape recorder—in those days they weighed more than ten pounds—wherever I went during my fieldwork in Amatenango del Valle, a Mayan community in the highlands of Chiapas. I recorded rituals, interviews, court cases, and off-stage behavior when people were drinking and relaxing. The tape recorder even went to events from which I was excluded, carried by Mariano Lopez Lin, who became my research assistant after he finished his term as mayor of the town. The morning after a marital reconciliation session to which I had not been invited, Mariano appeared with the recorder to help me transcribe and translate the tapes. The tape was twisted and somewhat damp. It was the reel-to-reel model that required care in its operation. After we unscrambled the tape we were able to recapture the last fragments before the trouble began. "Let's play it back to hear what we all said," one voice remarked in Tzeltal. Expletives ensued and then came the part that Mariano did not want to translate. I figured it out from McQuown's glossary of Tzeltal phrases and a key term I had picked up from a Twin Brothers story: "Let's take it out back and pee on it!" Apparently they had done just that.

Mayas are excellent listeners since they are trained to develop this sense from childhood. Service in the civil religious hierarchy promotes hearing the words of elder men and women who are the ritual speakers (*tatil k'op, me'il k'op*), and repetition in rhymed couplets of significant words in prayers cultivates their awareness of what they hear. The verb "to hear" is the same as that for "to feel," *sh'awayi*, and curer diviners can hear and feel by pulsing a patient for what the blood is saying. This allows them to understand the past and to anticipate the future. It is the best lesson an anthropologist can learn. I shall try to show later how their ability to listen prepares Mayas to live more successfully in the postmodern world than those who attempt to dictate the terms of survival to others.

HISTORICAL MATERIALISM AND FEMINISM

Our cohort of University of Chicago "structural functionalist" doctorates were beginning to get jobs, often replacing culturologists of the California Kroeberian School in the 1960s. Simultaneously the new broom of historical Marxism was beginning to sweep the eastern seaboard. Columbia

University graduates were exploring neo-Marxist propositions that had been closeted during the age of McCarthyism. In their revisionist views of hunters and peasants, we began to perceive these modes of production in greater complexity than the ways of life described by our predecessors. Eleanor Leacock reviewed ethnohistorical data proving that agnatic clans not only were not typical of northeastern groups but also would have sealed their fate at an even earlier age because they did not allow the flexibility of bilateral consanguineous kinship groupings, with women often playing central roles in the governance of communities as well as in hunting itself. Eric Wolf showed that peasants, far from demonstrating the idiocy of rural life as Marx caricatured them, were the revolutionaries of the twentieth century and, as Mintz demonstrated in Puerto Rico, the emergent proletariat and bearers of the new class struggle. Morton Fried deconstructed the term "tribal" to show that it was not a primordial unit of non-Western society but an invention of empire to mediate with the natives. Robert Murphy, who acted as mythmaker for the Amazonian hunter in the 1960s, became a collaborator with his wife Yolanda Murphy to give birth to the forest people in which the preeminence of women's horticulture was reclaimed in the new feminist climate.

My metamorphosis as feminist and Marxist—I do not feel that I am a part of either category but I have seen my name linked with these leanings—began in the 1970s with my fieldwork in Bolivia. My encounter with Marxism came in the field where Bolivian miners took upon themselves the project of educating me in their basic principles as well as the daily praxis of mine union activism. I came to know more about Trotskyism than I would have received in most graduate schools, especially in the United States where it was treated as a failed branch of Marxist-Leninist philosophy. I attended lectures sponsored by the Federation of Mine Workers Union given by Guillermo Lora, René Zavaleta Mercado, and other illustrious Marxists-Trotskyists of Bolivia, and I borrowed books from the miners' own libraries. To find a vibrant branch of a neglected philosophy put into practice in the periphery of modern industrial society is a lesson that I have never forgotten. Judging from my mentors, Trotsky was a more dedicated dialectician than Marx and provided a more appropriate theoretical formulation for Third World countries engaged in international exchange. Mineworkers invented dependency theory before it became a common substratum of development thinking among intellectuals associated with the Economic Commission of Latin American. The Thesis of Pulacayo, drafted by Guillermo Lora in 1946, maintained that commodity-producing industries of Latin America were increasingly expropriated of the value of their products, and the poverty of Bolivian miners was precisely due to their integration into world capitalist markets.

As an anthropologist working with a holistic frame of analysis, I spent as much time in the community listening to and talking with women, children, and the retired, as in the mines. They taught me, and underground workers confirmed, that all of their workplace struggles began at home, where the inability to meet life-work demands of consumption and fiestas was experienced and where women standing in line at the commissary decided when it was necessary to strike. Their labor heroes included housewives whose voices, like that of Domitila Barrios de Chungara, became increasingly important in the declining years of tin production when the mining communities were struggling for survival (Nash and Safa 1976). I considered my book, *We Eat the Mines and the Mines Eat Us* (1979), to be a critique of Marxism since his emphasis on wage-earning workers in the production site caused him and his followers to overlook the reproductive settings in which women predominated. But in the politics of footnoting, citing an author appeared to be committing oneself to an ideology, and I became categorized as a Marxist.

My awareness of feminist consciousness followed on the heels of the civil rights movement, but it remained a separate part of my life until I participated in a 1971 Social Science Research Council Planning meeting. In the opening session where I was the only woman among fifty or more social scientists, I listened to the men projecting the funding for research projects in the coming decade without reference to the gender or ethnicity of the researcher or of the population studied. That night I drafted a critique of the four dominant paradigms in Latin American social science: neoliberalism, neo-Marxism, dependency, and developmentalism from what I called a feminine perspective. When I presented it the next day, I concluded with a plea for inclusion in the research process of "women and natives of the cultures scrutinized . . . [who] not only find the old paradigms wanting, but the very construction of social reality . . . to be based on preconceptions that do not yield to a changing reality." When I finished not a word was forthcoming. The chairman called for a break. One of the men came up to tell me he wished his wife had been there to hear me. An economist asked me when I would be satisfied that a critical mass had been reached so that I could relax. Soon after I drafted a proposal for a conference on Feminine Perspectives in Latin America, and when it was funded, I called upon Helen Safa to help me organize the conference that took place in Buenos Aires in 1974 that led to *Sex and Class in Latin America* (Nash and Safa 1976).

Cartesian dichotomies came under criticism, as colonized subjects became their own ethnographers. Kathleen Gough (1969) led the attack with her incisive critique of anthropology as the "Child of Imperialism" and there was a growing literature (summarized in Nash and Safa 1976) critiquing the colonialist background of our discipline and calling for its decolonization. The opposition of civilized and primitive was no longer acceptable and even the euphemisms of simple and complex or developed and underdeveloped were anathema to the new cohort of anthropologists responding to a postcolonial world. Third World anthropologists—I include here the colonizers who had migrated from their "home" countries—also exposed the inadequacies of some of our most cherished assumptions. Max Gluckman (1947) launched one of the first and most severe attacks on functionalism as he criticized Malinowski for his ahistoricism and failure to see conflict as part of an integrated colonial picture. Talal Asad (1973) showed that the mystique of holism presumably encompassing all aspects of "tribal" life yet leaving out imperialist institutions "obscured the systematic character of colonial domination and masked the fundamental contradictions of interest."

The prevalence of Cartesian dualities was so deeply embedded in our subconscious that even while anthropologists were trying to escape the patriarchal-colonialist framework of thought they fell back on these props of earlier ideologies. Early feminist critiques drew on both Aristotelian and Cartesian dichotomies of women to essentialize the female nature in yet another mode. Simone de Beauvoir (1957) accepted Hegel's view of man as the active principle, thus assuming, in accord with Aristotle's law of contradiction, the opposite qualities of passivity ascribed to women. Lévi-Strauss (1969, 1970) persisted in affirming the characteristic of passivity in his updated Adam and Eve myth when he called women "the supreme gift" with which men set up the network of intergroup ties that provides a basis for exogamic marriage exchange, thus ensuring the dominance of the social over the biological in the family through the incest taboo.

Those marginalized from mainstream ideologies regarding society—women and the formerly colonized subjects of anthropology—became the major voice of criticism in the 1960s and 1970s. The decentralizing of the dominant Euro-American white male as the delineator of the objective world was for some so unsettling that the promoters of the new paradigm of postmodernism proceeded to reduce the scope of reality to a semiotic world of signs and symbols eliminating embodied representations. Significantly the first anthology reasserting their privileged position (Clifford and Marcus 1986) excluded any of the critiques from feminists and decolonialized subjects whose work they found "beneath their standards."

POSTSTRUCTURALISM AND POSTMODERNISM

Poststructuralism staked out its domain in a minefield of posthumous isms as the fox jumped blithely from postindustrialism to postmodernism, sometimes building on the very same propositions of earlier structuralists cast in a new language. What differentiates the poststructuralists from past post-hoc posturing is the skepticism fostered in the disengagement from the modernist projects. Few postmodernist anthropologists who situated themselves in the ideology and not just the landscape of late capitalism related their philosophy to structuralist propositions of the innovators of the new paradigm. Yet those like Alain Touraine (1971), Frederic Jameson (1981), and David Harvey (1989) who launched insightful comments on the postmodern landscape in the context of late capitalist conditions are now influencing a new cohort of ethnologists who relate the economic and political affairs of people until recently marginalized to the cultural identities they are formulating in a globalizing world.

Attempts to correlate the fragmentary lifestyles and identity issues of gender and ethnicity that dominated struggles in the 1970s and 1980s that coincided with declining capital earnings, the destruction of social welfare provisions, and the flight of capital into Third World countries without class-based union movements were shrugged off as examples of vulgar determinism. Once one relegates the positivist basis for an empirical social science to what Marx would call the dustbins of history, issues of gross national product and the demographics of work roles have little relevance. Yet when we approach these issues from our own ontological position as academicians, I have seen a marked correlation among my colleagues between the decline in grants, which do, after all, follow the decline in earnings at the Ford Motor Company or the reduced returns from corporate taxes to government-granting agencies, with the decline in the sense of progress that marked the modernist era. The denial of a world beyond the imaginings of social scientists may indeed be related to the very loss of the old props to Eurocentric and androcentric representations. It is no wonder that Steven Sangren (1988, 405) faults postmodernist discourse for the "misleading and surprisingly unreflective ways that diminish their own claims to 'reflexivity,' 'polyphony,' and 'dialogue' as core values."

INTERPRETIVE ANTHROPOLOGY
AND THE CULTURAL CRITIQUE

The hermeneutics approach as practiced by anthropologists raised even more doubts of the truth-value of our "texts" than when applied to literature. By exposing the artifice in ethnographic writing, Clifford Geertz (1973b) opened to suspicion the very question as to whether the understanding of humankind is advanced by fieldwork. Yet Geertz's skepticism that launched the interpretive paradigm was a mild antecedent to what has followed. From a position in which "facts" and "data" are understood

not as "objective entities" but rather "as social meanings attributed by social actors—including the fieldworker—in interaction with others" (Wilson 1983), there was often an indifference to validating by any means outside the text taken as the ultimate reality. Yet this vanity comes at a time
when growing wealth differences, measurable in an infinite number of in-
dices, are affecting the quality of life and the very fabric of society.

The involution of the discipline of anthropology in a cultural critique
that questions not just ways of representing the other, but of the very
process of representation, in the late 1980s and 1990s is more than coincidentally bound to the critique by feminists and anticolonialists of androcentric and Eurocentric models. This mood is reflected in (or possibly em-
anated from) the humanities where "Subjectivity, history and truth are
being questioned by white, male academics," Nancy Hartsock (1987)
points out, "at the very moment that such concepts are appropriated by
previously marginalized groups." The decline in the hegemonic position
of the core industrial countries in which anthropology developed has precipitated a decline in the position of male white elites that has led to this
soul searching. Identity takes precedence over class as the certainties of
class privilege are denied.

Once feminists and others who were colonized by it kicked out Aristotle's axioms from under the elite academic establishment, the self-
constituted leaders in the field proposed a savage nihilism that denies
the truth-value of any representation (Schremp 1989, 17). In their posturing I am reminded of the infant observed by Lacan (1977, 2) "still
sunk in his motor incapacity and nursling dependence," yet totally en-
chanted with his own image reflected in the mirror. Arrested in this
"mirror stage," the dominant discourse in the field now uses the world's
stage to confront anthropologists' own image as they check their own
pulse and mount their own infantile fantasies in an imaginary rendition
of what is out there. This self-image is then projected in literary references or the texts of deceased anthropologists that serve as a virtual field
site to elaborate, criticize, romanticize, or simply plagiarize. Paralleling
this in-textual analysis, literary critics frequently ignore context as the
"inner rifts and dissonances of textual system are privileged" (Przybylowicz, Hartsock, and McCallum 1985, 9).

Summing up our experience with past paradigms, I admit that an ongoing critique of our practice of anthropology is essential to the enterprise. Historical materialism of the 1970s indicated the vacuity of community studies viewed as timeless wholes, homogeneous and largely
unchanging. The critiques of functionalist studies that reified the status
quo under colonialism (Hymes 1974) led to an efflorescence of historically
situated and empirically grounded writing. The contributors' questioning
of the traditional/modern dichotomies made it possible to expand a the-

ory of process-situating studies of colonized cultures within a worldwide framework of capitalist advance.

Yet at the same time as we cultivate a critical reading of past ethnographies we might well pick up on positive insights that shed light on contemporary findings. Many postmodern discoveries were quotidian insights of ethnographers in the 1950s as they entered field situations that were rife with the conflicts and contradictions of formerly "tribal" cultures in the new nations of Africa and Asia. Lloyd Fallers's close association with Uganda chiefs enabled him to see in their role "the meeting point, the point of articulation, between the various elements of the patch work. . . . A man who was head of the Anglican church and the boy scouts was also a polygamist." McKim Marriott pointed to the paradox of overdevelopment as the basis for resistance to modernizing development programs in India. He found that the very overdetermination of cultural practices in highly interrelated customary practices made it of questionable merit if not impossible for Indian peasants to adopt changes considered more rational by the developers. In his introduction to his student Jomo Kenyatta's book *Facing Mount Kenya* (1961), Malinowski became his own critic in calling for an inquiry into colonial practices as well as the newly independent state of which his student became president.

A good ethnography can provide the basis for a completely new view of the people and processes studied. That is what Peter Worseley was able to do in his re-reading of Meyer Fortis's analysis of the Talensi. Using Fortis's own data, he was able to show that the fissioning of kinship branches was due as much to land policies of the colonial government as to inherent propensities in the kinship structure. Annette Weiner did not simply trash Malinowski for his failure to include women in his ethnographic field but, rather, showed the critical junctures in men's polities that depended on the show of women's wealth at funerals. Her ethnography deepened as it complemented Malinowski's picture.

These insights gained from anthropologists rethinking previous ethnographies in the light of subsequent studies are not cultivated in the new cultural critique. The tendency was to rediscover the same colonialist authoritarianism (Clifford and Marcus 1986) or blind spots to native ingenuity among developing agents (Escobar 1995) only to mount their critique on what is presented as a tabula rasa. Their own dependence on insights of their predecessors is ignored, as Sangren (1988) points out in the case of Said's antiorientalism.

The discovery of truth is not what the cultural critique is about. Truth itself is a suspect category, and the reality of the field is as much under question as the interpretations of it. In the words of one acolyte, "facts" and "data" are understood not as "objective entities" but rather as "social meanings attributed by social actors—including the fieldworker—in interaction with others," (Wilson 1983, 697) yielding an endless chain of imagery pointing to their own master image. Wilson concludes that researchers find it easy to discard the hypothesis testing, formulation of specifically defined variables, and concern with reliability of the ethnographic summary that marked scientific method. Textual analysis has shifted to another ism, as textualism is glorified, fetishized, and made an end in itself divorced from the experience of the self and the other. Fantasy takes over where empiricism ends. In his deconstruction of Chan Kom, the "village that chose progress" in Redfield and Villa Rojas's restudy, Castaneda (1995, 132), exhorts us to understand ethnography as the "presentation (not representation) of a culture, that is, a simulation in Baudrillard's sense. Thus we rediscover a culture that is invented in discursive and geographic space through an ethnographic complicity as Chan Kom . . . becomes the paradigm of Yucatec Maya culture in the guise of a modernizing Maya Folk."

PERIPHERAL VISION OF THE POSTMODERN FIELDWORKERS

In the wake of the representational crisis in anthropology, I would like to redeem the peripheral vision of anthropologists who have crossed the threshold opened by the cultural critique. I have found this project of redeeming the ethnographic vision among those who study "unstable places" where fragmented states release the curbs on violence within and beyond the realm of imagined stabilities (Greenhouse 2002; Warren 2002a). It is there that the door left open by postmodern inquiry allows us—in fact forces us—to transcend "the reification of settings as existing at a distance from personal life," as Carol Greenhouse (2002, 1) put it in her anthology of unstable places. In these settings that Victor Turner might have called "liminal stages," the differences between insider and outsider break down, and the need to find conscious expression of what is happening and why provokes an inquiry on the part of the subjects. Kay Warren (1998, 2002a) has shown the power of this inquiry in her study of Mayan cultural leaders in Guatemala and Charles Hale (1994) has shown it in Nicaragua. Like other anthropologists who are wildcatting on the frontiers of a predatory world system, they are the best antidote to the postmodernist retreat into armchair anthropology.

In this reassessment of fieldwork priorities, I have proposed the centrality of the word of the subject rather than the text of the anthropologist. Listening and hearing might then rescue anthropology from the nihilistic trend in the cultural critique, awakening us to the humanistic thrust that was central to Giambatista Vico and Gottfried von Herder in the eighteenth century. In the rediscovery of their lessons that the study of human society must differ in method and goals from that of the natural world because "man," as they put it, consciously struggles to define meaning in his own life, the postmodernists privilege the insights of the observer. Observation of nonverbal communication is, of course, still essential, but our stance as "objective observer" must be modified by greater heed to the interpretations of those who are the central actors in the event. When we enter into the imaginary construction of the data we observe there should be enough of both observation and self-representation on which to hang—and defend—our own representation. Fieldwork is essential since we lack the imaginative skills to capture the wide range of human possibilities that are still extant. I think this was what Sol Tax was suggesting when he tried to tell us how difficult it was to imagine anyone's conditions of being, even—and he used the analogy in class—someone of the opposite gender in our own culture.

In order to convey the significance of such a refocusing of our attention back to people we study, I shall draw on another allegory of the mirror, this one taken from the Zapatista seer, El Viejo Antonio of the Lacandón Rain Forest (*Expreso*, Tuxtla Gutierrez, December 30, 1994).

> There was a great stone where all those who were born in the world were walking in the paths of the first gods. With all that tramping above it, the stone became very smooth, like a mirror. Against this mirror the first gods blew into the air the first three words. The mirror did not withdraw the same words that it received but rather returned three other times three different words. The gods spent the time this way, throwing the words at the mirror in order that more come out until they were bored. Then they had a great idea, and they made a path over another great rock and another great mirror was polished and they put it in front of the first mirror and this returned three times three different words that they blew out, with all the force they had, against the second mirror, and this returned to the first mirror, three times three the number of words that it received, and so they were throwing out more and more different words, the two mirrors. Thus it was that the true language was born.

Zapatistas, like many indigenous people, are now disseminating their own words, but they now rely on international visitors and media representatives to help disseminate them. On the second anniversary of the Zapatista Uprising in January 1996, I participated in what Commander David called "The Fiesta of the Word." In this National Forum of Indigenous People, over four hundred indigenous people, along with leading Mexican intellectuals and international observers like myself, joined twenty-four Zapatistas to review the contents of the dialogue between the government and Zapatista leaders in the preceding fall. The proceedings took place in six sessions, each with about fifty to one hundred participants with four Zapatistas sitting quietly throughout each session, listening to what everyone said about the proposals set forth. For eight days the assembled group spoke and listened to each other's words. The document they produced, called the San Andrés Agreement, was presented and signed by the government representatives in the Commission for Agreement and Peace (COCOPA) on February 16, 1996. Even after the election of President Vicente Fox, who promised to solve the stalemate in fifteen minutes, the agreement has not been implemented by the Mexican congress.

The relativism of knowledge and the urgency of subjectivity is taken for granted in the pluripolitical, plurireligious, and pluricultural settings in which Mayas find themselves in the newly colonizing areas of the Lacandón Rain Forest and the urban barrios to which highland indigenous people who have dissented with caciques have migrated. There we can discover new understandings of what liberty, democracy, and equality might be as those who were excluded from the earlier dialogue begin to appropriate them: "Justice," El Viejo Antonio goes on in his allegory of the mirror to say, "is not to punish, but to give back to each what s/he deserves, and that is what the mirror gives back; Liberty is not that each one does what s/he wants, but to choose whatever road that the mirror wants in order to arrive at the true word; Democracy is not that all think the same, but that all thoughts or the majority of the thoughts seek and arrive at a good agreement."

The Zapatista call for autonomy of indigenous pueblos is not to isolate themselves from modernizing influences, but rather to embrace this diversity in governance that responds to a multiplicity of cultural traditions. They are the emergent "subjects of history" whose daily practice has prepared them to live in the postmodern world and who, in making their own history, are shaping a new moral community. Anthropologists can help bring this, and other visions of the postmodern condition from the people we study, to replace the mirror self-image of a skeptical and jaded discipline. Those who are focusing on these emergent autonomous communities find it necessary to engage in activist participatory research that goes beyond our participant observation. Since their subjects are under fire in the transformative social change they are bringing into being, their presence is not tolerated as it once may have been.

ACTIVIST ANTHROPOLOGY: PROMISE AND PERILS

Activist anthropology stems from some of the same values related to social justice that inspired Sol Tax to promote "action anthropology" with the Fox Indians a half century ago. While conducting a field research team with the Fox in 1948, he crystallized in a letter to the students some of his thoughts about introducing change for progress on the Fox Reservation. In the process of carrying out the agreed-upon action with the Fox, he felt that the students would learn more about culture and personality, social structure, and everything else. Action anthropology often meant specific involvement in projects usually conceived and managed by the anthropologist and carried out with Indians. Among those projects on the Fox Reservation were the production of TamaCraft industry, organization of a community center, and encouraging citizenship and active participation in democratic processes (Blanchard 1979).

A decade later the Cornell Anthropology Department carried out a similar project in Vicos, Peru, that was overtly directed toward overcoming the paternalistic codes of behavior in the feudal agriculture still persisting in highland Peru in the 1950s and 1960s. Yet because the initiatives were those of the anthropologists, who, in the words of one of the Vicos students, became the new *patrónes*, the Fox and Vicos projects were often criticized as "paternalistic." Nonetheless they satisfied the "citizen interests" as Tax called it (Blanchard 1979) of the anthropologists in contributing to the society by generating artistic talents of the people they studied and enabling them to earn much needed cash. Action anthropology was later called "applied anthropology" as development agencies expanded the range of their projects to rural and indigenous areas.

In contrast to the action and applied anthropologists who promoted the reproduction of a given status quo, activist anthropologists today take their lead from the people they study, adapting their talents and resources to the needs and interests of the people they join as they become engaged in transformative actions for structural change. The activist approach permits greater access to privileged sources of information than strictly scientific ethnography, but this comes with greater risks in representing one's findings. No matter how hard one seeks balance, some doors are closed at the moment others are opened since associations with those who are considered opponents will mitigate trust. It is rare to find an anthropologist like Charles Hale who was able to maintain a credible presence with protagonists of the Nicaraguan Revolution that found themselves on opposite sides of the table. As the conflict moved from that between Sandinistas and national elites to one between Sandinistas and the Miskito Indians, Hale (1994) was able to maintain open communication channels with both sides, thus enabling mediation of differences. Far from limiting the ethnographic stance, as some armchair critics maintain, this alliance with protagonists promoting distinct perspectives within a common cause generates the kind of discussions and actions that clarify an evolving process.

Activist anthropology grows out of the conflict situations that anthropologists encounter in field sites throughout the world where there is little tolerance for neutrality. Those who have engaged in it, as Barrie Thorne (1983) learned in her activist research with war resisters during the Vietnam War period, find that guilt mixes with euphoria as participation in events as an observer-collaborator often means sharing the excitement but not the full risk as others do. Thorne found that she was suspected of being a federal agent there to detect illegal activities of the draft resisters. Nonetheless protagonists of activism often value the role of observers in such crisis situations for itself, as I discovered when I joined a march of Bolivian mineworkers opposing the closing of national mines in 1986 (1992b). Since there were no immediate journalists on the scene when the army surrounded ten thousand marchers to prevent them from continuing on to La Paz, many came up to talk with me when they saw me with pen and paper recording the event. There was, as well, the anxiety as to what revelations would injure the movement once they were printed.

As a participant activist, the ethnographer finds himself/herself an instrument of the research, reflecting on feelings and emotions raised by the events in which she/he was involved as a participant. In the process of assessing the personal risk involved in participatory action, the ethnographer is sensitized to greater awareness of the implications of those who make up the social movement. Activist anthropology need not imply that the anthropologist renounces scientific criteria or the theoretical premises that inform the discipline. On the contrary, it means situating oneself in the field of social action, defining and often clarifying to oneself the particular perspectives that condition his/her research. I have seen greater transparency in the work of activist anthropologists than that of self-styled "objective" scientific researchers who have not felt required to divulge what motivates the choice of research topics or the relations with those who provide them with information. One direction of activist research is in collaborative work with the subjects of inquiry.

This kind of collaboration is cultivated as we enter into an intense dialogue during periods of crisis with people of a distinct cultural perspective yet one we are intent on sharing. Marco Tavanti, an Italian Catholic priest who worked collaboratively with the Tzotzil group that called themselves the Abejas developed collective discussions of the events that led up to the horrifying massacre of forty-five members of the community. He would raise issues to the diverse assembly of men and women, young and old, Protestant and Catholic, and government party Institutional Revolutionary Party (PRI) adherents and Zapatistas, asking them to reflect on this in common. He would challenge them to take their collaborators seriously and question their own premises, much as is done in a focus group (Tavanti 2003, 25–26). He maintains, and his monograph on the community that lived through this traumatic period and transformed the tragedy into a collective memorial proves, the positive advantages that can be gained from such a collaborative research design. The goal as he points out is as follows:

> Experiencing and welcoming diversity creates new cross-cultural and "syncretic" standpoints that are essential for interpreting our globalizing society. The point here is not just that foreigners interpret society from a standpoint of foreigners and indigenous from a standpoint of indigenousness. Rather, it is the experience of moving across localities and identities that generates new perspectives.

Collaborative anthologies such as *Women of Chiapas: Making History in Times of Struggle and Hope,* coedited by Christine Eber and Christine Kovic (2003), succeed in such a collaborative project by going beyond the usual network of the ethnologist to provide a broader scope for inquiry into the dynamics of social change in process. This is particularly marked by their inclusion of creative works that allow the writers to explore their inner psyche and its relations with a collective group as they imagine alternative scenarios. Plays, songs, prayers, life histories, and testimonials embody the experience of indigenous life and struggle that go beyond ethnographic representation. These creative texts draw upon everyday forms in which women express their sentiments and reflect on salient issues in their lives. Yet because the creativity involves imagination, the question of ethnographic validity arises. How do we know that they represent "the truth?" What are the criteria of validity when the usual canons of ethnographic authority are dismissed? The canons include long-term, intimate acquaintance with knowledgeable members of the group whose intelligent perceptions and honesty are probed in many different contexts.

Can we accept the texts on their own merit, or is the authority of the ethnographer still operating though not given authorship? Eber and Kovic answer some of these questions in the section overviews by providing the deeper layers of meaning for the texts. Prayers are the most commonplace yet most elaborated forms of speech in Mayan cultures. Their communities respect those chosen as collaborators, and their testimonies have stood up on many different occasions. As they participate actively in the social movements occurring in Chiapas, the contributors unite their voices with those of the women's cooperatives, church groups, political parties, and nongovernmental organizations with whom they work. In these collective actions, they connect their strategic needs as wives and mothers with their desire for structural change of their position as doubly oppressed.

This linkage of personal needs with the desire for change is characteristic of the processions and demonstrations of women supporters of Zapatistas in the Christian Base Communities in Chiapas. Their tendency to link their movement with strong ritual and religious symbolism was particularly evident in the Women's Day March in 1995 when the women all carried white flowers and candles as incense bearers accompanied them. These are the quintessential elements of the traditional festivals in indigenous communities. Although the march was a highly politicized event, with strong claims for peace and against militarism since it occurred a month after the invasion of Zapatista communities in the Lacandón jungle, the context was enhanced by these symbols to evoke the peace and justice. It was also validation for their appearance in public, since church and religious celebrations were the only events in which women participated publicly without men.

These symbolic references to the sacred and to the special relationship of women to Mother Earth often alarm First World activists who join the ranks of indigenous people. Yet we have much to learn from the anxiety raised in both these contexts. Our cultivated distancing from the spiritual sources of collective behavior may prompt in us disdainful reactions when we find the conviction of mobilized people expressed in religious terms. Yet Zapatistas draw upon these sources latent in the Christian Base Communities that thrived in the Lacandón Rain Forest during the ministering of Bishop Samuel Ruiz who drew from liberation theology in formulating his own theology of rebellion. Religion has always provided a powerful stimulus to the wretched of the earth, whether directing them to the world after death or before. Indigenous communities of the Lacandón Rain Forest drew from passages of Exodus in the Bible the message of liberation of the Israelis and applied it to their own condition of liberation from the slavery of the plantations in which they worked (Leyva Solano 1996). In Acteal, the Chenalhó hamlet where paramilitaries trained and financed by the Institutional Revolutionary Party massacred forty-five members of the Christian Base Community that called themselves "The Bees," religious faith fortified their commitment to resistance against the government and reconciliation with the community following the tragedy (Tavanti 2003). The strength of conviction in the justice of their struggle draws inspiration from the sacrifice of those who died. This was as prevalent in early Christianity when it appeared as the religion of slaves and poor people subjugated or dispersed by Rome as it was in the workers' Socialist circles in the nineteenth century (Engels 1959), and as it is today in Chiapas.

Just as the referential system of religion in the politics of indigenous peoples alarms the sophisticated outside observer, so too does the self-referential language of motherhood and identification with the earth often used by the women in these movements. In the postmodern, deconstructive mode, the very category of women is decried as essentialist.[1] Certainly a reductionist view of Third World women as people with "'needs' and 'problems' but no freedom to act" (Chandra Mohanty, cited in Escobar

1995, 8) merits criticism, but the critique should not end with the statement of the problem. We must go beyond deconstruction of the rhetoric to discover the incentives generating a common collective image among indigenous movements. Only then will we understand, as they do, how the struggle for dignity is essential to overcome their former subjugation at home and in public. As one Mayan activist put it when he spoke from the floor at an AAA meeting in the 1980s: "We were despised and subordinated as Indians, so we fought as Indians. Now we are not ashamed to call ourselves Indians." And as Juana de la Cruz, an indigenous woman in the actors' group *Fomento para la Mujer Maya* said on the tenth anniversary of their founding in February 2004, "We were despised as women in our homes and in public, and that is why we organize as women."

Cultural expressions provide a venue for formulating new conceptions of identity that are less threatening than strictly political settings. Warren's (1998) study of pan-Maya activists in Guatemala during the genocidal wars provides a case in point. By promoting the revitalization of Indian languages, cultural icons, and identification with territories, pan-Mayanists hope to transform their relations to the state and civil society. This represents only one of the many ways in which Mayas of Guatemala are reasserting their heritage in contemporary struggles. Communities of Populations in Resistance and Committees of Campesino Unity were other contexts in which indigenous people joined with mestizos to contest the genocidal attack on small-plot farmers of the western highlands and the colonizers of the Ixcán during the 1980s. Like Guatemala Mayas, Chiapas Mayan women are confronting the structural factors deriving from neoliberal policies that reduce social welfare and expand military budgets. To do it as women whose special responsibility is the care and nurturance of children is not to diminish alternative roles, but to complement them. The task of the activist anthropologist is to discover the alternatives posed by indigenous people, not to deconstruct their language as they seek common cause.

There is no doubt that activist anthropology involves us in greater risks as well as rewards. This may not be a matter of choice. In conditions of massive social upheaval, no neutrals are allowed for long-term participant observation. Collaboration promotes an awareness of the creative tensions involved in the processes of change, going beyond the events to clarify the conflicts and resolutions that enter into transformative change. As Charles Hale's monograph on the Miskito Indians in Nicaragua during the transition from the Sandinista revolutionary state to the neoliberal government demonstrates, activist anthropology does not preclude a critique of either side. The deepening of insights into the complicities of power and its contradictions is heightened as we learn in practice that there are no cookbook recipes for social transformation.

NOTES

This is a revised version of a paper prepared for the seventy-fifth anniversary of the founding of the University of Chicago's Department of Anthropology in 1995. It was presented at the 2004 Latin American Studies Association meeting in Las Vegas when Nash received the Kalman Silvert Award. An earlier version was published with the title: "When Isms Become Wasms: Structural Functionalism, Marxism, Feminism, and Postmodernism," *Critique of Anthropology* 17: 11–32.

1. Among those who have dominated this approach are George E. Marcus and Michael M. J. Fischer (1986), and Clifford and Marcus (1986).

2

The Notion of the Limited Good and the Specter of the Unlimited Good

George Foster shattered the codes of peasant ethnography when he published "Peasant Society and the Image of the Limited Good" in 1965. Peasants, who had just been discovered as ethnographic subjects, were invulnerable to criticism as oppressed and potentially revolutionary actors in history. By disclosing the assumptions that underlay behaviors that were otherwise explained in terms of traditional imperatives or fatalism, he opened up a debate that still kindles productive controversy. I argue that the empirically derived model of the limited good that Foster constructed to explain peasant rejection of modernization also cultivates conservation practices that benefit sustained development. I contrast this with development processes that cultivate a notion of the unlimited good. While opening up horizons that stimulate technological innovations and prolong the life span, neoliberal development may also promote practices of profligate credit card consumption, deficit spending, and inflated stock markets. Peasants, who have had to pay for the consequences of the debt crisis of the 1980s and the finance markets crisis of 1997, now face elimination in global markets in the third millennium. Now that the real limits of nonrenewable resources can be envisioned, some peasants are seeking alternative development programs to those of neoliberal market economics. The Zapatistas and their support bases in Chiapas are revitalizing collective behaviors oriented to conservation of land and resources. This more balanced outlook in which development for the collective good with redistribution of the rewards of production promotes sustainable practices provides an alternative to the specter of impoverishment fostered by unlimited growth benefiting only a few.

Foster's interpretation of peasant cognitive orientations was one in which "all of the desired things in life, such as land, wealth, health, friendship and love, manliness and honor, respect and status, power and influence, security and safety, *exist in finite quantity* and *are always in short supply*," [my emphasis]. This led to his conclusion that peasants operated in a zero sum game, in which they viewed any one person's advantage as gained at the expense of fellow human beings, thus inhibiting the motivation for growth (Foster 1965). Hence cultivating opportunities that would allow peasants to think beyond the closed system could enhance national development.

This hypothesis generated a flurry of criticism among his colleagues.[1] Peasants, who had just been discovered as ethnographic subjects, were for some anthropologists invulnerable to criticism as oppressed and potentially revolutionary actors in history. Others claimed that the peasant worldview of a limited good was justified in terms of their persistent poverty in the face of limited opportunities. Peasant notions of scarcity and the need for balanced reciprocity between human exploitation of nature and the gods that ensured its reproduction have remained a radical alternative to the predominant view of the First World that "natural resources" are unlimited, requiring only the knowledge and ability to exploit them.

The faith in science in mid-twentieth-century American culture as a key to providing synthetic alternatives to anything that was in short supply cultivated increasingly conspicuous modes of consumption in the 1960s and succeeding decades. It was only at the end of the millennium when the limits of nonrenewable resources became irrefutable that peasant understandings of the need to conserve limited resources emerged as an alternative mode of reproduction.[2]

The growing awareness of the finite nature of the good has transformed the expectations of unlimited possibilities into a specter of paradise lost for growing multitudes of impoverished people. Persistent waste of the world's resources by multinational corporations and the governments they control prevails in an expanding global market that consumes the gifts of nature and human labor. Those whose response is to declare war on all who compete for control of diminishing oil, water, minerals, and other resources are beginning to encounter resistance from social movements that seek to reinforce international covenants on the environment and the human rights of the poor. I hope to rescue Foster's insight on the peasant worldview and what that may offer for those concerned with a sustainable future for world populations.

LIVING WITH THE LIMITED GOOD

I was engaged in fieldwork in Mexico when George Foster's article was published (1965). The winds of change stirred by the Revolution of 1910–1917 came later to the state of Chiapas where I was working than in Michoacán where Foster worked. In Chiapas invidious actions of peasants were escalating as some benefited more than neighbors from the redistribution of land and power emanating from the central government. Foster's notion of the limited good helped explain a host of aggressions and ways of avoiding such encounters. These included witchcraft carried out by a professional, or simply evil eye cast by the invidious person on rivals. The idea was that, since everything was in short supply—land, capital, women, health, power—then anyone who had signs of greater affluence was suspected of consorting with evil powers and upsetting the common good. But this cognitive orientation was not consciously present in the minds of those who responded viscerally to the competitive presence of others in their environment. Foster was well aware that, as he put it, "in a rapidly changing world, in which peasant and primitive peoples are pulled into the social and economic context of whole nations, some of their behavior may appear irrational to others because the social, economic, and natural universe that in fact controls the conditions of their life is other than that revealed to them . . . by a traditional world view" (1965, 294).

What I was observing in the decade 1958 to 1967 in Chiapas was a change in the power relations governing the town as indigenous men replaced *ladinos* in township offices. The greater access of some indigenes to more powerful and lucrative opportunities favored the few literate young men who had attended government schools introduced during Cárdenas's presidency (1934–1940) in indigenous areas. The challenge of these young men to the decision making of the old curer diviners and elder officials upset the gerontocracy of *principales*—men who had served in all steps of the civil and religious hierarchy—that had ensured the power of elders.

Foster's thesis made sense to me as I pored over the homicide cases trying to figure out why there was a rise in the incidence of violence. From six cases of homicide in the twenty-year period from 1938 to 1957, the number of homicides rose to thirty-seven in the following seven years from 1958 to 1965. In the circumscribed world of small-plot peasant cultivators scratching out a living on land grants they began to receive in 1937, anyone who demonstrated even a modicum of wealth evoked intense envy. It was assumed that the wealthy must have gained their cattle or stores of grain at the expense of their neighbors. Either the wealthy person had stolen the spirit of his neighbor's crops, or he had gone to the Lord of the Underworld to seek stores of grain or cattle. If the first recourse was suspected, the wealthy man could expect to become the victim of witchcraft; in the second, he was ignored since people knew that he would have to work for the Lord of the Underworld forever after his death.[3]

In this process, young curers who had not served an apprenticeship with an older curer were being killed at greater rates than any others. Their claims to power, lacking the validation of their elders, were communicated to the *principales*, elders who had passed through all the offices in the civil-religious hierarchy, who would send out an order to jail them. Instead of processing the complaints with a court trial presided over by the president and *síndico* who responded to national laws, the elders allowed the prisoners to escape during the night, whereupon those who accused them of witchcraft rounded up a posse and set out to kill them. Analyzing the homicide cases, it was clear that charges of witchcraft were the means to redress the balance, as the new usurpers in the power structure were blamed for the changed order (Nash 1970). Envy, aggravated by the growing wealth distinctions in a society where the shared poverty of early colonial and independence times had been lost, provoked the recourse to violence.

Questions that had troubled me seemed resolved in a pattern related to daily conflicts stirred by envy and the notion of limited good. For example:

- Why did Simon's wife fear he would die if he purchased a radio?
- Why did Mariano organize a cooperative of five *socios* to help purchase a phonograph player for his bar when he could have afforded to buy it on his own and not have to share the income from his patrons?
- Why did Juliana take a circuitous route taking her a half hour longer to go from my compound to her own house?
- Why did Lucia not make the tourist type of pottery figurines her neighbor, the widow Petrona, sold so successfully?

Each decision involved a complex assessment of how to maintain equilibrium in social relations based on socially accepted levels of production and consumption. Those who tested out new modes of making an income usually sought associates in a cooperative that then shared the risk of making a profit. Simon defied his wife's fear of his buying a radio, and while he was not immediately killed, he was shot a half dozen years later when he defied codes of behavior defined by the limited good by taking on lovers. Mariano was able to survive his successful venture with the phonograph because his neighbors who composed the cooperative shared in the profits. He later went on to organize a cooperative with thirty-two members to buy the first truck in town, surviving this success until he flaunted it by taking on a second wife. Juliana avoided being seen when she came to work for me on the opposite side of the town by walking through cornfields far from the beaten paths so people would not accuse her of looking for a man from the wrong side of town. Since marriage partners were limited by endogamous moieties, young people of both sexes were suspected of taking advantage of available mates beyond their moiety. I also learned that young men could be, and were in two cases, killed for courting a woman from the opposite side of the moiety. The only potters who made innovations were past the age of marriage, like Petrona, who did not have to fear the envy and consequent infertility and ostracism that came from such challenges. Lucia, who was still young and of child-bearing age, restricted herself to the traditional styles of water jugs and containers, *comales*, and *nixtamal* strainers.

When I returned to Amatenango in 1987 after twenty years' absence, the changes I saw convinced me that the level of tolerance for the display of consumption had changed, and with it the collective mores that defined acceptable behavior. Many houses flaunted tile roofs and cement block siding instead of the wattle and daub exteriors. Some even had television antennas, and trucks were parked in at least a half dozen patios. In my recurrent stays in the next two decades, I saw an expansion of consumer spending with concomitant losses of subsistence activity. How had this come about historically in the European expansion? What is the impact on the collective practices of communities like Amatenango that only recently has expanded its exchange economy?

In the following section, I shall consider the ways in which the horizons of the limited good expanded historically and how this changes social relations. A process that may have taken centuries in ancient Europe had brought about a revolution in the expectations of Mexican peasants in two decades.

EXPANDING THE HORIZONS OF THE LIMITED GOOD

Credit, productivity increase through technological innovation, capital accumulation, and investment for development are the keys to unlocking the zero sum game that subsistence producers had followed in the ancient world. These constitute the basis for an expanding vision of the environmental potential, but they also enhance the risks. In early city-states, insurance was socially constituted in the moral economy of people bound by reciprocal ties of kin and community enhanced by religious solidarities. With the opening up of the scale and extent of the economy, the moral economy was diffused as institutional relations backed by the power of the state took over. Church and customary authorities mediated the uneasy tension between the exercise of greed by dominant economic powers and the redistribution of gains throughout the society. Their attempts to curb the impact of the powerful new tools provided by credit, productivity increases, development capital, and investment beyond the local community are described below.[4]

Credit

Rosa Maria Gelpi and Francois Julien-Labruyere trace the practices related to consumer credit back to Babylon where the Code of Hammurabi, chipped on a black stone stella, records forty-two years of credit spending from 1792 to 1750 B.C. These early accounts allowed agricultural villages to trade using currency or barley and borrow at fixed rates of 33⅓ percent for cereal and 20 percent for silver. Complex repayments in kind or labor allowed for expansion of the available quantity of resources to extend one's credit into the future. In case of default, these debts were secured by commitments of the land and labor of the debtor, his wife, concubine, children, or slaves (Gelpi and Julien-Labruyere 2000, 3).

Philosophers targeted credit as the beginning of serfdom, which, they claimed, was unknown to the Hellenic tribes in the Golden Age of Greece (Gelpi and Julien-Labruyere 2000, 5). By the sixth century B.C., personal enslavement, once limited to three years, no longer had a term limit, nor were acts of the gods—such as floods or scourges that impeded repayment as in the case of Babylon—taken into account. For this reason the Athenian Solon introduced reforms of 594–591 B.C. to relieve the enslaved and insolvent debtors and to allow them to become productive citizens. The legal reforms secularized notions of justice, and floods and other disasters were no longer considered the exercise of divine justice (Gelpi and Julien-Labruyere 2000, 6). Commercial loans became a factor in increasing commerce, but the rising debt structured new wealth hierarchies. Centuries later, Jesus condemned such practices, calling upon his apostles to "forgive us our debts as we forgive the debts of our debtors," as Saint Matthew, himself a former tax collector, records in the prayer that Jesus taught them.

The Roman Empire, from the beginning of the third century A.D. when its citizens enjoyed social stability, to the end of that century when trade declined and the lack of taxes weakened the army and the state, could be used as a cautionary tale for what is happening in America right now. By the fourth century A.D. the empire could not feed its citizens, maintain its administration, nor could its citizens pay taxes even under duress (Gelpi and Julien-Labruyere 2000, 11). Again reform movements concentrated on the issue of credit, with new religious faiths condemning usurious interest rates that rose as high as 50 percent. Reformers in the late Roman Empire believed that by fixing interest rates they could remedy the crisis of the empire (Gelpi and Julien-Labruyere 2000, 13). However, they reduced rates to such a degree that credit shriveled up, and with it the horizons of great expectations—a warning to the chair of the Federal Reserve.

By the twelfth century, these lessons were ignored, and credit for the burgeoning overseas trade resumed its course. Merchant traders embarked on ships with sails set with interest-bearing loans to cross the Red Sea into Southeast Asia and down the African coast. They gave birth to the bourgeoisie that rose up against the feudal trammels of conscience opposed to usury, as they strove to maximize the exploitation of capital in the quest to achieve rising expectations. The Catholic Church condemned the rising greed for profits, but Calvinism opened the era of capitalist advance in sixteenth-century England by giving theological legitimacy to wealth acquired by wise investments (Gelpi and Julien-Labruyere 2000, 54).

The American Dream is, as Lendol Calder (1999) argues, increasingly based on credit-card spending. However, when notions of the unlimited good intrude on public or personal assessment of repayment, the consumer forfeits his/her own future. This will be discussed below when I consider how the notion of the unlimited good, while raising the levels of expectation for a better life, may also cultivate behavior that raises a specter of doom for many.

Productivity, Capital Accumulation, and Redistribution

Credit was crucial to the expansion of early city-states that encouraged wealth differences and an unloosening of the ties to people and place that once constrained the borrowing and lending to local mores. With industrialization in the late eighteenth century to the present, productivity, based on technological innovation or changes in the organization of labor, became the key to capital accumulation.

An ongoing debate in political economy is whether the value added in production by technological innovation should be assigned to capital or to labor, a debate crucial to the assessment of the just redistribution of wealth created in the production process. The liberal political economist John Stuart Mill deduced that industry is limited by capital, and that "Every addition to capital gives to labour either additional employment, or additional remuneration; enriches either the country, or the labouring class . . . though credit is but a transfer of capital from hand-to-hand, it is generally, and naturally, a transfer to hands more competent to employ the capital efficiently" (1848).

At the same crucial moment in history in the mid-nineteenth century, Marx looked at the other side of the ledger, seeing the creation of value as uniquely produced by labor. The importance of this debate lay in the policy effects on the redistribution of the proceeds from production. Thus Mill would favor the capitalist who set the mills of industry going. Marx, on the other hand, would favor the worker who created value that was appropriated by the miller's exploitation of his labor. An oft-quoted aphorism reveals the material bias of Marx's theory of progress: If the water mill produced feudalism and the steam mill produced industrialism, what mill will produce Socialism? Some would fill in the blank with computer information, while others might reject the whole structure of inquiry as too pointedly materialistic.

Technological innovation fostered steady increases in productivity during the subsequent century of industrialization. Following World War II, U.S. veterans came home to an economy that doubled its productivity in twenty-five years. In 1965 when Foster's analysis was advanced, few of his contemporaries envisioned an era of diminishing expectations either for peasants or for themselves. The key to this optimism was increased productivity, much of which depended on the stimulus generated by innovation for wartime needs. Television, electronic devices, and medical advances in penicillin and other applications of these innovations rapidly entered into private consumption expenditures. The growth in population stimulated unparalleled consumption by households in the decades of the 1950s and 1960s, and even after the slowdown in productivity following the Vietnam War in 1973, consumption levels remained high, at least four times that at the turn of the century. This was made possible not because of rising wages that failed to keep up with inflation, but because of dual wage earners in households that were increasingly ready to go into debt to buy what they wanted.

Whereas the rise in productivity was highly correlated with the growth in living standards in the mid-twentieth century, that ceased to be the case at the end of the millennium. Employees rarely benefited from rising productivity levels, since the decline of trade unions and control over the media enabled the owners of capital to claim the rewards of technological innovation. Technology became an automated competitor that reduced the need for workers in production and actually drove down wages. Since automation represented the capital investment of the owner, workers did not realize the benefit in fewer hours or higher returns.

I was able to observe this process in the 1980s when I was doing research on the impact of industry on communities in Pittsfield, Massachusetts (Nash 1989). Computers were being introduced into many levels of production and clerical management of the General Electric plant. Arguing that the computer would allow the operator to access managerial information, managers eliminated any worker who operated a computer from the union eligible list, thus decimating the membership of the International Union of Electrical Employees (IUE). Hundreds of jobs in the secretarial and even production staffs were reclassified as adjuncts of management, and the productivity of these employees was henceforth attributed to management. This tipped the balance in favor of value added to the capital rather than to the labor side of the ledger. The union was at the same time taking a crippling blow from the movement of jobs overseas in the massive direct foreign investments abroad discussed below (Nash 1989).

Increases in productivity conduce toward growth in the economy when the balance between labor and capital ensures redistribution of rewards from production. What I found in the case of Pittsfield was the increasing control of capital over labor in the process of technological innovation. This was in effect what the Luddites had expressed in their sabotage of the machines introduced in the latter part of the nineteenth century. They were not so much opposed to technological innovation as they were opposed to the loss of control over the organization of production and with it their share of the profits from innovation.[5]

Again, as in the case of credit expansion, the expanding horizons of the available good come into conflict with societal norms for balancing productivity and redistribution. Instead of conducing toward greater leisure and increased income for all workers, the greater productivity accrued to the owners of capital. Therein lies the crux between advancing social horizons and the growing wealth gap. So long as labor was able to assert a share of the rising productivity, redistributive process operated through unions to create a new balance marked in the rise of social welfare states in the industrial countries of Europe, Canada, Great Britain, and the United States.

The uneasy balance between labor and capital that seemed to have been reached within national boundaries of the north after World War II succumbed to the movement of capital investment into the underdeveloped world in the 1970s and 1980s. Offshore production of goods in low-wage countries meant the loss of well-paid jobs in industrial countries. Faced with this competition, trade unions lost their power to bargain for a living wage with multinational companies that would shift production abroad. This was the third strategy that expanded the notion of the limited good for a diminishing number of global capitalists. I recount the growing gap between rich and poor within countries and between First and Third worlds below.

Development and Direct
Foreign Investment Overseas

Walter W. Rostow became the advocate for overseas development with his book *Stages of Economic Growth, a Non-Communist Manifesto* (1960).

Inspired by the cold war, he brooked no alternatives to capitalist development. Self-sufficient household production was not even considered in his agenda since it was assumed that it would collapse of its own inertia.

During the 1960s agro-industrial enterprises promoted the "green revolution," with chemical fertilizers, pesticides, and even herbicides. While the labor released from production in developed countries could be employed in other sectors, in Third World countries these laborsaving practices had a negative impact. Food supplies increased, along with the populations of the global south, but many small-plot cultivators lost their access to land and through this their control over production and their own reproduction. Competition in global markets required huge capital investments that drove out most small-plot producers.

In Latin America land reform programs that fostered the persistence of small-plot cultivation delayed commercialization of agriculture. But when Mexico developed its own petrochemical industry in the 1970s, the government offered farmers easy credit to use chemical fertilizers and pesticides. Within two decades small-plot cultivators were heavily indebted and beginning to experience the long-term destruction to soils and the environment caused by chemical fertilizers. Many farmers lost control over their *ejido* plots as development practices undercut the balanced traditional rural subsistence economies that promoted self-sufficiency in food production of the nation.

It was also during the 1960s that global financial markets were greatly expanded by the increase in oil profits promoted by the Organization of Petroleum Exporting Countries (OPEC). With petrodollars sloshing in global financial markets, direct foreign investment in capital intensive projects proliferated. Despite the caveats of conservationists and anthropologists who advocated grassroots development projects, the rapid movement of goods and people around the globe was intensified. Ecological issues became part of the discourse, if not the practice, of governments, but the emphasis was still placed on national advantages rather than global urgency.

Theodore Schultz was one of the few mainstream economists in the 1960s to challenge the strategy of development from above and to reevaluate semisubsistence household production. Drawing from Sol Tax's careful demonstration of the rational allocation of productive efforts by Guatemalan indigenous farmers in his book *Penny Capitalism* (1950), Schultz (1964) advocated the incorporation of peasants into modernization programs on their own terms. Few policy makers acted on his advice. I recall that one U.S. Aid for International Development (AID) official in Guatemala was fired in the 1960s when he succeeded in developing a native grain for highly bred pigs that substituted for the costly American feedstuff that was part of the AID package for raising pigs.

The notion of the unlimited good that underlay such policies was driven by profit motives originating in the industrial centers rather than needs assessment in the countries that received investments. The developing agencies, such as U.S. AID, often encouraged waste of the resource that was in greatest supply in Third World countries, human labor power. This was exemplified in a film *Rice*, which was produced in the 1960s by the Rockefeller Institute in the interest of promoting green revolution technology. It opened with scenes of peasants in the Philippines laying out rice terraces bordered with selected shrubs that prevented erosion, weeding intrusive plants by hand, and preparing compost from organic materials. Declaring that this "wasted productivity" of the farmers could better be utilized in broadcast cultivation using chemical fertilizers, pesticides, and piped-in irrigation water, the film then took the viewers into a "scientific" laboratory where chemicals were produced for "progressive cultivation." The immediate gains in productivity were offset by soil depletion that was only recognized a decade later. Ecologists saw the devastating effects of this revolution in the 1970s and began to advocate a balance between the new technology and earlier practices. But growing land shortages forced the increasingly desperate farmers to continue these intensive practices.

Despite warnings of these early critics of development, direct foreign investments (DFI) in highly capitalized enterprises, such as hydroelectric dams and super highways, multiplied as OPEC dollars washed up on the shores of developed capitalist centers. Finance capital took priority over investment capital as inflated notions of the unlimited good gained proponents throughout the world.

The persistent impoverishment and indebtedness of Third World countries disclaimed assumptions based on the trickle-down effect of capitalist accumulation. The neglect of the problem of a fair wage to labor or a fair price to the producer—which is basic to the notion of the limited good—was often explained on the basis of the difficulty in measuring the value added by labor and profits accruing to capital. A more pervasive impediment to addressing the problem of equitable redistribution came from notions of the unlimited good that cultivated greed. Once one accepts the underlying assumption that anyone could acquire wealth if they have the energy and intelligence to grab what is available, then the poor have only themselves to blame. Yet in the euphoria over rising fortunes of the 1970s, feminists were the first to shatter the assumption that income was shared equally among members of the same household, showing the greater leisure enjoyed by men and greater control over disposable income in expenditures. Studies of wageworkers exposed the falsity of a second assumption, that a rise in the GNP would benefit all families regardless of class and ethnic position. These studies showed a declining real income of wageworkers during the decades of rising growth in GNP.

Critics of globalization undermined a third assumption explaining the backward sloping curves of the global south as due to "feudalistic" practices or corruption, showing that the global north advanced with each crisis in the global economy. The critique of dependency grew in the 1960s as Andrew Gundar Frank (1965) and Cardoso and Faletto (1971) showed that capitalist economic development served to underdevelop the economies of Latin American critics of globalization. Like Samir Amin's analysis of African underdevelopment (1970), they emphasized the unequal basis for exchange between developed and underdeveloped economies, with industrial goods commanding higher prices than raw materials and agricultural products, and tied this to dependency on capital from metropolitan centers.

Critiques of development in both Latin America and Africa showed that the release of productive forces ensured the unlimited good only for a narrow cohort who benefited from capital-intensive development. The critique sharpened in the following decades, along with the increasing gap between rich and poor countries.

THE SPECTER OF THE UNLIMITED GOOD

The United States once offered the American dream to all its citizens and to the rest of the world. That was a dream of mobility, realizing the goals of home ownership, a college education for one's children, a dream that was for many realized in the unparalleled growth in productivity in the quarter century following World War II. Whereas World War II veterans were able to reap the rewards of an economy that doubled its productivity in a quarter of a century, these horizons receded with the Vietnam War (Krugman 1990, 9). Increasing disparities between rich and poor became more pronounced with the altered distribution of wealth in the Reagan-Bush era, when only a narrowing elite could achieve unlimited horizons. A struggling middle class continued to aspire to the old standards with both parents working and with credit-card spending, but low-wage sectors could no longer pretend that their horizons could broaden.

With the government resorting to tax-cutting policies and the reduction of social welfare expenditures while running up a huge deficit on overseas aggressions, the CEOs of major corporations enjoyed an explosion in their salaries to seven and eight figures. The public learned of this as the inflated lifestyle of corporate executives was brought to light in court as a result of corruption charges or divorce. Shocking disclosures about the multimillion-dollar homes, lavish parties costing hundreds of thousands of dollars, and payoffs to friends of Enron and World.com executives came to light as the principals were brought to trial. We learned of the former CEO of General Electric receiving more than $220 million in retirement benefits when his divorced wife brought him to court to gain $13 million, and we caught a glimpse of Tyco's CEO accompanied by his trophy wife as they appeared at his trial when he was accused and finally condemned for looting the company of $600 million.

Yet as the favored few indulge the greed promoted by the image of an unlimited good, the expanding horizons fostered in the decades following the Second World War have turned into a specter of impending doom for the majority. Not even those who appear to benefit from the unequal distribution of rewards can enjoy their privileged position. Citigroup, a private bank with a "family advisory practice" (read: how to avoid paying inheritance taxes) professes to enable the affluent to "bear the burden of wealth." Their advisers not only give advice on where to invest one's wealth, but also grapple with issues beyond the technical: what is the effect of inheritance? How do you instill a sense of responsibility in children who may never have to work? The answers they provide address responsibility to a narrow band of kin-related people that will be the beneficiaries of wealth accumulated in the client's lifetime. The capitalist barons of the early twentieth century appear as giants of philanthropy in building cathedrals and museums that validated their wealth compared to Microsoft's Bill Gates, who hastily set up his foundation when faced with a congressional inquiry into his monopolistic practices.

How have easy credit, rising productivity, and overseas development, which served as the keys to expanding the horizons of the limited good, narrowed to become a specter of the unlimited good? My basic argument is that distortions in the economy and society arose as access to the goods of life became limited to a narrow elite both at home and in the developing countries. Credit-card spending by those who aspire to unlimited consumption but do not have the means to satisfy their desires encourages personal debt, adding to the vulnerability of an economy in which the government is fast becoming the major debtor of all time. Productivity increases without yielding rewards to those who work within the economy fail to promote future investment. As the flight of capital seeking low wages and low or absent taxes progresses, the social welfare sector is reduced and the gap between rich and poor increases globally. I shall briefly review these processes in the United States and overseas areas to which the privatized capitalist mode of production was exported.

CREDIT-CARD BUYING AND ADDICTIVE CONSUMPTION

With ever more available credit-card lending, consumption became an addictive habit rather than a means of survival. Lendol Calder (1999, 9) shows the expansion of debt in graphic terms: In 1928 consumer debt was $6.5 billion on the eve of the stock market crash. Three decades later in 1958 it was $45 billion. Only seven years later it had more than doubled to $94.8 billion. But in 1988 it had increased sevenfold to $666 billion. The burden of these high-interest loans is carried particularly by low income, minority people, who are not able to acquire bank loans at non-usurious fees. As Robert Manning (2000, 19–20) tells the story, the expansion of credit-card consumption at usurious rates is a new aspect of class warfare that is not perceived as such.

But problems also confront the affluent, particularly in the second generation born in the decades from 1950 to 1970. Whatever remained of Victorian premises of thrift in the parental generation was filtered out in a booming economy that promoted high expectations and a willingness to go into debt on the part of their children. When the boomers came of age in the 1970s and 1980s, 68 percent of Americans carried credit cards; now when their children go to college, they are targeted long before graduation. The greatest surge in credit-card spending and bankruptcies came in the late 1980s when charges for the average cardholder debt carrying interest of 18 percent per year increased from $395 to $2,355. By 1994 revolving debt averaged $4,000 per household, and the nation's total consumer debt had risen to $603 billion (U.S. Bureau of Economic Analysis, National Income and Product Accounts of the U.S. 1929–1995, cited in Manning 2000, 13). Seventy percent of students now carry more than a $2,000 debt that is typically maintained in a revolving account for which they pay an annual interest rate of 17 percent.

With each life crisis, credit-card debt expands. Keeping up with the availability of credit, retailers have developed new and more finely tuned ways of promoting purchases. Each day the postman stuffs my mailbox with sales catalogs, anticipating each life cycle change, and with each purchase I become a new persona to target. When I purchased a child's toy for a new godchild, I began to receive granny books with toys and clothing that would befit Little Orphan Annie when Daddy Warbucks arrived in her life. A purchase of a fairly modest flannel nightgown from Victoria's Secret promoted a rush of catalogs offering risqué underclothes from Boston Proper to La Redoute. After I purchased a set of self-watering planters for my small New York apartment there arrived gardeners' manuals and lawn furniture catalogs advertising teak benches and sun-energy lamps for improving my "country estate." When I signed up for Medicare, I was deluged with catalogs for chair assist lifts, support stockings, and antiwrinkle cream. Competitive spending on life crises has escalated. A New York Times article (July 13, 2003:1, 17) indicates that couples take on an average of $25,000 in debt for elaborate weddings. The inflated spending neither adds to the security of the marriage, nor to domestic fealty, since the aggravation of the debt burden assumed with the wedding often leads to a breakup within two years of the marriage.

With the return of inflated spending and tax cutting in the current Bush regime, the "debt industry" is the most flourishing enterprise, with the marriage of banking and credit branches facilitating unparalleled domestic and national indebtedness. What do we face with the looming fiscal crisis caused by debt? We have already seen the stagnation of consumer production in the United States, and personal savings have declined to depression-era levels. The rise in stock market indexes in the last few years has done little to improve employment prospects of U.S. workers. The tax breaks to the top income group are not invested in domestic production but, rather, in China and other overseas ventures. WalMart remains at the top of the Forbes 500 list of corporations and is the major employer, providing minimum wage jobs for retirees and teenagers at less than minimum wages for youthful and aging workers who do not receive medical and social benefits. And retail companies do not offset the growing trade imbalance.

PRODUCTIVITY INCREASES
WITHOUT GROWTH IN EMPLOYMENT

Even the good news brings with it a worsening of the crisis for those who are marginalized by these trends. The "burst of strength" marked by the U.S. economy in the last quarter of 2003 when the U.S. economy rose by 3.3 percent was attended by a rise in poverty from 31.6 million to 39.3 million (U.S. Census Bureau, reported in the *Berkshire Eagle* December 13, 2003, 1, 2). Productivity increases in the same quarter also failed to generate increased wages or employment to make up for the 2.7 million jobs lost in the recession from March 2001 to the belated surge late in 2003. This led some economists, notably Paul Krugman (*Berkshire Eagle* August 13, 2003), to question the tax cuts that have dominated Republicans' crusade for the past twenty-five years and to call for "fiscal sustainability." Meanwhile the cutback in government services in education, health, and national security at home threatens our way of life in ways that add to future costs in crime, destruction of whole communities as in New Orleans, and declining prospects in leading-edge technology. Tax cuts serve only the rich in the game of shrinking government in the social sector while expanding militarily throughout the world.

The failure of wages to keep up with productivity is due in part to the decline in unionized jobs. The eight-hour day remains fixed in the standard employment schedule and wages and welfare benefits have shrunk with privatization of government services. In the first three years of the third millennium, the loss of jobs has affected not only the United States, which runs a huge trade deficit with China, but also countries of the global south—especially Mexico and the Caribbean—that had, in previous decades, received U.S. direct foreign investment. With each job lost, the vision of the unlimited good is further restricted in its potential to improve the general welfare of society.

THE UNDERDEVELOPMENT OF DEVELOPING COUNTRIES

The export of capital overseas was the solution of classical economists to stagnation in the profit rate for domestic investment. Following World War II, direct foreign investments in Europe through the Marshall Plan stimulated the economies of the United States as well as Europe. Yet when the same strategies were applied to Africa and Latin America, the development programs backfired. In this situation the critique of development as a means of expanding the social good gathered force. This occurred during the debt crisis of the 1980s when the national economies of Mexico, Brazil, and Argentina were on the brink of bankruptcy until they were "rescued" by the International Monetary Fund (IMF) at the price of accepting crippling conditions. Criticism spread when the financial crises in Indonesia and Thailand were exacerbated by the conditions imposed by the World Bank and the IMF.[6]

Africa has become an extreme example of the failure of Adam Smith's dictum that man's self-interest can lead to the best of all possible worlds (Morton 1994, 244). Morton attributes this to the fact that elites of the countries that gained independence following World War II pursued self-gratification without any compulsion to "paying the corresponding development price of sacrificing their authority" to the state (1994). Nor do they respond to the "ceremonial fund" that traditional societies once provided in the form of celebrations for the small holders and wage earners who lack the political power to claim their due share in the common good. The lack of a legitimized governing authority deprives such nations of accountability for their own expenditures or the aid provided by nongovernmental organizations (NGOs).

The increasing disparity between rich and poor nations and segments of populations within nations contributes to the social dislocations and rising incidence of violence in the new age of diminishing expectations. When Joseph Stiglitz, chief economist of the World Bank, wrote his summary of the economy in the last year of the millennium, he called for a more serious evaluation of poverty indexes as an indicator of economic stability or disruption (Stiglitz 2000, viii). Since then he has become an emissary for the critics of globalization, denouncing the global financial institutions for their failure to ensure a just redistribution of wealth as he did in the Mumbai Forum in January 2004 (*La Jornada* January 20, 2004, 27). Deploring the economic dogma of his discipline prioritizing competitive advantage in neoliberal global markets, Stiglitz criticized the trends of globalization resulting in unemployment and demonstrated their links to insecurity and violence.

Ultimately the failure of development within the nation and beyond is a result of the dissolution of the social contract between the state and the people. This in turn evolves with the cutoff in the connection between wages and spending, between production and distribution, and between investment and needs. The distortion in these basic political economic equations conduces toward a greedy appropriation of the unlimited good by the powerful and the marginalization of the vast majority. The result is not a zero sum game in which the winner gains at the expense of fellow players, but rather a no-win game with everyone the loser.

FINDING A BALANCE

In Foster's terms, the shared cognitive orientation in every society provides the members of any society with basic premises that guide behavior (Foster 1965, 293–94). In Tzintzuntzan the notion of the limited good as one in which all desired things existed in short supply and in finite quantities promoted invidious behaviors since people could progress only at the expense of another member of the same community. The negative impact of this constricted vision led to punitive action against anyone who exceeded culturally condoned limits to consumption and investment. Foster's solution was to promote economic opportunities that would provide a way out.

Shortly after George Foster left his field station in 1963 the Mexican bank Banrural made credit available to allow peasants to take advantage of technological innovations of the "green revolution" introduced by Mexico's petrochemical industry. These credits allowed peasants throughout the country to transgress the old limits imposed by their cognitive orientation. At the same time, the cognitive connections between work, available resources, and standards of consumption that were deeply embedded in previous generations of peasants were often lost, along with the land that ensured their livelihood.[7] In the long term the loss of an ethic of conservation and personal independence based on thrift and concern for the future poses a threat to the nation. Since the early 1980s, Mexico has become dependent on corn imports as well as other foods, and with the North American Free Trade Agreement (NAFTA) of 1994 even the most resistant rural indigenous peasantry is beginning to succumb to the intrusion of imported, often biogenetically altered, food crops.

Mayan cultivators, pastoralists, and artisans who have migrated from the coast and highland communities to settle in the Lacandón Rain Forest are now marking an alternative path. The revolt in 1994 of the Zapatista Army of National Liberation (EZLN) was a rejection of their marginalization from the national project defined by neoliberalism. Government funds at the local level promoted a dependent relationship between indigenous officeholders and federal agencies—called *caciquismo*—or bossism that deprived the majority of democratic representation. In the intervening decade, indigenous leaders succeeded in negotiating the San Andrés Agreement with the government of President Ernesto Zedillo in February 1996. Since the Congress failed to implement the agreement, and the administrations of both President Zedillo and President Vicente Fox have instead maintained a repressive army of occupation in the territory where they were promised title to lands, Zapatistas and their support communities have asserted their autonomy in the *Juntas de Buen Gobierno* (Gatherings of the Good Government). In the proceedings of these governing councils, which they call *caracoles* (snail shells), that are a metaphor of the Mayan theme of cyclical time, they seek continuity of the past in the present.

Those indigenes who have chosen to support the Zapatistas bring to the world they are trying to create a profound sense of their own vision of the natural limits of the good things in the world.[8] By communicating their knowledge of the real scarcities that exist in that world to the rest of "civil society"—the national and international visitors who come to the jungle to listen and learn—the Zapatistas and their supporters hope to promote an understanding of the need for sharing the scarcity rather than fighting a war against the poor.

Zapatistas are not alone in seeking an alternative to global capitalism. When the *Congreso Nacional Indígena* (CNI) met in March 2004, there were, in addition to the Juntas de Buen Gobierno in Chiapas, representatives of indigenous people in Guerrero, Oaxaca, Morelos, Michoacán, the Distrito Federal, and Veracruz. All reached a consensus to support the San Andrés Agreement, and many joined the discussion of how they should defend their lands and forests against the depredation of hydroelectric power and lumber companies through illegal confiscation and sales by the government. Rejecting political parties as a route to achieve their distinctive goals as indigenes, they called for general assemblies that would operate collectively as the maximum authority for the recognition of diversity and for vindication of historical memory and identity.[9]

Their pleas have not been heard in international circuits. In the summer of 2005, the Juntas de Buen Gobierno were closed when the Zapatista leaders perceived a threat to their alternative practices. As yet, the leaders of a globalizing economy have failed to seek a balance in the expanding horizons of development, behaving as though the resources of the world are indeed unlimited. They have instead exploited resources at ever increasing rates of depletion, often using military force to facilitate their activities. As their awareness of the danger to their ways of life grows, it is the semisubsistence cultivators, fisherfolk, and the remaining hunters and gatherers of the world who are leading the crusade to retain small-plot cultivation, organic farming, the preservation of wildlife, and conservation of forests. The alternative global dialogue that began in Rio de Janeiro in 1992 followed by meetings in Brazil a decade later confirmed the reality of a multicultural force united in defense of the distinct heritages that contribute to diversity and survival in the world.

The World Social Forum meeting in Mumbai, India, in January 2004 was a showcase of culturally distinct people who gathered together to discuss alternatives to neoliberal globalism. The meeting united the tribal people of India with refugees from Buthan and Tibet, the fisherfolk and hunters of Thailand concerned with punishing industries that contaminate their rivers and forests, and cultivators that rejected transgenic seeds that destroy ecological systems of biodiversity. Citizens of Mandra Munda in Bihar, who for seven thousand years guarded their sacred food of rice for their god Simbonga and for humanity, shared the story of the miracle of this basic crop with Indians of Anáhuac in Mexico who spoke of the gift of corn from their god Quetzalcóatl. Their sense of the value of the gifts that each group preserves is heightened by the awareness of the fragility of the scarce resources that ensure survival. Hopefully their lesson will penetrate the specter of greed cultivated by the image of the unlimited good.

NOTES

This paper was presented as the Fifth Annual George and Mary Foster Distinguished Lecture in Cultural Anthropology, Southern Methodist University, April 5, 2004.

1. David Kaplan and Benson Saler (1968: 202–5) attacked Foster's thesis of the notion of the limited good as a tautological inference from observed behavior that lacks reference to a coherent group. The very term "peasant" has had a fraught history that need not be adumbrated here, except to recall their status as semisubsistence cultivators often having access to collective lands and resources that maintain communal identity. This attachment to an increasingly scarce and dwindling resource in itself promotes a parochial view of their access to the world that is captured in the image of the limited good.

2. See summaries of peasant alternatives to global integration in Nash (1994, 2003a).

3. For Tzeltal-speaking Mayas of Chiapas, the Lord of the Underworld is the counterpart to the Me'tiktatik, Mother-Father creators embodied in the Sun and the Moon, present in the *Popol Vuh* account of the origin of the world. In Amatenango people equated the Lord of the Underworld with Don Klabil, a recently deceased ladino, Don David, who lent money to Indians at high rates of interest (Nash 1970).

4. Karl Polanyi (1957) analyzed the transition from substantive economies relying on kin and personal ties to market economies with formal economic claims in commercial exchange. The moral commitment in substantive economies is captured in James Scott (1977).

5. See Eric Thompson (1963) for an assessment of the historic role of the Luddites in England.

6. Jeffrey Sachs, who instituted IMF conditions during the 1985–1986 debt crisis in Bolivia, later turned against tactics of the fund during the 1997 crisis in the economies of Indonesia and Thailand.

7. Cf. Barkin (1987) and Bartra (1982) for the history of the loss of food self-sufficiency with the introduction of capitalist practices into the countryside.

8. Carlos Monsovais (*La Jornada* January 15, 2004, 15) calls the Zapatista vision "the truly mysterious: the world of scarcity without limits (*escasez sin limites*)."

9. See Duncan Earle and Jeanne Simonelli (2005) for a discussion of the Juntas de Buen Gobierno and the way in which they function with civil society.

3

Women in Between

Globalization and the New Enlightenment

Women's perspectives have attained the significance of a new enlightenment, overtaking the seventeenth-century Enlightenment. In the Cartesian view of nature as something to be controlled and dominated, women were relegated to immanent positions in a world of transcendent male philosophers, scientists, and conquerors who defined, categorized, and ruled a society made rational by their civilizing mission. Women's everyday work in reproducing society was invisible until recent decades, when feminist scholars and activists began to explore women's contribution to society and the survival of the human species. Women's mediating positions linking families to communities, and communities to larger political, economic, and social circuits, become crucial to survival where global development processes have undermined social reproduction.

I shall argue that the multilateral and resilient approach that women and other marginalized populations manifest enables them to assess more clearly their personal situation in relation to global issues. Whether their marginality stems from social, ethnic, gender, or class positions, their consciousness of injustice provides a baseline for understanding global trends in embodied terms. This kind of knowledge, cultivated in the immanent roles assigned to subordinates in the world system, promotes a new enlightenment based on gender-balanced and multicultural understandings. Once collectively mobilized, it could become strategic in providing an alternative to domination by global corporations. The danger lies in the erosion of such a collective perspective when women gain success as actors equivalent to men in an individual-ized and privatized global society.

Those of us who have survived the transformative decades since the 1970s, during which women's perspectives were introduced into scientific discourse, can now evaluate critically the contested discourses of early feminism. Some feminists drew on the rational, scientific paradigm exemplified by René Descartes, including his identification of women with nature and men with culture—and, by extension, civilization—and the assumptions that women were everywhere subordinated to men.[1] Simone de Beauvoir (1957) targeted the problem, but her desire to join the ranks of transcendent males occluded the importance of female roles. She despaired that the "second sex" was biologically doomed to imma-nent roles. By that she—and her transcendent mentor Immanuel Kant—meant biologically determined reproductive roles. Her escape was to deny maternal functions and the nurturing roles imposed by "nature" on women. Contesting this conclusion, a feminist critique of Enlighten-ment rationalism began to expose the fallacy of universal gender roles based on dichotomized oppositions and unilineal evolution that en-dowed men, particularly European men, with the roles of philosophers and kings. Pointing to evidence from missionaries, conquerors, and trav-elers, ethnographers began to construct historicized accounts of how women's roles in the Western hemisphere changed with the advent of colonization (Etienne and Leacock 1980). Others analyzed the transfor-mations in women's roles from egalitarian or complementary roles to fe-male subordination within New World empires (Nash 1978; Silverblatt 1987). The breakdown of gender hierarchy based on naturalized differ-ences opened up research into women's domains of knowledge and methods of discovery.

Today the Kantian pole of immanence in the world of lived experience is no longer the Cinderella hearth of a society dominated by transcendent males. Everyday experience is being examined, extrapolated, and extolled as the fount of social science insights and the touchstone of reality. The task remains to incorporate these understandings in collective action. By reclaiming cognition from the transcendent cerebral sphere and inserting it into the daily interactions of people through communication systems, Jürgen Habermas (1984) opened the door to admitting reflexivity and cog-nitive thought in the lived world. Michael Billig et al. (1988) expanded the study of interactive communication, which allowed both practical and re-flective responses that enable people to act in common. This gave greater impetus to the analyses of narratives as ways of exploring people's con-sciousness in spontaneous and uncensored discourse.

It is in this immanent field of consciousness that Dorothy Smith (1987, 1990) produced a feminist methodology in which the everyday world became problematic. As a second-generation feminist who learned to understand the subordination of women from Beauvoir but rejected Beauvoir's selection of the transcendent sphere, Smith accepted her own immanence in the world of practicality. This allowed her to explore a range of experience ignored by theoreticians of her day. Speaking of her contemporaries, women who came of age in the 1950s, she found that they excelled in communicative interactions. She herself acquired her fundamental notions of what constituted women's work as a wife and secretary, but instead of rejecting these premises out of hand, she recognized their value in social reproduction. In the social sciences, women's culturally constituted perspectives direct our attention to an embodied subject located in a particular historical setting (1987, 110). Smith says of the feminist methodology she was forging with other women in the 1980s:

> Instead of constructing theories that will explain, I am concerned in how to contextualize or how to constitute the textuality of social phenomena where conceptual practices remain salient . . . preserving the presence of subjects in our accounts. (1987, 106)

This brief digression into feminist ways of knowing serves as a bridge to address what has become visible in the ethnological field as women become both the chroniclers and subjects of social science discourse. This new enlightenment rivals that which occurred in the seventeenth century when Descartes and his colleagues exercised their prerogatives as transcendent males to consign peoples of the world to appropriate places in a hierarchical order of men over women, managers of labor over workers, and the civilized (presumably European) nations over the primitive and/or feudal orders. The seventeenth-century Enlightenment opened up universal visions of liberation, but only elite males could realize these. The rest could aspire to join the enlightened only by rejecting their incarnation as women or as primitive others. In mid-twentieth-century Europe, Beauvoir criticized the intellectual elites of a rational Enlightenment but could not accept an alternate life. Smith also engaged the intellectual life but embraced the embodiment of knowledge.

The new enlightenment promoted by the opening up of civil society to women, indigenous groups, and others excluded from the chambers of the elect was not immediately realized. The distance between third-world feminists and those who were socialized in the first world grew from distinct premises that were fomenting in the mid-twentieth century. I became aware of this when Helen Safa and I co-organized the first conference on feminine perspectives for the Social Science Research Council in 1974. After traveling for a month throughout Latin America, visiting universities and research centers to find people doing research on gender, we felt we had succeeded in getting a representative group. But when we arrived at the conference site in Buenos Aires, we found ourselves confronted with a picket line of women charging us with yet another imperialist takeover, this time by U.S. feminists. When we were able to enter into a dialogue with the picketers, all of whom were dedicated activist researchers, we recognized the basis for the difference: whereas we had been challenging the gated entrance to academia and the limited vision this portends, these women were fighting for control over reproductive practices, for family welfare issues at the grass roots, and against the militarization of society. Former Argentinean president Juan Perón had just returned from exile in Spain with his new consort, Isabella, and the contest for power in the nation exacerbated the tensions that Argentinean women were challenging us to address. We invited the picketers to participate in our sessions and to raise these issues in the plenary meetings.

Although I was personally transformed by the experience, the tension between theoretical and activist social science remains, and the distinct commitments of first- and third-world feminisms persist. The feminist movement has given prominence to women and to those who share their concerns as mediators between theoretical concerns and activist applications in their nongovernmental organizations (NGOs) and grass-roots organizations. In a global society where the threat of nuclear war-

Figure 3.1.   Indigenous women of Chiapas join men in the march to protest government withdrawal of social services, 1995.

fare looms closer than ever since the end of the cold war, it is important to assess how specific commitments to living in the world that are characteristic of women, and particularly third-world women, can mediate ideological differences.

The new era of enlightenment is a product of social movements calling for greater participation by those who were marginalized from the civil society constituted by elites of the earlier Enlightenment. The feminist and civil rights movements cultivated the cultural diversity that was suppressed in nations constructed on the model of eighteenth-century Jeffersonian or French revolutions.[2] Feminists who inspire or join such movements are saying that they were never a part of the empires or democracies that were constructed in the five hundred years of conquest and empire building. They point out that the revolutions inspired by the earlier Enlightenment were fought in the name of liberty, equality, and justice for all men and that women (like slaves) were not included. Yet women's complicity as reproducers of life—socially as well as biologically—often meant a commitment to the status quo in which they were subordinated. The distinctive knowledge gained by balancing these commitments to life with commitments to progress and advancement in the world is what gives focus to the new enlightenment that I propose to identify and to nurture.

What changes are wrought in the new enlightenment? The division of labor that sustained the Kantian dichotomy between the immanent world of nonreflective subjectivities and the transcendent world of thinking and postulating actors is breaking down. Sharing in what had been roles strictly limited by gender and ethnicity such as childcare and housework tends to undermine some of the hierarchical structures based on the separation of such roles. More important, women and other subordinated people are beginning to redefine the division of labor and how that should change. At the same time, women in working families are losing the security of stable households and the income of a male provider along with the dependency that entailed. The imposition of flexible regimes of accumulation translates into job instability as production is shifted to overseas sites and as technological innovation makes people obsolete along with the machines they serve.[3] Gender antagonism develops and explodes in these settings, as I shall describe below. Yet at the same time alternatives to role dichotomy are opening the possibility of a mutual engagement in the project of living. The awakening of consciousness among indigenous women in the third world expands the horizons of feminist and humanistic thought regarding the potential of humankind.

I shall discuss three instances of rapidly changing gender roles in globalization and how feminist activist researchers perceive and analyze them. The first is in Nicaragua, where women were part of the armed rebellion of the Sandinistas; the second is at the U.S.-Mexican border, where export-oriented assembly plants, or *maquiladoras*, were introduced in the neoliberal regime of flexible production; and the third is on Mexico's southern border, where Zapatistas and their supporters are confronting the neoliberal Plan Puebla Panamá proposed by Mexico's president Vicente Fox. By juxtaposing issues raised by feminists with issues affecting both ethnic groups mobilizing for their rights and workers who are losing their rights of citizenship in global enterprises, we can assess the advances in theory and practice developing among populations who were not part of elite social discourse in the early Enlightenment. I shall argue that the contribution of these groups is the key to a new enlightenment addressing changes in global society.

NICARAGUAN FEMINISTS AND INDIGENOUS RIGHTS

Feminist and indigenous rights movements are central to what are called new social movements based on issues of identity. Theorists are correct in recognizing these alternative sites of social activism (Alvarez 1998), but in their analyses two qualifying conditions must be kept in mind. First, multiple social positions complicate social interpretations, as Ernesto Laclau and Chantal Mouffe (1985) maintain: a woman is not only a woman but may also be an underpaid maquiladora worker and/or an Indian. Second, in the multiple social positions they occupy, people are also responding to historical changes in the conditions that affect their lives, as Alaine Touraine (1988) argues.

With these qualifications in mind, I shall try to show how structurally based inequalities motivate movements identified as feminist and indigenous in Nicaragua during the Sandinista and neoliberal periods of the 1980s and 1990s. But because both feminists and indigenes shared an identity as poor people and as citizens in the Sandinista revolutionary government, they were also responding to exogenous changes that affected the country in ways that did not correspond to exclusively feminist or indigenous interests. Nicaraguan women who had been engaged in neighborhood committees to care for victims of the 1972 earthquake and who were angered by the misappropriation of relief funds began to participate in the armed struggle against Anastasio Somoza (Molyneux 1985, 228). This "combative motherhood" role promoted by Sandinistas began to wane as casualties rose in the U.S.-backed action that engaged the country in a fratricidal war. Maxine Molyneux recognizes the government's success in promoting social welfare throughout 1982 and much of 1983 but shows that, as the war made demands on the impoverished nation, the emancipation of women was sidelined (1985). For women, who constitute 60 percent of the poorest Nicaraguans, state welfare assistance could not replace the social insurance provided by husbands or sons who might be killed in the war. Diane Molinari (1988), who carried out field-work in Nicaragua during the early years of the Sandinista victory and returned when the Contra rebellion was well underway, noted that, just as the women of Managua's poor barrios had mobilized against Somoza in 1979, so did they turn against the Sandinistas by voting for Violeta Chamorro in 1990. Molinari contends that in both instances the women's inability to fulfill their domestic roles defined their political commitment.

I witnessed some of the contradictions based on conflicting identities of gender, class, and ethnicity when I joined a group of academics organized by the Committee in Solidarity with the Peoples of El Salvador to investigate the Contra war in Nicaragua in 1982. While we were in Nicaragua, educated women of the middle class were engaged in their attempts to write a new constitution that would include the rights of women. The Nicaraguan Women's Association, or Asociación de Mujeres Nicaraguenses "Luisa Amanda Espinosa,"[4] was calling for greater control over their lives and their bodies, the right to divorce, to have the number of children they wanted, and to manage their own wealth, whether inherited or earned. Women of the barrios, in contrast, shared a growing apprehension about the deaths of their husbands and sons in the war against the Contras, an apprehension that made some question their loyalty to the revolution.[5]

The degree to which the Sandinistas forged the construction of women as nonpolitical subjects—ceremoniously making them official members of the Mothers of Heroes and Martyrs—perpetuated the dependency of women's groups on the Sandinista party. But after the Sandinista defeat in 1990 the state could no longer contain a radicalized feminist movement that resisted the neoliberal changes ushered in by Violetta Chamorro in 1990 (Babb 2001, 206). The Nicaraguan women who became an essential part of the government's maquila industrial program as cheap, expendable labor sustained one of the longest strikes since the North American Free Trade Agreement (NAFTA) went into effect in 1994. In this struggle they defied state authority, the apathy of trade unions representing the male workforce, and the threats of foreign-based firms as they asserted the rights of workers to organize. This new independence in the gender struggle must be theorized along with women's rejection of the demagoguery that confines the parameters of their struggle to a single facet of maternity.

At the same time feminist issues were beginning to surface in the early 1980s, the Sandinistas had just begun to relocate indigenous Misquito communities inland from their coastal habitat, where they had developed a semisubsistence economy based on fishing and commercial exchanges.

This had allowed them to be independent of the Nicaraguan government from the colonial period through independence. The Sandinistas justified the relocation on the basis of "security reasons," since some of these communities had joined the rebel forces or assisted the counterinsurgency effort. With the mediation of a research institute established by Charles Hale, an anthropologist working in the southeastern Nicaraguan region of Bluefields, the Sandinista government was able to reestablish contacts with the Misquito of Sandy Bay. The resulting dialogue between the Contra and Sandinista positions allowed both sides to come to a resolution recognizing autonomy and allocating a territorial reserve in 1984. As Hale points out in his book, *Resistance and Contradiction* (1994, 13–15), this compromise was achieved when Sandinistas rejected the economism—or class reductionism—endemic to Marxism, on the one hand, while the Misquito opened their ranks to more radical trends, on the other.

Comparing these two distinct but parallel instances of actors responding to identity interests—women threatened with the loss of their sons and husbands and natives threatened with the loss of subsistence base and way of life—we can perceive the importance of identity politics but also its inadequacy as a holistic explanation. Cartesian dichotomies are not predictive of beliefs and behavior; larger structural issues are at stake than those made explicit in the discourse about the demands of women or of indigenes as actors in defense of their identity. Women, especially those in the barrios who were asked to sacrifice their men and children to the revolution, were questioning the course of militarism and what some considered to be an intransigent position in Nicaraguan relations with the United States. If gender interests are to be realized within the larger context (Babb 2001), as Molyneux (1985) hypothesizes, then the political institutions charged with them must eventually respond to the women's specific interests as well as to class demands. In the case of the ethnic revolt, strategic intervention and the cultivation of a dialogue that resulted in autonomy legislation resolved the larger issue that had threatened the allegiance of the Misquito. Responses to these specific demands of women and of indigenes proved to be transformative for society as a whole.

FLEXIBLE PRODUCTION AND THE MAQUILADORAS

Turning to another site of global capital advance, this one on the northern border of Mexico, Patricia Fernández-Kelly's (1983) study provided a landmark case of the expansion of export-oriented production in Mexico as foreign direct investments (FDI) increased exponentially in low-wage areas in the Americas. With unusual clarity and foresight Fernández-Kelly shows how foreign capitalists were able to gain entry into the low-wage Mexican labor markets at a time when restrictions on Mexican migration to the United States were imposed. Because of the desperate economic situation, investors were able to gain tax-free production sites with few environmental restrictions, where they could avoid costs related to social reproduction. They also gained assurances from the Mexican government that labor unions would not be permitted. At the same time the owners of the *maquilas* gained access to the huge U.S. market with a U.S. congressional act allowing for tariffs to be calculated on the basis of value added (i.e., the low wages of the women themselves) rather than the total value of the product.

Women were drawn to the border by illusory promises of secure jobs and access to consumer goods beyond their dreams. Fernández-Kelly shows the growing contradictions in a distorted labor market where women, as the major wage earners, challenged the culturally constructed image of men as breadwinners.[6] The promises were illusory since the women were subjected to uncertainty because of high turnover and the lack of benefits that could provide security to them or their families. Gender antagonism was present from the early years. Men who were turned back in their attempt to cross the border into the United States still had better access to organized labor unions, and they, along with state and national politicians, pressured the maquilas to open some positions to male workers. Since it was assumed that the men would be "permanent" workers, in contrast to the necessarily "temporary" female workers, they were able to enter training programs for the few supervisory and managerial positions available in the maquilas. In these positions they could impose control over the sexuality as well as the work performance of the workers. Fernández-Kelly reported the required use of birth control pills and the firing of women who got pregnant. Gender antagonism combined with class antagonism flourished in a sexist and racist environment that cultivated misogyny (Fernández-Kelly 1983).

If we fast-forward to the late 1990s, we gain another perspective on the tangled story of women on the northern frontier. In the decade from 1993 to 2003 more than 4,476 women and girls have disappeared, and 303 were murdered in the vicinity of Ciudad Juárez, Chihuahua. They had in common the characteristics of being poor, young—between teenage and thirty years of age—and dark skinned, and many were workers in the maquilas. The owners of the maquilas refused to take even the minimum precautions advocated by women's rights groups during the decade of phenomenal growth in maquilas. The cases, which were ignored or treated in a desultory fashion by Mexican border police, attracted the attention of the Interamerican Commission on Human Rights and women's groups. These groups put pressure on the police, especially at the time around International Women's Day, to carry out more extensive investigations (*La Jornada* March 8, 2003).[7]

The maquilas are a classic example of an institution structured on Cartesian principles of gender. First, there is consistent pressure from the start against political organization of and by female workers in the maquilas. Second, the conjunction of male-dominated trade unions with male-dominated government agencies, which provide the institutional basis for the hiring and training procedures of maquilas, ensured male prerogatives in the Mexican borderlands. Trade unions on both sides of the Mexican-U.S. border have historically neglected women workers because they have been considered temporary or, even worse, competitively destructive of the higher wages men could command. Lacking the support of government representatives who might respond to the labor unions, women are further cut off from wage-earning opportunities. Until recently women's only alternative was to turn to human rights commissions in international courts less responsive to the patriarchal system that operates in the local settings.

The other key to women's vulnerability in the rapidly expanding industrialization of the border area is the fragmentation of society and the precarious household economy. Here we can learn more from activists than from a postmodernist deconstruction of discourses. Melissa Wright (2001) uses an extended metaphor of women's precarious employment to connect women's stilled lives to the reproduction of value in maquilas. However, she fails to come to grips either with the power issues that promote the managers' negligence in introducing security precautions or their lack of commitment to pursuing justice when violations occur. These wider conditions reinforce the lack of job security and the lack of mobility that women experience in flexible production regimes. Chávez Cano, founder of the Casa Amiga (House of a Friend), a group whose members are mothers of disappeared or murdered daughters, points to the fragmentation of society that erupts into mass psychosis. The sexist tradition allows misogynist practices such as violence against women in the home to be carried out with impunity. Records of interventions made by Casa Amiga in 2002 indicate a rising incidence of such violence in Ciudad Juárez, with 973 cases of domestic abuse, fifty-five of incest, and forty-nine of rape of adult women. In 85 percent of these cases, women relate a family history of incest. Chávez Cano indicates that "here the social fabric is so damaged that the danger is as great in*side* the house as outside" (*La Jornada* March 8, 2003).

The murdered women share not only the characteristics that they are young, that they work principally in the maquilas, that they are dark skinned, and that they are of poor, working families but also the fact that they were systematically raped before their death by strangulation. Forensic examination shows clear signs of torture: cigarette burns to their bodies and genitals, the twin-pointed injuries made by electrodes used by police, and in one case, wrist injuries suggesting that the victim was handcuffed and forced into submission.

Police called this case a "crime of passion" and attributed other cases to drug overdose. Although there is no specific link between the maquilas and the murders, the practices of the managers—their delay in introducing safety measures and their prerogatives in disciplining workers—add to the vulnerability of the women. For example, some managers reserve the right to lock out any worker who is late in reporting to work. One seventeen-year-old girl who was later abducted, tortured, and murdered was not admitted to work because she was three minutes late.

Law enforcement authorities blame members of bands calling themselves *los Rebeldes* (the Rebels), *los Choferes* (the Drivers), *la Foca* (the Seal), and *el Cerrillo* (the Untamed) or suggest that a serial murderer committed the killings. Activist groups such as Casa Amiga and Nuestras Hijas de Regreso a Casa (Our Daughters Must Return Home) charge authorities in the investigation with negligence and false arrests. They also charge the authorities with aggravated assault against lawyers defending those falsely accused and on forensic detectives who undermine the cases police construct to protect those in powerful positions.

Can we develop a new enlightenment theory linking local misogyny to the disintegration of social structures, a theory that will contribute insights to liberation struggles of peoples in a globalizing world? We can start with the insights of those striving to overcome the disadvantages of working women. Rosario Acosta, director of Nuestras Hijas de Regreso a Casa, states: "The maquiladoras are a big part of the problem. Here the transnational corporations have all the rights and no obligations. Up to now they do not ensure the safe return of their employees to their homes. Local companies are also responsible; they are the first to experience the crisis like a boomerang" (*La Jornada* March 8, 2003). The systematic lack of responsibility on the part of the maquila managers and the instability forced on the workers account for a great deal of the fragmentation of society.

Women's labor is the principal component of the new "flexible" regime of capital. These workers' very vulnerability as women alienated from patriarchal homes and as workers with scant government regulation or union representation makes them especially desired in the flexible organization of production. The general invisibility of women's work in the domestic sphere is perpetuated even as these women became wageworkers, further distancing them from benefits that male workers can win. This is due in part to their government's concessions to the investors in the maquilas that did not allow any access to trade union organizations. It is also due to the shame associated with married women who work. Since these women lack institutional and emotional support for their position in the workforce, the owners of the maquiladoras can operate with impunity in laying them off peremptorily, thus destabilizing the household schedules of thousands of women who support families in the frontier zone.

The instability inherent in the export-led development programs is not coincidental; it is a programmed part of flexible production introduced in the 1970s and modified in the 1980s. At the height of the debt crisis from 1983 to 1986, when Mexico was forced to devalue its currency, managers perfected the system of flexible labor employment that responded to changes in production schedules and increasingly gave priority in hiring to women in lower-level jobs. Since the women lacked both labor unions and government regulations, they were forced to accept home assembly work at lower rates when there was a downswing in production. This subcontracting furthered their invisibility and exclusion from labor unions and public agencies. The so-called flexible regime of production characteristic of neoliberal development is based on the forced acceptance of uncertainty by women in increasingly precarious household situations.

Supporting this hypothesis is the fact that the stable growth that began in the 1970s decreased in the 1980s and was followed by a crisis of unemployment for male wage earners with increased employment of women in services and commerce as well as self-employment.[8] A similar trend occurred in the United States in the nineteenth century. Charles Babbage elaborated the principle named after him, which called for the segregation of lower-paid, "unskilled" labor in categories that were often socially discriminated against because of the worker's gender or status as recent immigrants (Nash 1989).

The context in which this situation develops lethal consequences is one in which men and women are held at the border subject to the whims of U.S. immigration officials. Some accept work for drug trade operations, and others, particularly women, are forced into prostitution. These illegal operations are also tied into big business interests. In Ciudad Juárez this means maquila operations, landowners, construction barons, and energy suppliers—all of which are connected within a group of families (*La Jornada* March 8, 2003). The impunity for the deaths derives from the intervention of these powerful figures in local investigating teams that subvert information coming in, even from police across the border.

The very processes that promote globalization also give hope for a resolution of the discrimination women face in border communities. Human rights organizations working with grassroots coalitions are promoting transnational cooperation between police and courts in addressing the deaths and disappearances. The 1997 *Human Rights Watch World Report* included a report of the Women's Rights Project on sex discrimination against female workers in the free trade zone of northern Mexico, indicating that some maquilas fired pregnant workers. This resulted in charges against North American maquilas, charges that can now be directed to the National Administrative Office of the United States, which oversees regulations in the North American Agreement on Labor Cooperation. However, the practice of firing pregnant workers continued among Mexican maquilas despite the fact that the National Administrative Office stated in 1998 that doing so constituted an extensive violation of human rights (Human Rights Watch 2005, 5). Other charges of violating workers' freedom of association are being adjudicated at a multinational-owned auto parts plant in Ciudad de los Reyes (Stevenson 2003). These networks now operating among the three countries (Canada, Mexico, and the United States) involved in NAFTA promise to give women a greater voice in their workplace and community. Even more important, the growing outcry against the crimes has resulted in a proliferation of human rights groups that are putting in place the institutional networks to address these problems. They too are a product of globalization processes and cannot be forgotten in assessing changes in the gains and losses of globalization.[9]

PLAN PUEBLA PANAMÁ:
INDIGENOUS RESISTANCE AND FEMINIST VOICES

My final case is drawn from indigenous people of Chiapas, where many pueblos support the Zapatista movement. For semisubsistence farmers and housewives who are forced to compete with subsidized agricultural products in the world market, the future is clear. Without protection from foreign exports, they must expect ever-diminishing returns for their subsistence crops or join the streams of migration to urban centers in Mexico or the United States. On January 1, 1994, when NAFTA was to go into effect, the Zapatista National Liberation Army (EZLN) said *¡basta!* (enough!) to neoliberal development and took up arms against a government that had ignored its members' claims to land titles in the colonized area of the Lacandón Rain Forest and their need for protection against the dumping of subsidized U.S. crops.

The alternatives offered by the neoliberal regimes of Mexico and Central America stress exogenous development of export-oriented production. In 2001, during his first year in office, Fox's administration launched a major hemispheric development scheme, Plan Puebla Panamá, designed to promote modernity in the southern sector of Mexico. It projects a new vision of Mexico's place in the hemisphere by directing attention to the southern border with its Central American neighbors and away from the northern border where maquilas abound (Fazio 2001, 3). The scheme promises the integration of sectors in the basic infrastructure of the state through education, the growth of productive enterprises, and protection of the environment. Promoters claim assets that include the abundant labor supply available at competitive costs at the global level (i.e., below most wages in the world labor market), a privileged geographic position, political democracy, and commercial agreements already in place.

The plan, which is now being discussed in Zapatista circles, denies the central concerns of this new revolutionary movement. Zapatistas have called for endogenous development for the advance of human subjects who are agents of their own enterprises. They seek expansion of traditional industries such as organic foods, including coffee and honey (the latter is already being marketed by an indigenous cooperative). In order to accomplish this, they need credit and access to domestic and foreign markets. In contrast, the plan promotes direct foreign investment in enterprises exploiting the rich resources of the region, including oil, hydroelectric power, the biodiversity of fauna and flora, and the tourist attractions provided by the indigenous populations.

In their statement of purpose (*Plan Puebla Panamá* 2001), government planners devote pages to the improvement of roads, communication, and port facilities and to the further development of highway, rail, and canal facilities that will parallel the Panama Canal through the Isthmus of Tehuantepec. Yet nothing is said of the institutional means to draw indigenous people into the planning process. Even more ominous for small-plot cultivators who seek sustainable development (Fazio 2001) is the fact that there will be no restriction on remissions of profits to foreign capital. Based on the history of foreign capital investments on the northern border, we can expect that similar commitments will extend to labor practices, fiscal regulations, and environmental considerations in Chiapas.

Women are suspicious of a plan that talks about invigorating the local economy but intends to send the men to distant areas where they work on constructing the infrastructure for bigger and more costly enterprises. They have heard bulletins about the existing maquilas in Central America and are not enthusiastic about having their own "underutilized labor" allocated to working ten to twelve hours a day with no time left to tend their families (Earle and Simonelli 2005). Faced with similar projects in Oaxaca, campesinos are concerned that their lands will be seized by eminent domain and that the region's archaeological zone will be affected. The highway between Mitla and Oaxaca runs through the sacred Zapotec valley that may have generated the religious discourse that was the founding nucleus of Mesoamerican civilization. As one spokesperson saw it, these new enterprises threaten the fabric of society: "We want to continue being administrators of our resources, we want a social corridor that supports our pueblos, we do not want projects that make our culture yield, we want to be actors in and not spectators of the CBM [*Correador Biológico Mesoamericano*, or Mesoamerican Biological Corridor], we want a corridor of campesina enterprisers, not a maquila corridor" (*La Jornada* March 4, 2003).[10]

In the colonized areas of the Lacandón Rain Forest and in the Christian Base Communities of the highlands of Chiapas, women in the Zapatista movement are seeking a new way of relating to their families and communities. In their cooperatives and collective work groups, they try to promote egalitarian relations that deny the hierarchical order based on gender and wealth that were their destiny in the plantations or highland pueblos from which they come. In my limited stays in the rain forest, I could sense remarkable transformations in gender relations, as Duncan Earle and Jeanne Simonelli (2005) discuss. Men often engage in childcare and cooking, just as women participate in public arenas. These are the conditions that both men and women want to replicate in any development enterprises, just as they are putting them into practice in their daily lives.

The growing uncertainty in a changing world shows a gender and class bias. Men find themselves displaced in the wider society by other competing workers and even by technological innovations more than do women. This is due to the nature of the work in which they are customarily engaged as well as to the place in which it is carried out. When women's work in the home becomes commoditized, their service jobs play on skills that are part of deeply ingrained socialization. They cannot easily be replaced by machines in the fields of building interpersonal communication networks, nursing, childcare, education, and other gendered activities. The innovative work of rural women migrants in creating income-generating jobs processing and selling food in the markets and streets of Latin American cities ensured the survival of their families throughout the political and economic crises of the 1980s.

Women's acceptance of these necessary adjustments is, I would strongly emphasize, a correlate of their living in the world. In contrast, men's vulnerability in economic crises stems from the very transcendence of their roles in normal periods. By training and acculturation, men are not expected to respond to daily needs; rather, they expect to be waited on by family members or servants. Young men are finding it increasingly difficult to find and hold a wife. When they lose the services of wives and daughters, they lose a sense of themselves in the world, and when they abandon their families, they rarely send remittances to support their children (Ehrenreich and Hochschild 2003).

This vulnerability is also characteristic of indigenous male campesinos insofar as they have capitulated to the dominant patriarchal models of the household. Jacinto Arias Pérez, a Tzotzil-speaking scholar who has a master's degree from Princeton in anthropology, gives us an insider's view of the disorientation he and other Indians experience when confronted with many alternative choices in life.[11] He writes:

> We have doubts about how to live. . . . In the early part of the twentieth century, the objectives were clear. This may be my limited vision, from experiences in my life. What Indians considered to be domination by ladinos (non-Indians) was outside of their world but now it is within their world. The boundaries of Indian-ness have widened and are less definable in themselves now that many of those who were considered Indian have much of the same outlook as the conquerors or invaders. (Arias Pérez 1994, 379)

The conflicts that once separated Indians from ladinos now operate within indigenous communities. "Traditionalists" (made up of the *caciques,* or native leaders, who were co-opted in seventy-one years of Institutional Revolutionary Party [*Partido Revolucionario Institucional*] hegemony) oppose those who introduce change through religious conversion and political party competition. Gender hostility, cultivated in a setting where young men with little chance to gain land and without wage-earning opportunities are unable to find a wife or keep her, aggravates the usual competitive hostilities faced by people in a situation of limited opportunities (Aubry and Inda 1998; Garza Caligaris and Hernández Castillo 1998). Gender hostility is rising as well because women no longer accept as natural their subordination, abuse, and confinement in the home. Women are marrying later, and some choose not to get married when they have alternative economic opportunities (Collier 1990; Nash 1993). When women of indigenous communities in the Lacandón Rain Forest and highlands of Chiapas break their isolation in the domestic unit and demand a voice in change, they emphasize their roles in the transformations they can make in their lives and in their society. They have one strong factor in their favor: they are not as implicated in the co-optive strategies of the state and political organizations as are men because fewer women have voted or entered public office.

Women who were engaged with men in the armed takeover of four cities, the military barracks, and the state prison on January 1, 1993, voiced their demands from the first week of the rebellion. Their attempt to change the subordination of women in the home as well as that of indigenous people in the nation highlights the broadening of social movements with the participation of what were subaltern voices. The statement of purpose drafted at the First State Convention of Indigenous Women in Chiapas reveals the strength of their conviction about women's participation in changing the world:

> Take up the word of women, what we have been saying, demanding, reclaiming in our communities, *ejidos* [lands held communally by indigenous

townships], assemblies, and houses to our husbands, brothers, fathers, authorities and to the government that does not listen to our voices, so that the words do not remain within the four walls of our houses.[12]

They speak not only of their oppression and discrimination but of the participation of rural women in the seizing of land and the struggles of the Zapatistas that give an example of struggle and rebellion. The voices include the women of civil society, the NGOs, the teachers, and the students involved in this process of search for utopias toward a more just and equal society.

Indigenous women and men in the autonomous communities of Chiapas are joining together with mestizos and transnational NGOs to help bring about the changes needed for a democratic society. Women are now calling on men to shoulder some of the child rearing and other domestic responsibilities in the autonomous communities. In turn, women seek greater public participation in the decisions that affect their lives. By sharing these everyday tasks, they may promote a consciousness that gives priority to life. If this consciousness were to prevail in national and global centers of power, we might hope for peaceful resolutions of internecine and international hostilities.

The Zapatistas' attempt to gain a multilateral engagement of all members of the society on many fronts exemplifies the resilient approach to social change. The concept of resiliency is taken from environmentalists who demonstrate the survival value of nonlinear dynamics by which ecosystems maintain themselves in the face of changed circumstances. Susan Walsh demonstrates the effectiveness of such policies in her study showing the success of multilateral coordination among subsistence-based communities in the Bolivian highlands (Walsh 2003, 49). Their self-sustained economy based on the genetic diversity of their potato crops and on reciprocal exchanges reinforced by ritual and kinship ties contrasts with the unilineal, hierarchical control advocated by modernization theory, which has dominated development circles for the past half century.

CONCLUSION

In the beginning of the third millennium we find ourselves in the midst of a new enlightenment, yet we are still trapped in the limitations of outmoded structures of intellectual and social life. Women in the social movements that have expanded their horizons through the inclusion of feminist, civil rights, and indigenous goals emphasize that they do not seek power but rather a free space where a democratic society can emerge. The emerging paradigm that Ponna Wignaraja (1993), editor of *New Social*

Movements in the South, highlights is that of a positive synthesis of ideas and sentiments with social praxes, promoting sustainable development that embraces all life (see also IUCN 1997; IWGIA 1998).

These goals and the approach to realizing them are emblematic of the new enlightenment, emphasizing an all-inclusive civil society that embraces the social welfare of all humans. The goals seem elusive in a world where an emerging empire threatens nascent democracies and where those who claim ownership of the technological progress created in the age of enlightenment use it for destructive ends. In the neoliberal world in which the precarious existence of more than one-third of the people hangs in the balance, bodies, as Florence Babb states, "function as a battleground in discussions that center on how quickly adjustment measures may be introduced and how much the population can withstand before irreversible damage is done—or before political protest grows stronger" (2001, 197).

Nicaragua, the maquila zone, and Chiapas serve as testing grounds as women working in maquilas hotly contest these propositions and as indigenous peoples pose alternative development programs in their autonomous territory. The global assembly plants have increased the intensity of labor exploitation using predominantly female labor. While indigenous people at Mexico's southern frontier are seeking a cultural renaissance and liberation from the racist subordination to which they were subjugated, what some have called a hybrid society at the northern border is enmeshed in a nightmare of neoliberal development. Women trying to maintain their families with low-paid jobs in a flexible labor force are subject to the violence brought by narcotic and sex traffickers at the same time that men are held back from labor streams to the north by U.S. immigration policies. The development program known as Plan Puebla Panamá for the southern border threatens to introduce the combination of flexible production for low-wage women workers with men forced to migrate, join the military, or engage in narcotic trafficking that is found at the northern border of Mexico and in Nicaragua. Indigenous people and the NGOs that support their claims for sustainable development offer an alternative that springs from immanent sources against the destructive path of universalizing free market initiatives. Despite the dismal prospects faced by workers in global assembly plants, women are joining in union organizations, as Jane Collins (2003) documents in her study of garment workers in the United States and Mexico. The efforts of workers organizing unions to counter world trends toward low-wage labor are paralleled by the efforts of indigenous people striving for a sustainable autonomous development that includes all people.

As they gain a sense of their right to exist in the world, indigenous and poor working women and men, joined by middle-class professionals, religious activists, and other grassroots activists, are changing the way that revolutions are mobilized and the ends for which they struggle. Just as they have done during crisis periods throughout history, women are bringing the knowledge and skills they have acquired in building mutual assistance networks into a political arena. There they call for dignity and increasingly for peace, as entrenched interests turn to war in a last-ditch effort to ensure their dominant positions. Working collectively with men, they might overcome the gender and class hostility that shred the fabric of society.

The conjunction of class, gender, and ethnicity in today's social movements can be analyzed only in holistic terms. Whereas Cartesian oppositions classify social actors in unique categories, only some of which are expected to exercise power, the dynamics of global processes must take the multiple visions of all social actors into account in order to analyze and propose changes that embrace all social sectors. Thanks to our developing feminist heritage, we can now envision that goal with clarity and pursue it with enthusiasm.

NOTES

This was the keynote address for the Women in Development Conference organized by the Center for Latino, Latin American, and Caribbean Studies of the State University of New York, Albany, in Costa Rica in March 2003. A version of the paper was published in *Signs, Journal of Women in Culture and Society* 32, no. 4: 145–67.

1. So pervasive were these assumptions that early feminists (see articles by Rosaldo and Ortner in the anthology edited by Rosaldo and Lamphere [1974] accepted Descartes' assumption of the universal subordination of women along with de Beauvoir (1957) who was further burdened with Kantian categories of the immanent and transcendent. Leacock and Nash (1977) and Etienne and Leacock (1980) drew upon ethnohistorical and ethnographic accounts to question the spurious basis for such universalizing categories.

2. Ponna Wignaraja (1993, 7–8) spells out the vision of a democratic polity in her anthology, *New Social Movements in the South*.

3. "Flexible" production regimes are those that followed the demise of what were called "Fordist" production regimes predicated on a stable workforce, and protected by government regulations and union contracts. In global markets the emphasis on swift responses to consumer demands required that firms respond quickly to the knowledge on the demand trends in order to maintain their competitive edge. This required flexibility in production schedules, which ultimately meant that workers must bear the social cost of movement in and out of the workforce and that they have little control over their jobs.

4. Luisa Armanda Espinosa was the first armed woman fighter killed by the Contras.

5. CISPES and other groups in the United States were trying to get the U.S. Congress to stop appropriations for the Contra war. Yet on the eve of the vote, Daniel Ortega made an inadvisable trip to Russia where he was photographed in a meeting with the Soviet leaders that appeared on the front pages of newspapers throughout the United States, thereby diminishing the impact of efforts to gain a negotiated settlement.

6. Comparative studies of export processing labor carried out two decades ago can be found in Nash and Fernández-Kelly (1983). Safa's (1996) study shows how the preferential hiring of women and the loss of male breadwinner roles affects gender roles in Caribbean society. Anru Lee's study (2004) of the changing relationships within families with the restructuring of the economy from offshore production to services has freed women from oppressive labor with little inheritance rights. In these transformations, gender antagonism is often exacerbated.

7. The data on murder and abuse are provided by the leader of Casa Amiga, Esther Chávez Cano, in an interview published by *La Jornada* on March 8, 2003: 48–49, 53. I am indebted to Sarah Hill for sending me the *Observer* magazine article by Ed Vulliamy, "Murder in Mexico," March 9, 2003.

8. Orlandina de Olivera (1987) assesses the cycles of expansion and recession attendant on the employment of women in twelve areas of Mexico. Correlating these trends, we find a growing instability in family income related to higher rates of female employment in comparison with that of males.

9. As Saskia Sassen (2003, 260) reminds us, there are two distinct dynamics emerging in the lives of migrant women workers. Though their invisibility and disempowerment as a class of workers remains, they still have access to wages and salaries, however low.

10. "Queremos seguir siendo administradores de nuestros recursos, queremos un corridor social que apoye a nuestros pueblos, no queremos una suma de proyectos que hagan sucumbir nuestra cultura, queremos ser actores y no espectadores del CBM, queremos un corridor de empresas campesinas, no un corridor de maquilidoras."

11. Florence Babb (1989) describes the ingenuity with which Peruvian women managed complex processing and selling operations in the sale of food items, maintaining low costs and carrying out childcare operations that ensured the survival of low-income families during the 1980s.

12. Flier distributed at the meeting of the First Chiapas State Convention of Indigenous Women, March 1995; my translation.

II

REFLECTIONS IN THE ETHNOGRAPHIC MIRROR

4

Multiple Perspectives on Burmese Buddhism and Nat Worship

In the mid-twentieth century, anthropologists doing fieldwork in Burma and historically grounded religious studies scholars specializing in Burmese Buddhism were both developing operational models that took into account the relation between Buddhism and *nat* worship. The authors consider the themes developed in this parallel mode of scholarship grounded in the postcolonial situation. Anthropological observations of situations rising in 1960 from the tensions between still-present guerrilla movements and the independence government of U Nu indicated that recourse was being made to both Buddhist and nat traditions in novel ways. Historically grounded religious studies reveal the importance, complexity, and persistence of this coexistence and interaction throughout the course of Burmese history. The authors also consider the changes in their respective fields that open up the possibility of developing new models for the interpretation of this important aspect of Burmese life.

In 1960, when I first traveled to Burma, the country was on the threshold of defining a postcolonial form of governance wavering between U Nu's conciliatory policies and Ne Win's sword rattling. U Nu held daily "tension relieving breakfasts" with prominent personalities involved in the many conflicts that still prevailed more than a decade after the assassination of Maj. Gen. Aung San and some of his cabinet members ended the first independent government in 1947. The Burmese government had just rejected the U.S. Aid for International Development (AID) project for paving a highway from Rangoon to Mandalay as well as other development projects proposed by Western nations eager to take advantage of a new field for investment. The Burmese government reasoned that the highway was to be converted into an aviation runway for B-52 observation planes flying into China.

We went by train to our chosen field site in Mandalay, where the United States had opened a consulate and information service. The British presence was still manifest in the Indian professionals they had brought to fill posts in the colonial administration. English was widely spoken in the city and even in the nearby township of Patheingyi where I worked, and where the town officer and monks who taught in the monastery school spoke excellent English. My research proposal was to study the ethnic groups that were pouring in to Mandalay from the surrounding villages and hills. However I soon discovered that the plurilingual river ports on the banks of the Irrawaddy River that I had chosen were too complex for someone with the limited Burmese I had acquired in preparing for the field. They also exceeded the paradigm of community studies that I was methodologically prepared to work within. I therefore decided to work in the township of Patheingyi. Even these areas, only ten miles from the center of Mandalay, were still plagued by dacoits and guerrillas. Without the validation of an armed victory against the British to warrant their taking power, guerrillas who lived in the Shan hills survived by preying on tribute rice they extorted from peasant cultivators. I was amazed how readily they seemed to accept me until my interpreter, a young woman who studied at the University of Mandalay, said they identified me with a member of the U.S. and British troops that had freed them from the Japanese.

During my daily tours of three hamlets in Patheingyi I became well acquainted with the spirits as well as the monks and peasants that inhabited the region. At the entrance to each village, a nat shrine box enabled one to leave an offering so that no harm would befall the visitor. Each major tree was the abode of a nat spirit that had to be mollified by offerings and protected from those that might attempt to cut them down. Each house held a representation of the nat favored by the family. Min-Maha-Giri, the blacksmith who defied the king's rule in ancient times, was the most common. His representation as a coconut was placed as far away as possible from the hearth, since he would become enraged at this reminder of his death by being burned at the stake by the king. On very hot days the woman of the house might fan him.

I learned in the course of my year of fieldwork that these beliefs in nat spirits were in no way contradictory to Buddhist beliefs and practices. Buddhism and nat spirit worship were, in fact, expressions of a single system of beliefs, as I learned in the ceremonial and customary behaviors witnessed in my fieldwork: *pongyis* or monks visited nat shrines along with the rest of the populace, removing their thong sandals to show respect; politicians made offerings at nat shrine boxes when they visited their constituents. Thieves offered food and drink to the nat shrine box to gain their acceptance of their plundering. The linkage of the Buddhist and the animistic belief system was most dramatically revealed at the *shinbyu* (initiation rite into Buddhism) of a headman's sons in one of the hamlets I visited frequently. Guerrillas had killed the headman because he had revealed the tribute dropoff place to the authorities, and his restless spirit was appearing in dreams by many villagers. In order to create instant *kutho*, or merit, his widow arranged an elaborate shinbyu in the monastery, attended by all of the monks in the region and all of the villagers. The widow extended each offering to the monks with her hand wrapped in the *longyi*, skirt, or the headscarf of her husband. When I visited her after the shinbyu, I asked her whether the spirit had appeared since then, and she replied that no one had seen or heard from him.

Our operating paradigm was that of structural functionalism, a model that Stanley Tambiah (1970) brought to a pinnacle with *Buddhism and the Spirit Cults in North East Tailnad* in 1977. It was a powerful approach to studying things as they are in a frozen time-space continuum, and in those days we were focused on phenomenological reality. We were almost discouraged from getting too engrossed in ancient texts since this would contaminate our vision of what was still extant in the culture. Yet some of the old Burma hands—a retired British engineer of the Burma Oil Company

Figure 4.1.   A shinbyu, *Buddhist initiation ceremony, enabled Burmese villagers to hasten the spirit of their father, killed by guerrillas, to the afterlife and avoid his becoming a* nat.

who was a history buff and historians who were once part of the British colonial administration—also found a bonding between so-called Buddhist and animistic spirit worlds.

In Burma we soon discovered that the system of beliefs in animistic spirits coexists within the framework of Buddhist religion not as a distinct cult, but as a deeply integrated constituent of identity and society. In the township of Patheingyi near Mandalay where I carried out fieldwork in 1960, belief in animistic spirits called nats,[1] is a complementary part of Buddhist belief, integrated in the daily and seasonal religious rituals. The origin of nats and the historical situations giving rise to their belief has been the subject of inquiry and speculation for several scholars of Burma.[2] In those analyses the historical origins of nats have been captured, but at the time of my research in 1960 no one had raised the question of the persistence of the cult and its significance in the everyday life of the villages and region. Burma had just emerged from a devastating war of occupation by the Japanese. My appearance in Patheingyi evoked vivid memories of the American and British liberation, with some asserting that my husband, Manning Nash, was among those in the allied forces.

The essay included here, based on narratives of many of the women and men with whom I visited during my stay, was formulated as a structural functional analysis. The analysis provided a frame for my very first impression of nats as familiars with whom people lived in an uneasy accommodation. This differed from the dominant views of established scholars as well as those who came later to the same region, who related nats to a domain distinct from Buddhist orthodoxy.[3] An incident that I used to buttress my structural functional orientation occurred when a headman was killed by insurgents who had retreated to the Shan hills rising from the Mandalay plains. Since independence was granted by Great Britain after World War II, the rebels under British rule had no validation for assuming official roles and so were demanding tribute from the rural peasantry. The headman was doomed when he revealed their pickup depot where federal police captured a few of their members, and his fate was sealed when the Mandalay governor proceeded to proclaim him a hero. In a postmodernist era, this would have been the focus of the story, but for me it was an epiphenomenon to the main thrust of defining how these irksome spirits cultivated behaviors that strengthened social structure. They were as abhorrent yet as necessary as the devil in medieval Christianity when theologians had to create an anti-Christ to explain evil in a world created by God.

In this prefeminist era, I described, but did not elaborate, the significance of gendered spheres. This division of responsibilities enabled men to profess to be strictly Buddhist in belief and practice, and at the same time to maintain their equanimity since their wives and other female relatives were in charge of the nats. Since women could never reach nirvana in this lifetime, they did not have to be as scrupulous in their behavior as men and could carry out the daily and annual propitiations that ensured the safety of the household. Although I had heard many stories of nat wives I never seriously dealt with a theme that has preoccupied current researchers in the area (Brac de la Perrière 1998).

Yet within this rigid framework of a structural functional analysis, ethnographic description enabled us to go back over the data to capture structural regularities. We could also rely on the brilliant insights of what we then called informants that crept in. One man quoted in the conclusion summed up the nats' relation to Buddhism: "When we do something for Buddha, we do it for the next life, and when we do something for the nats, we do it to help us in this life." As a serious practitioner of Buddhist meditation, he claimed that he could ignore the nats since taking the five precepts each day gave him power over them.

The following text was written in 1963 (Nash 1966).

LIVING WITH NATS: AN ANALYSIS OF
ANIMISM IN BURMAN VILLAGE SOCIAL RELATIONS

Here I shall examine the role of the nats, not as a distinct category of experience, but as it affects everyday social relations. This approach follows that of Simmel (1959, 11), who saw the immanent sources of religion in the relations of men to the world of man, and of Firth (1959, 131), who defines religion as "a concern of man in society with basic human ends and standards of value, seen in relation to non-human entities or powers." Through this approach I hope to show (1) how the nat cult is perpetuated through obligations inherited at the structural level of the family, village, and region, (2) how the relationships between the nats and their spirit relatives and spirit mediators tied together villages in a subsystem of ritual and spiritual identification, and (3) how the adjustment of these Burman villagers to the subsociety of nat spirits living among them parallels the adjustments they make in ordinary human relationships and in interpreting catastrophic events. Finally I shall show how, in the villages today, concern with soul crises is resolved in Buddhist ritual rather than in the development of new nat cults.

ORIGINS OF THE NAT CULT

There is no single definition of nats since the designation covers a wide variety of distinct categories. The major division the villagers recognize is between the *ahtet nats* and the *auk nats*—that is, the upper and lower nats. The ahtet nats, who are big nats awaiting Buddha in the sky, have no personalities or legends associated with them in the Burmese villages. The ahtet nats correspond to the *devas* who figure in Hindu myths as the kings and virtuous people who are rewarded with happiness in the six seats of heaven (Scott 1927, 232). These spirits appear in the cosmology of all Buddhist countries. The king of these nats is Thagya Min, and the Burmese count their New Year from the day he descends to earth, celebrating the occasion with their annual water festival.

The auk nats belong to a different order entirely, and the villagers never confuse the two. It is with this group only that the paper is concerned. The auk nats include both named and unnamed spirits drawn from indigenous pre-Buddhist cosmology as well as from Hindu or other outside sources. The core of the nat cult is the Thirty-Seven Lords, or Thirty-Seven Nats.

The leading figure in the cult of the Thirty-Seven Nats is Min-Maha-Giri, or Einzaung Nat. This nat has been officially recognized by Kin Kynaungha in an attempt to give symbolic unity to the Pagan kingdom (Scott 1900, 20). The pantheon of Thirty-Seven Nats was first officially recognized during King Anawrahta's reign about the beginning of the eleventh century. In an attempt to establish Buddhism as the religion of his kingdom, King Anawrahta first tried to suppress the cult but, failing that, took the images of thirty-six nats worshiped in the Pagan kingdom and placed them in the compound of the Shwezigon pagoda. In order to regularize the cult, Anawrahta established as the overlord Thagyn Min, the Buddha nat.

Since that time the list has varied: Some old nats have been displaced by new and the personalities of later nats have become merged with earlier. But the number of nats associated with the cult of the Thirty-Seven Nats has not been changed (Htin 1956, 81). Villagers differ in their account of what nats are to be included in this list, and even specialists concerned with propitiating the nats are not consistent. Most of the nats were legendary figures either of royal blood, or associated with royalty, who died sudden and tragic deaths (Htin 1956, 99). Their deaths were, in many instances, ordered by a king jealously guarding his throne against real or imagined rivals. Major nat figures have associated with them a cluster of relatives who died of sorrow or sacrificed themselves on the nat's death. Some of the nats were granted overlordship of certain regions by the reigning king and towns in these regions became the center of annual celebrations.

The language surrounding the village and cultivated fields is alive with nats. Among these are the Earth Guardian, Bonmazo the paddy land-owner, Ashingyi, and a host of spirits inhabiting woods, mountains, streams, and rivers. The tree nat, Yokahkazo, occupies every large tree, and most of the village Burmans show respect to Yokahkazo by removing their slippers when they approach a large tree. The villagers honor the Rain Nat, Mogaung Kyawawe, during times of drought with a tug-of-war ritual. Merchants offer flowers on their weighing scales to the nats concerned with commerce (unnamed) before beginning the day's business. When a Burman makes a trip beyond his own locality, he almost always takes the precaution of placing a bunch of *thabye* leaves on his cart, boat, or even his truck as an offering to the nats who may occupy the regions through which he travels.

Nat propitiation enters into every significant phase of the villager's life. I shall explore below the occasions for these ceremonies and the different structural responsibilities involved in the propitiation of the various categories of nats.

HOUSEHOLD, VILLAGE, AND REGIONAL NATS

The responsibility for propitiating the nats is transmitted at three distinct structural levels: the household, the village, and the region. The household nats are selected from among the Thirty-Seven or a local nat or even a "village nat" without name or personality; the regional nats include any of the Thirty-Seven Nats who have attained some eminence as well as those omnipresent nats of the field or trees who are recognized throughout a wide area.

The Household Nat

In the crowded disorder of the Burmese village house will be found, almost universally, a coconut slung from the southeast pole of the house, in the upper level if it is two-storied. This offering to the house-owner nat, or Min-Maha-Giri, gives a sense of security to the house owner, who looks upon him as a guardian against thieves or unwanted spirits. Members of the household are constantly aware of the presence of Min-Maha-Giri in their house. As the house is being built, as soon as the *udaing* or southeast corner pole is raised,[4] an offering of bananas is made to Min-Maha-Giri, and 1.25 kyats (about twenty-five cents) is sometimes placed in the posthole by the carpenter in the name of the owner. Min-Maha-Giri dislikes the presence of birth or death in the house. Therefore, when a baby is born, the coconut that represents his presence is taken out of the house, disposed of, and replaced with a new one after the New Year celebration of Thingyan. Similarly, when a member of the household dies, the coconut is removed, sometimes hung in a tree in the compound, and replaced after the seven-day period during which the house is thought to be unclean. Even during a serious illness of a member of the family, the coconut is removed in order not to offend the sensibilities of the house-owner nat. Min-Maha-Giri is also offended by sexual intercourse, and the house owner usually will keep his bed far from this pole if he is sexually active. Since Min-Maha-Giri was burned to death while tied to a tree, he dislikes the sight of fire. If the householder does not have a separate kitchen, he tries to locate the hearth as far from the sight of the coconut as possible, and some say that Min-Maha-Giri does not like the offering of cooked food because of the association with fire.

Along with Min-Maha-Giri, every household offers one or more nats known as the *mizaing-hpazaing*. Mizaing refers to the nat spirit inherited through the mother's matri-line, hpazaing to the nat spirit inherited through the father's patri-line. The two nouns used collectively refer to the Thirty-Seven Nats as a group from which personalities become the inherited responsibility of female lines of descent and of male lines of descent.

How the responsibility for nats originally became assigned in certain families is unknown and no historical research has been done in this area.[5] The mechanism for passing on the responsibility was, however, ascertained in the villages under study by interviews and census.[6] Some say that women receive their nat obligations from their mother, men from their father. Others say that they received their nats from their parents. If this latter statement were true, there would be an accumulation of many nats for each household. However, there are conditions that counteract this tendency. In the first place, men and women from the same village frequently have the same nat and each child would receive just one. If the parents' nats differ, the woman's nat is the one likely to be inherited. Women are more concerned than men about the propitiation of the nats and are the ones who give all the food offerings on all domestic occasions for all nats. Men are more frequently serious Buddhist meditators, attending the *pongyi kyaungs*, or monasteries, and maintaining the five precepts. This activity sometimes gives them confidence that they can overcome the power of the nats or leads them to erase believing in the nats' power. The woman's nat is, in consequence, the one most attended in the family and the one most likely to be perpetuated.

Women make large ceremonial offerings to their own and to their husband's nats once a year. Sometimes the offerings are given simultaneously; sometimes the family may give a contribution to an elder female relative who knows better how to give the offering. This contribution ranges from twenty-five pyas to one kyat (four cents to twenty-one cents), and the elder relative calls the names of all who have contributed as she makes the offering. It is the gift and not the giver that is of importance to the nat. "The nat," said one informant, "is interested only in the offering, not in the person giving it." The amount of the offering is set by custom and the nat may become insulted and cause trouble if the offering is short of the traditional sum.[7] Women assume the responsibility for this offering when their mothers, on their deathbeds, plead with them to carry on the propitiation or beware of the wrath of the nat.

At almost every life crisis, offerings are made to the mizaing-hpazaing, the thirty-seven officially recognized nats from the time of Anawrahta's reign. Seven days after birth, a naming ceremony, called *kinbun tatte*, is held. At this time a food offering is made for all Thirty-Seven Nats of the mizaing-hpazaing, along with the nat or nats that are the special responsibility of the house. Thus thirty-seven small fish are fried and offered along with, for example, betel nut, which the Taungbyon brothers favor if they are the mizaing-hpazaing, or duck egg, which Ma Negale, the niece of Min-Maha-Giri, likes if she is one of the mizaing-hpazaing, as well as the red food and white food, *monni* and *monbyn*, which all nats like. Relatives of the father and mother of the child are invited and actually consume the food first offered to the nats.

Before a wedding ceremony, the couple offer bananas and pineapple to the mizaing-hpazaing at the bride's and the groom's houses. This offering is similar to that made to the elders of both the boy and the girl during the ceremony. The nat offering is essential, even if there is no other ceremony attending the marriage of a couple.[8]

The household is not forgotten even at the shinbyu, the initiation of boys into the Buddhist monastic order. For the shinbyu, which is a reenactment of Buddha's own renunciation of the material pleasures of life in taking on the robe of the mendicant monk, the boy is dressed in rented silken clothing recalling the elaborate robes of a royal prince of the past century, and, to complete the likeness, is rouged and powdered and decked out with golden ornaments. Along with his male siblings or cousins, he sits on velvet cushions before his parents, relatives, elders of the village, and most of his own and neighboring villagers. Because of the elaborateness of the ceremony and the fact that the children are the center of attention, parents fear the wrath of the nats whose envy is so easily aroused. One woman commented, "At the shinbyu, the mizaing-hpazaing will harm the children if they are not offered something." Throughout the ceremony, three large platters of bananas and coconuts remain in place before the initiates—one for the parents, one for the Buddha, and one for the nats. The *beiktheik hsaya* (the master of ceremonies hired for the occasion) ties a white thread in the children's hair, asking that the nats protect them. After making the offering of fruit to the Buddha and to the elders, the beiktheik hsaya offers the red and white food to the Thirty-Seven Nats. This is done so that they will become guardians of the ceremony.

The offering to the nats at the very time that a child is introduced into the Buddhist order indicates the thorough penetration of animism in Upper Burma village life. Some monks claim to have raised objection to nat offerings at a shinbyu only to have the village elders refuse to eliminate this part of the ceremony because the parents would fear for their children.

When sickness strikes a member of the family, the villagers suspect they have aroused the anger of the household nats. Certain ailments are typically caused by nats—skin diseases, sudden falls, madness. The housewife may confirm her suspicions by going to one of the nat shrines and lifting the *pwè shidè*, the fortune-telling stone placed before the nat: if the stone appears heavy when lifted, the trouble is felt to be caused by the nat. She may check the diagnosis by going to the *hse hsaya*, or curer. In all his consultations, the first question the hse hsaya asks is whether the patient has kept up the offerings to the household nats. The first course of treatment often is an offering to the house-owner nat and the mizaing-hpazaing.

In talking to the villagers about the nats with whom they live one discerns that these nats are petty and irascible tyrants, quick to take offense or to feel jealousy if any member of the household or the other household nats receive special attention. Nats require constant attention—some housewives even fan them during the hot season as well as keep their water offering and flowers fresh. In return they give nothing but appeasement of their wrath and the sense that their presence keeps strange nats away. The house nats do not control decisions, but their wishes are taken

Figure 4.2.   The Taungbo twin nats are fretful spirits appeased by Upper Burma villagers.

into account whenever the household acts. Their presence is made known through disaster, not through success.

The Village Nats

The villagers say that the nat looks after the village as a grandfather looks after his family, that is, he is concerned with their general welfare rather than, as a father would be, their daily maintenance. By his presence he guards the village against strange nats and even human invaders, just as the house nat, like a sentry box, serves as a warning to anyone who wishes to do harm to members of the household.

In a survey of seventeen of the villages in Patheingyi Township, the following nats were identified:

Nat	*Character*	*No. of villages*
I. Bobogyi	No legends	5
II. Myinbyu Shin	White horse owner	4
III. Personalized nats	Lived and died in immediate area of village	8

None of the village nats were found as household nats in the three villages in which a survey of the latter was made. This suggests that different categories of nats may be associated with the village and with the household, but the negative instances are too few for generalization. About a third of the villages did not personalize the nat, simply calling him *bobogyi*. The personalized nats (III) were identified immediately with geographical features of the landscape such as a hill or stream where they had lived or met an untimely death. Only one of the eight—the Lord of Aungpinlè—was identifiable in Temple's (1906) list of Thirty-Seven Nats. Except for the third category, the characteristics of the nat did not give a clue as to the basis for selection by the village.

In those villages with personalized nats, greater attention was paid to them. Sometimes the nat houses in these villages were elaborate shrines with large figures of the nat and associated figures in the legend, such as Ingyin village's series of shrines for Me' U, the beloved of the Taungbyon brothers who was killed by them for having refused their love. In the village of Hsèdawagie is enshrined the nat Aserotakima, the queen who committed suicide in order to become guardian nat of the dam her husband was constructing on the river running past the village. So sacred is this shrine and the area surrounding it that until eleven years ago the people residing in this village never wore slippers, carried umbrellas, or rode horses. Since she was pregnant at the time of her suicide, pregnant women are particularly fearful of disturbing her and carefully avoid the waters in which she killed herself. However, eleven years ago the *natkadaw* (nat wife) charged with care of the nat at a village *pwè*, or celebration, for Aserotakima divined by certain signs that she would be less demanding of these observances if she were given a three-day pwè instead of the usual two. And so it is said that from that year on the people have worn slippers and carried umbrellas, but they still dare not launch a boat on the waters near the dam.

In addition to the annual pwè, not always observed by all villages, offering to the village nat is made whenever disaster strikes or threatens to strike a village. This may be combined with the efforts of the monks to exorcise evil spirits through the special prayer session called the *payeit yuttè*. After a fire in Zigyogon, which demolished only one house but threatened the entire village, the village natkadaw and four other women made an offering of water, fruits, and betel nut to the village nat, at which time they asked for his protection against fire in the future.

When the village must change its locale, as happens frequently to the island villages of the Irrawaddy River, the monks are called upon to rid the place of any resident devils or spirits with the payeit yuttè, a *natsin*, nat shrine, is erected on the east side of the village, and a special offering is made to the village nat. Only then is the village thought ready for occupancy.

An offering is made to the village nat preceding the celebration of the shinbyu. The day before the celebration, the *shinlaung*, or Buddhist initiate, goes in a cart drawn by white bullocks to make offerings of fruit to the village nat as well as to older people of prestige in the village. As in the case of the offering to the mizaing-hpazaing during the shinbyu, this offering is made from fear of the nat, whose envy would be aroused by the attention and interest the village folk focus on the initiate.

The village nat has been cast in the role of the lord protector of the village. When people migrate from their village they frequently use the annual *natpwè* as an occasion for visiting their relatives. If they are unable to return, they send a contribution to one of their relatives living in the village to make an offering to the nat. In this sense, animistic faith ties the Burman more strongly to his village than does the village pongyi-kyaung since, on moving, he becomes identified with the kyaung in his new neighborhood, whereas he retains the obligation to propitiate his hometown nat.

The Regional Nats

Three types of nats will be considered in this category:

1. nats whose personalities are so strong that they are honored throughout a region encompassing several towns;

2. nats with special functions to perform who are honored throughout a region on special occasions when their services or powers are called into play; and
3. generalized spirits of the paddy land, of the stored rice, etc., who have no locality or village but are recognized as powers throughout a wide region.

A geography of nats, tying them to particular villages or regions, would clarify questions concerning the spread and persistence of the animistic cult. This work remains to be done for Burma. However, the limited survey I did suggests some aspects of village-regional nat relations. The regional nats include both village and household nats. Certain villages in the Mandalay district have become centers of regional nat cults. In Aung-pinlè, there is a large nat shrine with lineages of the nats most frequently honored throughout the area. Taungbyon is another center for the celebration of the nats.

The Taungbyon brothers, Shwebyingyi and Shwebyingge, are the two most popular nats of Upper Burma (Temple 1906, 25–26). The legend associated with them does not in itself explain their popularity:

King Anawrahta, accompanied by the brothers, who were the offspring of an Indian adviser to the court and an ogress of Popa, went to China to secure a tooth of Gotama Buddha. The Chinese emperor treated the Burmese king with contempt, and so the two brothers, who could become invisible, entered his chamber and wrote on the wall asking the emperor to meet the Burmese king. The emperor did, and apparently handed over the tooth. But on the return trip, the tooth disappeared. Later the brothers were asked to superintend the building of a pagoda that now can be seen in Taungbyon. During the construction, the brothers got drunk on toddy palm wine, and two bricks were missing from the entrance arch. The king had them executed for their failure to carry through the job. The king tried to return to his palace, but encountered many difficulties on the boat trip. His ministers advised him that the spirits of the brothers who felt that their execution was unjust, particularly after they had served the king loyally in the attempt to get the tooth, caused his troubles. Therefore the king ordered that regular offerings were to be made to the nat spirits of the two brothers.

In one of the songs commemorating the brothers, the final verse says, "Now all ye pretty maidens love ye us, as ye were wont to do while yet we were alive." Apparently this plea was taken seriously, and the nats have a coterie of nat wives (natkadaws) attached to them. The younger brother is the most favored and has the greatest number of wives. It is a standing joke in the villages to suggest that he shares his wives with his older brother.

The widespread popularity of the Taungbyon brothers can probably be explained by the devotion of their natkadaws. The natkadaws go from town to town, offering dances and prayers to their images. They are frequently, but not always, the daughters of natkadaws. Two of those interviewed said that their mothers had asked them on their deathbeds to undertake the responsibility of dancing for the nat and making offerings to him. When they ignored this request, they became seriously ill. They were advised by nat wives to join their ranks, and they were then cured.

The natkadaws attached to a particularly favored nat, such as one of the Taungbyon brothers, have an internal hierarchy through which they are related to the nat. The most important natkadaws are called *natmayagyi*, or big nat wife. Others who do not devote full time to the cult are known as *hnama aya*, sister of the nat. The lesser wives give offerings to the big wives in thanks for the instructions given by the latter on how to please the nat. There is some rivalry between the natkadaws in attracting the attention of the nat who visits them in dreams or reveals his presence by a kind of bodily seizure, which may cause them to shake when they offer him food.

The natkadaws gather in the centers for the nat festivals. Some travel in professional troupes along with their own musician and images, which they set up in villages that have called upon their services for the annul pwè. With their battered images and contorted dances, they perpetuate the legend of their nat's powers, and the nat who commands the largest number of natkadaws has the largest reputation and following.

Some of the nats in the Mandalay district are remembered only during special events requiring their appeasement. Among such nats is Anauk Mèdaw (Lady of the West) who is said to be "owner" of the mother and child at birth. Amegyan, a rough-speaking nat who can cause harm to either mother or child, serves her. To prevent this, an offering of 1.25 kyats is made at birth. Those who are unable to give the money make a special request for a credit extension until after the harvest. The money is actually collected by the midwife. Before the war, Anauk Mèdaw was given only 14 pyas, but the offering has since increased to five times that amount because, as the people explain, the price of rice has increased by that amount.

The nats of the paddy field and the stored rice are directly concerned with the basic crop. Even men who are serious meditators and who scoff at the idea of nats see to it that the paddy field–owner nat is propitiated. This nat, sometimes called the *lè nat* (paddy or rice field nat), or Ashingyi, or even the frequently encountered term "Bobogyi," must receive an offering at the time of transplanting the rice and at the harvest, the first of these offerings to ask that a good crop result and the second to give thanks for the harvest. The work gang leader, usually the eldest of the women who do the work of transplanting and harvesting, makes the offering on the east side of the field. A female nat, Bomagyi, is guardian of the stored rice bins. She was a spinster who, while working for a rich landowner, was killed by a co-worker. After the harvest, when the rice is threshed and in storage, an offering of sticky rice is made to her, along with *thanahka*, a skin cosmetic, mirror, and comb (since she was a spinster she was concerned with beautifying herself and had the leisure time to do it). Because of the circumstances of her death (i.e., while winnowing the harvested rice) people say she does not like the sound of threshing and they endeavor to be quiet when giving her an offering.

Beyond the village and paddy field limits, the woods and fields are thought to be inhabited by a host of named and unnamed spirits. Those who venture daily into these regions as woodcutters or fruit gatherers always offer some of their lunch first to these nats.[9] If a village is established on new territory an offering is made to the earth owner, Bonmazo (given as "Burmese" in Temple 1906).

These nats are the lords of all that is important to the village Burman, and it is by their sufferance that he is permitted to use the fields, or enter the forest, or even to store the grain he has harvested in safety. In making offerings to these nats, he gains some sense of security and nobody with whom I spoke, even the most devoted meditator, was so foolhardy as to risk the anger of a nat concerned with the basic needs of himself and his family.

The world of the nats is, then, tied to the structurally significant units of the society through responsibilities inherited in familial, village, and regional contexts. In assessing the strength of the three levels of animistic belief, the word of the informant strengthens the conclusion based on structural analysis. One village Burman said that he might ignore all the nats except those he acquired as his mizaing-hpazaing. The fact that the obligation to propitiate the mizaing-hpazaing nat is acquired through the strongest kinship bonds, that of mother to daughter and secondarily that of father to son, assures that these nats will be perpetuated. A housewife's failure to carry out this responsibility is a source of gossip and criticism. Negligent as the average village woman is about her housekeeping duties, the only thing I have ever heard neighbors criticize is failure to propitiate the nats. At the village level, the responsibility of the elders to the village nat is evoked less frequently and there are fewer incidents to indicate failure in fulfilling this responsibility. Nat worship at this level might easily succumb if it were opposed. Regional nat cults will probably survive as long as the natkadaws are convinced they have been called upon for this mission in life and as long as they receive sufficient profit to pay the musicians who inspire them.

NATS AS A SUBSOCIETY IN BURMAN VILLAGES

The village Burman is from his earliest years introduced to the world of nats. While the nats do not control decisions or impose patterns of action, all the exigencies of daily living and the crises in the life cycle are interpreted in terms of them. Marriage alliances are not determined by the mizaing-hpazaing preferences of the families involved, but if the marriage violates other customary preferences it is feared that the nats will be displeased. Their presence is honored at those ceremonial occasions attending naming ceremonies, Buddhist initiation, and marriage; their representations are removed at birth, sickness, and death conditions, which make the house "unclean."

This constant awareness of the nats and the interpretation of misfortune in terms of their known likes and dislikes are illustrated by the response of the people of Patheingyi to the fact that the headman became insane. All agreed that his insanity was caused by the nats, but accounts differed as to which nats were ultimately responsible and as to how he had failed in his responsibility. One account went as follows:

> U Chan, the headman of Patheingyi center, was ordered by the township officer to chop down some large trees in order to straighten the streets of the village. He called forth from the village a voluntary work group and set to cutting down the trees. This angered Yokhkazo, the nat who lives in the big trees. He in turn roused the anger of the village nat against the headman. Within a short time, the headman became insane, wandering about the village and talking wildly.

According to another account told to me by a village elder in the township:

> Even though U Chan was just carrying out the orders of the township officer, it was his own responsibility to advise the nat of this before cutting the trees. The village men who were ordered to do the work along with him went with an offering to the tree nat before they set to work. They said to the nat that it was the headman who ordered them to cut the trees and they were just doing as they were told. It was the headman's own fault that he had not shifted the blame to a higher authority. U Chan was always a hasty and aggressive man who often failed to confer with the elders before going ahead and doing things. His failure to explain to the nats that he was cutting the trees only because he had been ordered to do it caused them to turn against him.

The headman's nephew made a different claim of responsibility:

> About three years ago, the headman bought some pigs which he intended to raise and breed. Now Htibyuzaunga is the mizaing-hpazaing of the head-

man, and this nat does not like the presence of pork even when not slaughtered for human food. Of course he caused the headman to go mad in his anger that his tastes should be ignored. The headman lost a lot of money on the pigs, many of which died because he could not take care of them properly. It was evident from the start, then, that the mizaing-hpazaing nat objected to having the pigs.

U Chan was himself responsible for his sickness because he failed in his role of headman to placate the village nats when undertaking a project that would displease them; he neglected, as a subordinate of the higher government authority interested in the township officer, to explain that he was not responsible to the tree nat; and, even before this, he had incurred the displeasure of his mizaing-hpazaing nat by harboring pigs, which are detested by this nat.

Thus any misfortune in the lives of the villagers evokes this kind of interpretation, which, in turn, reevaluates and redefines the responsibility to the nats in terms of the role in which one is acting. Since each individual fills more than one role and, in enacting these roles, is required to make offerings to different nats, his misfortunes are interpreted in a variety of accounts.

The villagers' relations to the nats have parallels in other social relations. Wives show the same consideration to their husbands; one woman said that having a husband is like having a nat in the house—he must be cared for, deferred to, and any impingement of his *hpon*, or male power, must be avoided. Most adults tend to treat children under the age of understanding as they do the nats: they cater to every wish of the child constantly, as they do the nats, constantly appeasing him and attempting not to frustrate him.[10] The avoidance of conflict and the considerations for sentiments and interests of others evident in the treatment of nats is a characteristic of all social interaction, expressed in the term *a nadè.*

SPIRITS AND NAT CULTS

In the villages today, the concern with spirits persists, but it is no longer the basis for nat cults. As we have seen in the legends, nats originated in spirits of the dead who died a violent and unnatural death and whose souls failed to become incorporated in a new life. Because of the annoyance these spirits caused to people of a region they were granted overlordship of an area by the kings and were thus appeased by annual and intermittent offerings and celebrations. Since the kings were overthrown, no new cults have been established. The problem of laying to rest the restless souls of those who died a green death—*aseinthe*—is now resolved through Buddhist ritual offerings for the dead so that the spirit will enter a new life. This resolution indicates the thorough integration of animistic and Buddhist tradition, as I shall illustrate in the following case:

> The headman of Kangyi, Patheingyi township, was killed by Communist insurgents along with his brother. The headman had been giving tribute of rice and supplies to the insurgents in order to gain the villagers' security from their raids. Government authorities forced the headman to reveal the nature of the insurgent leaders and to forewarn the military police the next time they were to come for tribute, threatening to beat the headman if he failed to do this. The headman complied, and the leaders were caught. Shortly afterward, the headman and his brother were killed in an ambush by the insurgents, one of whom was the headman's brother-in-law. The mutilated bodies were taken to Mandalay and buried without village ceremony. The knot of hair from each of his surviving children was cut and put in the coffin, along with a length of string measuring each child's height. This was a substitute for the child so that the soul of the dead man would not be tempted to take his children with him.

In the weeks following the headman's death, some of the people of the village had dreams in which the headman and his younger brother appeared. The younger brother's wife was pregnant, and his restless spirit indicated in the dreams that he was worried about her. The younger brother said to one dreamer (not a relative) that the headman was leading the life of a devil.

The widow, concerned for the life of her children and for her dead husband's spirit, consulted the elders of the village who advised her to hold a shinbyu for the children with the money she would receive from the government as widow's compensation. The shinbyu would be held in the name of the dead man so that, with the final offering, the kutho, or merit, would add to whatever merit he had acquired in his lifetime of offerings and ensure him a new life.

The shinbyu was held at the pongyi-kyaung to avoid the expense of a mandate. The day before the shinbyu the headman's wife made her offering to the village nat at the natsin and to her own and her husband's mizaing-hpazaing nat in her house. She offered a pot of water to the spirit of the hill, asking him to come to the shinbyu. The night before the shinbyu, a villager dreamed the headman appeared in a tree outside the town wall; the dreamer asked the headman why he appeared in his dream, and the latter replied that he had come to see his son's shinbyu.

Throughout the shinbyu the widow wore her husband's scarf at her neck. As she offered the gift of a robe, matches, rice, and fans, with money to the monks, she held the scarf at her cheek and gave these items in her husband's name. The eldest of the monks who officiated prayed, saying that the widow made these offerings for her husband so he could continue on the path to Neikban (Nirvana). While he prayed, the widow poured water, catching it in a plate. (This ritual, the *yeizet chadè*, is symbolic of the Buddha's custom of pouring water on the ground when making an offering so that the ground should be witness to the good deed.) The widow then said:

> I am offering the monks food and clothing. I am making my two sons *koyin* [monks]. That which I am now doing will cause the five enemies of man to disappear. For this life and for the afterlife we assemble here to get rid of bad luck and worries.

The headman's clothing lay folded on the mat on which his widow sat before the monks: his sleeping rug, longyis, and *eingyis*. The longyis were later made into curtains for the kyaung windows, and the shirts cut into table doilies.

On the day following the shinbyu, the mother went with the children in their koyin robes to the fort where her husband's spirit had appeared in the dream. She took his clothing along and called upon his soul, telling him what she had succeeded in doing. About three hundred villagers, friends, and relatives attended her, along with one monk who did a payeit yuttè, a recital of prayers to rid the site of devils. He said to the dead man's spirit: "It is not your duty to remain here any longer. Your spirit is free to go (*ameint pyandè*)." He then gave the people present the five precepts.

The ceremony was successful—nobody had dreams in which the spirits of the dead men appeared in the two-month period that followed the shinbyu, according to my last inquiry.

Even natural death is attended by a danger period of seven days in which the spirit of the deceased hovers near his home. The wake carried on at this time is a period in which villagers, friends, neighbors, and relatives guard the body and keep off evil spirits, as they while away the time gambling, eating, and drinking. During this period the entire village is unclean and all offerings to the nats are postponed until after the final ceremony in which the priests offer the five precepts. The offering of food to participants in the wake, and the offering of rice, candles, etc., to the monks who give the five precepts at the burial, is the deceased's last chance to gain merit.

On the seventh day after the deaths, in the late afternoon, a spirit caller, usually a young male relative of the deceased who is not afraid of spirits, calls the spirit at the grave while holding a piece of the deceased's clothing in a ceremony called the *leitpya kwedè*. If the deceased has young children, particularly in the case of a mother of young children, there is some danger that the soul of the children will accompany the parent to the grave. In these cases, a string measuring the height of the child or a knot of the child's hair will be put in the coffin as in the case of the murdered headman. As a further precaution, two bananas are taken, one ripe, which is given to the child to eat in the house and the other, an unripe one, which is thrown to the west of the village in the direction of the graveyard. The final act is for the monks to gather on the morning after the soul calling to give the five precepts to all those who participated in the wake and burial.

The concern for the soul contradicts the Buddhist doctrine of denial of *anatta*, or the ego-identified soul substance. However, the one solution of the soul crisis now lies in the Buddhist doctrine of reincarnation. If passage to the next life is interrupted because of the circumstances surrounding the death or appearance of the restless soul in dreams, the traditional Buddhist ceremonial is resorted to as a means of acquiring merit for the deceased, which will make the transition possible.

CONCLUSION

Animism, since Tylor first defined it, has been a grab-bag category of all forms of spirit worship. In Upper Burma, however, the animistic spirit cult has a specific content with distinctions in the kinds of spirits worshipped that are related to the structural units of the society through which this worship is carried on. The nat cult is tied to the family, the village, and the region, and these different ties affect the strength and persistence of the cult. The mizaing-hpazaing nat, which is transmitted directly from parent to child, is the most consistently honored and the last to be given up. The village nat, though he is of less importance to the individual than the household nat and has no direct transmission of responsibility for his maintenance, is nevertheless an important link with the whole village and must be propitiated even if one moves away. The regional nats are those of the household and village nats that have attained fame in a wide locale and whose popularity depends upon the natkadaw and other specialists associated with the cult. Misfortune resulting from failure to meet the responsibilities to the nats, which the villager inherits and acquires by virtue of being a member of a family and living in a village, meets with little sympathy from his fellow men, for this is felt to be a basic obligation.

The nats are an extension of the human society in village life, and propitiation of them affects one's fortune in this life. In the words of one informant, "When we do something for Buddha, we do it for the next life, and when we do something for the nats, we do it to help us in this life." As a subgroup in the society, their presence is feared and honored in almost every house and in special shrines. Crises and misfortunes are interpreted in terms of the nats' likes and dislikes. Serious Buddhist meditators ignore nat offerings, but they too admit their presence in saying that their taking the five precepts daily gives them power over the nats.

Nats, when analyzed in the social context of belief, emerge as integrated figures of the society, existing in an order that never competes with Buddhist ideology. They have survived the monarchs who established their domain and continued to receive their tribute during the rule of the British. They have persisted in the period of independence, their survival due in part to the chaos that followed the war (personal disaster still being attributed to their power). The social aspect of religion, negated in the Buddhist ideal of the monastic life (Durkheim 1915, 67), survives in the nat cults, and the relations with the nats reflect the conventions of social interaction. No new nat cults have emerged, but the soul crises of transmigration, which gave rise to belief in them, persist. The resolution now lies within Buddhist rites of gaining merit through giving.

POSTSCRIPT

The optimistic conclusion to this essay written in 1963 could never be expressed today. Ne Win succeeded U Nu in a military coup in 1962, a year after we left Burma. Economic and political ties were ended with world powers and even neighboring countries. The military junta has refused to seat Daw Aung San Suu Kyi, who won the 1990 elections, and the country is squeezed by economic sanctions imposed by most countries because of severe human rights violations.

I returned to Burma, now renamed Myanmar by the military junta, in January 1998 when Myanmar opened a crack in its door to the East. We returned to find the capital city of Yangon, formerly Rangoon, much like we remembered it, still dominated by pagodas and parks. Its trees have been saved from annihilation by traffic that devours the landscape and skyways of Bangkok. Both men and women, still wearing the classic longyis draped across their sinuous bodies, slip gracefully on their thong sandals through city traffic. The major class distinction is in the quality of the cloth: beautiful silks in iridescent shades for the wealthier people, cotton plaids or flowered patterns for the less so, and parasols blooming with flowers that shade women from the midday sun.

In the fiftieth anniversary of its independence, Myanmar is still close to the insurrections that threatened the country with fission along ethnic and ideological lines in the early years of its independence. The suppression of all public expression other than that condoned by the State Law and Order Restoration Council (SLORC) allows the rogue government to remain in power despite the loss of the 1990 election to Daw Aung San Suu Kyi's National League for Democracy. The ubiquitous presence of government troops, now even more widely visible because of their entry into "social welfare" tasks, is matched by troops of pongyis who go out in their saffron robes each morning to beg for the monasteries. The government, seeking ideological support for its waning power, is courting the legions of monks who inhabit the temples dotting the landscape. SLORC gives major funding to the four hundred thousand monks, novices, and nuns that are found in the national population of 45 million, and generals and officials have been responsible for building major pagodas in recent years as they try to legitimate a tottering government.

We were well advised on how to prepare ourselves for the trip by a Buddhist scholar who had survived a few years' stay. "Bring many small American bills," we were told. Currency exchange is highly controlled by the government which gives an exchange rate thirty times less than the black market rate. We changed the required amount of three hundred U.S. dollars into foreign currency equivalents (FCEs)—crudely printed paper that looks about as legitimate as the currency for a Monopoly game. These could then be cashed with considerable difficulty in the few banks found in the countryside, whereas American dollars were enthusiastically received.

"Stay in government approved hotels; the police are less forbidding in accommodations where SLORC has set its mark of approval." So we stayed in the very British Liberty Hotel in the outskirts of Yangon where tea was available at all hours of the day and the Chinese attendants all spoke English. "Contract a guide and a driver for your trip." We arranged to be met at the airport by a guide, Ramesh, an Indian born in Myanmar who had just been forced by the financial crisis in Thailand to leave his post as tourist agent for the greater Southeast Asian locales where he had served until a few months before. He conducted us to the van and our driver, who became our courier to the interior of Myanmar.

Without their services we probably never would have survived the week's trip. They knew where to go and when, to whom we could speak with candor and who might have us expelled, what we could buy and what we ought to pay for it. The very next day we set off on the road to Mandalay, carrying George Orwell's *Burmese Days* and a used copy of Wheeler and Cummings's *Burma Travel Survival Kit*. Three decades before on our first trip to Mandalay we went by train. It was either that or Kipling's road to Mandalay, the Irrawaddy River, since the road was pockmarked where paved, and a dusty track in most of its expanse. U.S. AID agents offered in 1960 to construct a highway from Yangon to Mandalay, but the government refused that development plan as well as others offered by Western powers. "Why should the U.S. want to do the construction?" the press asked rhetorically back in 1960. In order to fly reconnaissance planes to China was their own answer. So the road was never built and to this day remains a mostly dusty track once beyond fifty miles of the capital.

Our driver kept up a constant communication with his horn, a special beep for each of the different modes of transportation from pedicabs (motorized three-wheel cabs), bicycles, bullock carts, buses, trucks, and the vans that service local passengers, overflowing with people and products hanging to the rear ladder of the vehicle and piled atop the roof. Chickens, ducks, and *pi*—pariah—dogs, kept partially alive by the food offerings to the Buddhist temples, flapped or draggled from our path as we tooted through tree-lined streets in villages en route. Each of the big trees has its own nat spirit I was told in 1960, and surely they must have kept guard during my absence since enormous trees encroached on both sides of the widened road. Some of the more venerable trees were bound with silk sashes that people offer periodically to show their respect to its nat.

The enchantment of the road trip also lay in the views of people and their activities: paddy fields, some flooded for seeding and some in growth; rice being threshed in villages; and houses near the Irrawaddy River still constructed on poles that raised the rattan thatch walls and roofs from the dust or mud depending on the season. We occasionally stopped to buy fruits sold on the side of the road, and in one of the larger towns and at Gyobindauk we saw livestock as well as the artisan products, vegetables, fruits, and grains that were visible spilling out of shadowy markets. The road was an extension of their homes and paddy fields, with women and children in bullock carts, their faces caked with thanahka, holding bright parasols, and men with palm straw hats as broad as umbrellas shading their bodies.

The ceremonial life of Buddhist Burma was also on display along the highway. We witnessed a shinbyu party loading up a jeep with children as they prepared to ride around the village before entering the pagoda in Shwedaung where the road ran parallel to the Irrawaddy River. Each boy reenacts the life of the Buddha, dressing in royal finery before entering the pagoda where his head is shaved in an initiation rite that marks their humility as he becomes novitiate priest with saffron robes. Girls also have an ear-piercing ceremony to mark their passage of initiation as nuns. Although they are now driven through the streets of their villages in jeeps, as well as in bullock carts as we saw in 1960, the celebration is still an important rite of passage as a citizen of Myanmar as well as a novitiate in the Buddhist faith. We saw a natkadaw preparing for his transvestite role by caking his face with thanahka and outlining his eyes with mascara.

As we approached our evening destination of Bagan, we saw people congregating in teahouses smoking cheroots as they curled up on wooden benches that spilled out to the highway. In Taungwingyi, gamelan music and dancers notified us of a nat festival in process. A woman, apparently in a state of possession, wove across the flower-petaled floor. A handsome young transvestite with his eyes enhanced with mascara and wearing his longyi in the women's fashion (draped and tucked on the side instead of bunched in the middle) lounged on the sidelines until he too, would join the dancers. When we asked about the nat who was being honored, he happily responded that it was in recognition of the Thirty-Seven Nats recognized in Upper Burma and was ready to spell out all of their names when Ramesh, our guide, advised us that they were all in the revised edition of Temple's book. As an anthropologist I did not want to take that without questioning whether the roster of the Thirty-Seven Nats still included those in the pantheon that King Anawrahta authorized when he reigned from 1084 to 1113. When he introduced Buddhism to help unify the many distinct races with diverse spirit animistic worship, he constructed a pantheon for them in his capital city of Bagan since he was unable to eradicate the pervasive nats. Cloistered in a wing of the main pagoda, they still receive offerings from devotees, who also consider themselves to be Buddhists. We planned to follow our tour of Bagan the next morning with a trip to Mt. Popo where a pagoda constructed on the peak is a showcase for the still-popular nats.

Our hotel was within the compound of Bagan, and it took us only a few minutes to arrive by car at the pagoda where we could best view the dawning sun. A few other tourists, mostly Burmese and some Australians and Japanese, climbed the three-tiered pagodas. From the summit we could see the bulldozed area where SLORC plans to expand tourist facilities, and the ruins where workers, both men and women, were working on reconstruction. Brick making was a fine art conforming to the architectural needs of the thousands of pagodas built almost a millennium ago. A few white-faced pagodas loomed in the early morning sun out from the orange-red glow of the ancient pagodas.

By early afternoon we arrived in Mt. Popo. Climbing up the stairs, accompanied by chattering monkeys and even more devotees and tourists than we had seen in Bagan, we found the Thirty-Seven Nats. The image of Bo Ma Gyi, the princess exiled by her father for her marriage, with her consort and their two children is ensconced with their many offerings of flowers, fruits, and coconuts, in the center of these restless spirits who still are honored in many households as well as in their shrines. Nats are treated much like the Burmese rulers who have extorted so much tribute and given so little in return. In the centuries that these highly differentiated people—the Mon, Shan, Karen, Kachin, Arakanese, and Chins, as well as many distinct dialects and beliefs within these groups—have been welded together as a colony and nation, people appeased their overlords as they attempted to retain their own customs.

We found Mandalay to be a far more bustling city than Yangon, with its commercial enterprises benefiting from the proximity of Chinese industrial growth just to the north. Small family-run enterprises making beautiful longyi materials, lacquer trays, boxes and images, and embroidering tapestries have a ready market among the prosperous Chinese of the city and in the export trade with China. The government here suspects Buddhist monasteries of harboring greater dissidence. A rumor that the gem lodged in the stomach of the Buddha image in the Mahamuni monastery on the outskirts of Mandalay was stolen by antigovernment monks set off a police crackdown and became a national incident. In retaliation, Muslim mosques were burned by what the government claimed was a gang of Buddhist monks, but what others claimed was the government's own agents stirring up trouble among the religious groups.

It was still forbidden to go much beyond Patheingyi, the township just to the north of the city where I had worked in 1960. Much to our surprise, the officials in Patheingyi said that the township officer at the time I was there came in frequently to consult with them. They sent an officer on motorbike to bring him to the town hall and within fifteen minutes he arrived, looking as vigorous as I recalled him to be. He remembered my interpreter, whose husband, he said, had become a professor in the University of Mandalay. When we returned to our hotel, we consulted with the owners about how we might find them. He looked for the professor's name in the telephone directory in vain, and then offered to take me to the university. He secured a taxi with darkened windows—it was forbidden for foreigners to even visit the university—and I crouched down in the backseat as we entered the gates of the university grounds.

What had been a bustling center for Mandalay youth as they embarked on professional careers was now grown over with weeds and all the classrooms closed. In the chemistry building we found a chemist who said he knew a physicist and would take us to his house. He mounted his motorcycle and we followed him out of the gates. When a policeman stopped him, we thought we were in for trouble, but we were greatly relieved to learn that he was reprimanded only for failing to wear his helmet, a law in Mandalay that all motorcyclists had to be properly helmeted. After he had retrieved it, we proceeded to the house of the chemist but were not successful in our mission. The physics department had closed years before and the faculty had dispersed.

Sagaing, the legendary site of dazzling pagodas topping the range of hills rising from the shores of the Irrawaddy River and dark recesses of hermits' caves, is only a half hour by boat from Mandalay. It is the site of one of the most extensive Buddhist monasteries, where the world-renowned monk, the Venerable Ashin Nyanissara, presides over the Buddhist Academy with its library, hospital, and classes for monks. It is one of the few windows to the West that offers the Burmese knowledge of the rest of the world, and where travelers can enlighten themselves. The monks' attempts to bring potable water to the town nearly backfired when the runoff leaked into the hermits' caves.

We returned on the alternate route to Yangon, stopping overnight at Taungoo. A smiling Chinese couple operated the Beauty Bed and Breakfast where we stayed. It was January 3, the eve of the celebration of the fiftieth anniversary of Burma's independence. We thought of joining the crowds that were congregating where gamelan music was playing, but the tea-shop owner on the main street said that it was just a government-ordered celebration. The next morning the owners of the pension joined us for a magnificent breakfast with all kinds of fruits and delicious cakes. They told us that both of them practiced medicine, and that their daughter was studying medicine too; but, knowing that the university campuses had been closed for a decade to prevent antigovernment protests, I questioned where she attended classes. They ruefully admitted that classes in the Yangon University had been suspended for the past two years. The woodcutters logging teakwood not far from the city were too poor to be able to buy mosquito netting, so the most prevalent diseases they treated were malaria, followed by dysentery. But they had found an effective herb for the treatment of malaria that was much less expensive and had fewer side effects than the imported medicines.

As we approached Yangon the road was being paved, a lengthy process since pulverizing the gravel was done by women using hand mallets. Men stoked an infernal machine fired by logs of wood to boil the tar that was poured onto the surface with an improvised barrel. Dozens of trucks passed us, bearing teakwood. This confirmed rumors that SLORC was extracting all of its resources in teak, gold, rubies, and oil to make up for dwindling reserves in the government treasury. Myanmar is now the largest exporter of heroin to the world market, and there is an active internal trade.

In the capital there was no evidence of an independence-day celebration. Some guessed that the government had forbidden any congregation in fear of demonstrations against SLORC; others attributed it to apathy brought on by ten years of government repression since the army refused to turn over power to Aung San Suu Kyi's democratically elected National Coalition Government of the Union of Burma. The monks, who enjoy a prestigious position in society and with the government, could be crucial if they assume moral leadership, an Anglican priest told us. He has responsibility for social action projects in the Chin

Hills where the Chin people, like the Keren and other minorities, have already chosen a separate path for the future since a high majority has converted to Protestantism.

The vital presence of the nats confirmed my earlier impression of their importance in dealing with the social strife in Burmese society. They are still the mediators in a pluricultural society that has withstood tyranny in the many changes of rule. The functionalist paradigm discarded in the postcolonial world along with the governments that pretended to control this vibrant society still captures some of the enduring cultural paradigms that survive military rule and provides the templates forging a new national identity.

NOTES

This paper, based on fieldwork in 1960, was published under the title "An Analysis of Animism in Burman Village Social Relations," in Manning Nash, ed., *Anthropological Studies in Theravada Buddhism* (New Haven, Conn.: Yale, Southeast Asian Studies, 1966), with a new preface and postscript written in 2005. I am indebted to Frank Reynolds for many helpful comments in elaborating these reflections.

I use "Burma" throughout, the English name of the country before it was changed to "Myanmar" by the military after its takeover of the government.

1. Research for this study was carried out in three neighboring villages in the township of Patheingyi, Mandalay district, Patheingyi center, Nyaungbintha, and Zigyogon. Surveys were made in twenty of the sixty-five villages of the township. I am indebted to the National Institute of Mental Health for money in support of the research.

2. See especially Langham-Carter (1933), Brown (1915), Htin Aung (1955 and 1956), Scott (1900 and 1927), and Temple (1906).

3. Melford Spiro (1970), who arrived shortly before we left Burma, was the most adamant in identifying spirit animism as a distinct sphere from Buddhism. Subsequent scholars (Lehman 1972 and especially Brac de la Perrière n.d.) remark on the nat spirits as intrinsic to Buddhist identity.

4. Compass points are significant orienting points for the Burmans in all their activities, and particularly in reference to the nats. The significance is based on the reckoning of Indian astrologers who formerly were advisers to the kings. East is the direction of good fortune, west of misfortune. In the east of the village, therefore, the natsin is located, offerings are made, and the coconut is hung in the east of the house; the west is the site for the cemetery, refuse dumps, and in the west of the house is located the birth room.

5. In fact, in the studies cited, no mention was made of the mizaing-hpazaing in discussing the Thirty-Seven Nats. It is not, however, an obscure feature of the communities, and I was made aware of it in the first week of my study.

6. The majority of the people have the same nat in any one village, or a nat favored in the neighboring towns, as the result of a census taken in Nyaungbintha shows: twenty-six of the fifty-nine households were questioned about their mizaing-hpazaing; sixteen of these, or 61 percent, had the relatives of Min-Maha-Giri; three had Htibyuzaing, the white-umbrella owner; five had two Taungbyon brothers; one had Badone; one had Hodawgyi, the Mandalay district nat; one, whose grandparents were from Lower Burma, brought one of the Lower Burma nats with him; and another family, from Shimbogale, had the *komyoyin eindwin*, the nine-village nat. Five of these families had another of these same nats along with the nats counted above, and in the remaining cases, the spouse's nat was the same or the nat was not mentioned. The census I carried out, though inadequate in that questioning about second nats was not pressed, shows that the mizaing-hpazaing nat is linked to a locality.

7. One woman tried to give a smaller contribution than usual to her mizaing-hpazaing nat because of her poverty. She was seized by a violent illness during which she seemed to be bound by invisible ropes, with water and froth coming from her mouth. In order to cure her, her family offered rice and *lahpet* (pickled tea leaves) to Htibyuzaung, the slighted nat, and she recovered. She subsequently took the responsibility for nat offering when her mother died.

8. The family of one girl who was marrying a man separated from his first wife had neither the money nor the inclination to have a large ceremony (because of shame in the face of the deserted first wife and her children). However, they made an offering to the mizaing-hpazaing nats in their house so misfortune would not result from the wedding.

9. One man, who gave some of his pork curry to the nats when he was in the mountains, returned to find his cow missing. He realized immediately that the Taungbyon brothers, who are his own mizaing-hpazaing, were insulted by the offering because their father is a Muslim.

10. Leach (1954, 173) saw in the relation of the Kachins to the nats an extension of the *huan* class hierarchy to a higher level. The way in which people deal with the nats parallels the way in which they deal with human superiors.

5

The Limits of Naïveté in Anthropological Fieldwork

The 1954 U.S.-Instigated Coup in Guatemala

During my graduate student days in the 1950s, rebellions, domestic violence, alcoholism, drugs, and corruption in public office were considered peripheral to the field project; today they have become central themes in ethnography. Fledgling anthropologists went into field situations innocent of counterinsurgency plots spawned in the emergent globalization system, and of the role that we might unconsciously play. Now too much is known about undercover plots to ignore or deny U.S. intervention in the field sites we choose. When I was invited to a conference on Fifty Years after the Guatemalan Coup of 1954, I wrote for the first time about my experiences in Guatemala in 1953 and 1954, reflecting on how they set the stage for the decades of civil war that followed. In the interim since the coup, some ethnologists ignored or even denied the genocidal reign of terror; others have made the violence a central focus of analysis. Its lasting effect has been to force us to see ourselves in the mirror of our work and to relinquish the pose of objective observer divorced from the moral implications of the encounter. Comparing the resurgence of ethnic identity in movements on both sides of the Mexico-Guatemala border, I return to the question Max Gluckman raised: What are the limits to naïveté in fieldwork? Comparing the political crises in Mexico and Guatemala, I conclude that, in the context of ethnocidal policies promoted by an indigenist policy of integration in Mexico and the genocidal policies pursued by military leaders that ruled Guatemala for three decades, it becomes ever more relevant that we become more conscious of the role we play in analyzing, ignoring, or denying the political context of our work.

Who is going to benefit by what we do or fail to publish, and who might be compromised by our interpretations? What role can we play as activists, both to reveal what we learned about past errors and to try to bring about a change in direction?

An incipient critique of such ethnographic exclusion can be found in Max Gluckman (1958). He noted the importance of social conflict in his "Analysis of a Social Situation in Modern Zululand," in which he voiced a strong critique of segregationist policy in South Africa and the importance of recognizing conflicts and dysfunction as part of the field analysis.[1] This early essay provided a more poignant glimpse into the structural problems of colonization seen through the window of apartheid than the book he edited late in his career, *Closed Systems and Open Minds* (Gluckman 1964). Yet the subtitle to that anthology, *The Limits of Naiveté in Social Anthropology,* suggests a key issue in the development of anthropology that I will consider here.

We went into field situations innocent of these undercover plots spawned in the emergent globalization system, and of the role that we might unconsciously play. Now too much is known about coups engineered by secret agents and the mundane actions of financial institutions foreclosing on debts to ignore or deny U.S. intervention in the field sites we choose. In waging the cold war, precursors of the U.S. Central Intelligence Agency (CIA) engineered the overthrow of Mossadegh, prime minister of Iran, in 1953 and then the overthrow of President Jacobo Arbenz in Guatemala in 1954. Other covert operations followed in the Dominican Republic, in Brazil, and in Bolivia resulting in the replacement of populist democracies in 1964. Chile lost another experiment in democracy in 1973 when U.S. secretary of state Henry Kissinger instigated the coup that overthrew the democratically elected government of President Salvador Allende. In the 1980s more sophisticated tactics involved International Monetary Fund (IMF) conditions imposed on indebted countries that debased national currency and denied social programs in order to redeem debts incurred by the military dictators put in power in the previous decade.[2] The Reagan administration resorted to earlier tactics when it recruited rebel troops in Honduras to destabilize the Sandinistas in Nicaragua.

My first venture into fieldwork was in 1953 when the discipline of anthropology was still a field of discovery and we approached the world with naïveté born of adventure. Our concerns were limited to those of fending off the diseases common in third world countries—dysentery, hepatitis, malaria—or of feeling estranged in settings where we were thrust back into childhood, learning a language that was not written. We were not concerned with paramilitary or guerrilla operations, nor did we feel that we had to justify our presence. America had just won a war against Fascism, and had not yet embarked on our own imperial campaigns. The ethnographic frame was on the functioning of traditional societies and the structures that maintained coherence in the face of modernizing changes.

I arrived in Guatemala in 1953 when the country was still experiencing the spring of democracy brought about by the revolution of 1944. The chosen place was Cantel, and the timeless people were workers in the Cantel Textile Factory, one of the few factories operating in Guatemala.[3] Our professor, Sol Tax, had passed through Cantel in his survey of indigenous communities of the Western Highlands in the 1930s. He was impressed by his view of a workforce made up of indigenous men and women working in a modern factory that employed some eight hundred hands. When we arrived fifteen years later, we were also awed by our view of men and women wearing regional attire pouring out of the factory gates to cross the Samalá River on a hammock bridge and climbing up to the town center five hundred feet above. There at least half the workers lived in adobe brick houses with tile or thatched roofs, typical of those found throughout the Western Highlands, and as many more lived in housing near the factory provided by the Basque owners, the Ibarguen family.

In our first week we learned to appreciate the intricate balance between Indians and *ladinos*, a term that included acculturated indigenous people and *mestizos*, or mixed-bloods. In the months that followed we also began to perceive distinctions among social classes, which spanned the ethnic strata. Finding a space to live in was part of the learning process since rentals were as scarce as in New York City. People built houses only to live in, but as we became accepted while temporarily living in the schoolhouse while the children were on vacation, the local pharmacist mentioned there might be one available. Thus we met our landlady, an Indian woman who was the first in her family to make the transition to ladino (non-Indian) status. She was a traditional curer, and (as we learned later) the lover of the pharmacist, so with her acquaintance we had the full gamut of medical lore open to us. We also learned that the plant manager was the illegitimate son of one of the Basque owners of the factory. As a mestizo, or child born of indigenous and ladino parents, he had spent his early years living in the village with his mother until his father's wife spotted the resemblance. She brought him to live in the big house near the factory, where he was put in charge of labor relations. This had become a problem for the owners with the advent of a democratic government since the workers had organized a union. The heads of each factory department—the weaving, spinning, and dyeing operations—were foreigners, with a Yorkshire weaving master and a Lancashire spinning master at odds with each other, and a German dyeing master. Paternalistic practices that included physical abuse with which they had exercised control over the labor force were no longer acceptable, and the bastard son served as an excellent mediator in the growing number of labor disputes.

Looking back on the imposed categories of traditional and modern that shaped our research design, it is now clear to me that the mediators in our small world of Cantel were those marginalized by miscegenation and illegitimacy and these were not part of our ethnographic frame. Other divisions in the workforce and in the village governance were more predictable in terms of structural factors in the traditional to modern paradigm defined by ethnicity, religion, class, and education. The revolutionary government of Juan José Arévalo Bernejo had succeeded in its objectives of educating many indigenous youths, and literate young men were working as mechanics and maintenance crews. They were the leaders of the first union ever allowed in the factory. They were also challenging the *principales*—elders who had fulfilled all the posts in the civil religious hierarchy in governance of the pueblo. As a result of his army experience, the mayor of the town, Santiago Xitimul, was literate. A practicing Protestant before his election, he found himself forced to drink during his tenure as mayor because of the many ceremonial occasions in which he was officially engaged, but vowed to return to abstinence after his term.

Our year of research was coming to an end in the summer of 1954 when rumors began to circulate about a rebellion led by Col. Castillo Armas with five hundred armed soldiers, including former soldiers of the Wehrmacht, who had returned to claim the lands taken from families of German plantation owners during World War II. Castillo Armas had, as he later acknowledged, benefited from a Fort Leavenworth course in preparation for his role as liberator. Radio Voice of Liberation broadcast ominous reports of the battles fought by these rebels, the body count, and tales of poisoned lake water, but we tended to ignore them since such reports often proved fictitious. We were somewhat more disturbed when government security agents arrived one day when we were visiting a hamlet, inquiring about our activities in the town. The mayor and chief of police told them there were no *gringos* in town and offered no information regarding where we might be. This made us feel accepted by the villagers, but still uneasy about national developments.

People became alarmed in June 1954 when airplanes began to circle overhead, apparently observing activities in the factory compound and the village. Cantel was suspect because of its union of workers, and the union represented a Communist conspiracy. Daily broadcasts from Radio Voice of Liberation warned of the massive rebellion forming in Honduras that was moving toward Guatemala. The workers camouflaged the new steel and concrete bridge, which had only recently replaced the precarious hammock bridge, with evergreens in fear that this newly finished link from the factory to the town center would be bombed. Later one day in June 1954 when we had just returned from Quetzaltenango, about ten kilometers from Cantel, Radio Voice of Liberation announced that there had been a skirmish between rebels and government troops. Yet we had seen no signs of disturbance or any military troops.

On June 25 we decided to break the monotony of village life by going to a movie in Quetzaltenango. Youths with whom my husband, Manning, played soccer joined us in our secondhand yellow jeep. When we found ourselves alone in a nearly empty theater, we suspected that the uprising was something more than a contrived rumor of Radio Voice of Liberation. We sat through the film despite the freezing cold, without the body heat of the usual scores of Indians and ladinos. On the road back to Cantel we saw trucks parked bumper-to-bumper as they loaded up *campesinos* recruited to defend the revolution. Because he wanted to give an account of recruitment levels to his superior officers, a lieutenant hailed a ride with us in our overloaded jeep. We were afraid the army might commandeer the jeep because of the woeful scarcity of vehicles, but he simply thanked us and took off, allowing us to return to Cantel center.

The next morning we learned that the war was over. President Arbenz had met with Jack Purifoy, the U.S. ambassador who had just returned from a successful eradication of Communism in Greece, the night before and had pledged to avoid a bloodbath by leaving the country. The arms that Arbenz had ordered from Czechoslovakia remained in a ship unable to dock because of the threat of U.S. fighter planes hovering over the port. We could verify they were never delivered to the countryside, where peasants mounted in trucks on the road to Cantel had only their machetes to defend *la patria*. The presence of a Soviet-allied ship loaded with arms provided the motivation for the Dulles brothers, who occupied the positions of secretary of state and head of the CIA, to trigger the coup. Castillo Armas was seated as president on July 8, 1954.

One of our friends who was a union representative left Cantel the following day. We heard from reporters in Guatemala City that Arbenz left the country, declaring he took nothing with him. The next day *El Imparcial* published a photo on the front page showing him passing through customs, his chest bared and his hands raised over his head as he was being searched. Not long afterward, our friends in the press corps indicated that a leading figure in Arbenz's diplomatic corps had used diplomatic immunity to take out one million dollars in small bills from the national bank of Guatemala. It was one of many stories never published. *Time* magazine ran a story by their stringer, Harvey Rosenhouse, relating that Castillo Armas was reselling at high markups corn bought from the Mexican government at a low price. The corn was to provide relief for peasants whose crops had been trampled when the former owners took back the land. In retribution, the government sent out an order to beat up a Herbert Rosenhouse. Harvey had a twin brother Robert, and Guatemalan intelligence had confused the target, calling him Herbert and capturing Robert. The latter was happy to report that he survived the beating since the clubs were made in Guatemala.

It was the beginning of low-intensity warfare with the assistance of a U.S. naval blockade and CIA bombing runs out of Managua (Hersh 1992, 353). The coup was a testing operation for future interventions that continued throughout Central America. Each day following the coup, rumors circulated about who was being jailed and who had fled. The jails were filled with five thousand suspects when Richard Adams received a grant to study the penetration of Communist ideology in the countryside. He asked us to assist him, assigning Manning and a number of Guatemalan students to the jail interviews and me to compile the results. Among the prisoners was a student who advised the team about the prisoners' interpretation of the questionnaire. Convinced that the interviews were part of a scheme to distinguish militant Communists from those who were apolitical, the prisoners had worked out responses that minimized their involvement in the revolutionary government, and indeed, our summation of the interviews confirmed this. But the moderate views they expressed reflected a well-grounded support for the Arévalo-Arbenz government that was not based on fomenting a violent revolution. This was the allegation of the U.S. National Security Council when they approved plans for a coup against a government that had for the first time in Guatemalan history made strides in advancing rural education and health, and that had permitted democratic participation in unions and cooperatives.

In the following months the factory managers returned to their old practices. The weaving and spinning masters resumed their abusive labor practices, even hitting workers as they had done in the past before there was a union. The weaving master denounced us as Communists to the U.S. Embassy, but with the intervention of friends we were not forced to return home earlier than planned. The entire embassy changed in the early months after the coup. No longer were there Spanish speakers knowledgeable of the country and of indigenous culture, but bridge-playing monolinguals who did not venture far from Guatemala City.

When we returned to Chicago we had an unexpected visit from a CIA agent on a hot July morning. He waited in the stifling heat of our basement apartment for Manning to rouse himself, only to be told that he could read whatever Manning might publish, but that he (Manning) had nothing to say. Although the agent had not tried to debrief me, it was then that I began to realize our research might fit into a larger domain of state intrigue that may even have influenced the funding of our research. The book, *Machine Age Maya* (M. Nash 1956), probably had little that would have interested the CIA, then or even later. It was, as some called it, a functionalist argument for an existing industrial accord, extolling the benefits of modernization. Although I had contributed maps, interviews with women workers, missionaries, and protestant converts, as well as census materials I conducted in the five hamlets, the township's center, and factory housing, I had little input into the ideological formulation of the book since I came down with lingering case of hepatitis.

MAYAS ACROSS THE MEXICO-GUATEMALA BORDER

Mayan linguistic groups of both Mexico and Guatemala were united in the governance of the Province of Guatemala. Indians on both sides of the border were subject to tribute payments that forced them out of self-sufficient agriculture and into the market, to sell their products or labor (MacLeod 1983, 89–214). The Spanish expropriated lands granted to indigenous populations and thereby acquired a labor force of the expropriated Indians for their haciendas and workshops (MacLeod 1983, 194; Carmack 1983, 214; Wasserstrom 1983). In both areas, the liberal period, especially after 1870, brought about the loss of communal lands, forced labor, and pressure for ladinoization. Communities in the more isolated areas of the highlands on the slopes of the Sierra Mountains were able to retain their traditional culture until the revolutionary period, but the price was seasonal labor in coastal plantations (Carmack 1983, 217; Wasserstrom 1983; Rus 1986). Rebellions occurred when indigenous people were pressed beyond their ability to sustain the culture of their ancestors or when corruption of Spanish and ladino intermediaries exceeded the norms. Thus the Rebellion of Cancuc broke out in Chiapas in the township of Cancuc in 1712 when tributes rose in a declining economy, during the droughts that affected the townships of Yajalón, Petalcingo, Tila, and Tumbala in 1771, and in 1867–1869 in Chamula. As capital intensive exploitation intensified in Guatemala, revolts occurred in the mid-nineteenth century in Ixtahuacán, in 1876 in Momostenango when liberals seized the lands of Indians, and in Ixcoy in 1898.

I carried out fieldwork with Mayas in Chiapas from 1957 and in summer sessions in the 1960s, returning twenty years later to view the changes that had occurred. The growing opposition to President Carlos Salinas de Gortari and President Ernesto Zedillo's neoliberal policies erupted in the Zapatista uprising of January 1, 1994. This gave me a perspective on both sides of the Guatemalan-Mexican border when they were under fire from their governments. Similarities in culture and society persist, but historic changes following independence from Spain when the frontier was established in 1824 led to differences in the relations of indigenous people with the state on each side. Both areas experienced the opening up of trade and liberal "reforms" that divested Indian communities of much of their communal lands. And throughout the countryside *caudillos* (strong-armed men) retained control until the revolutions that took place in Mexico from 1910–1917 and in Guatemala in 1944.

In Guatemala ethnic relations were expressed in a continuum of cultural and economic strata (Adams 1964) with the indigenous majority subordinate to a dominant white elite. In the post–World War II era contact with missionaries of a reinvigorated Catholic Church, agents of the United Nations, the U.S. Peace Corps, and a variety of NGOs ignited the sense of injustice among Indians and the fear of rebellion among ladinos, or acculturated indigenous and mestizo populations. Guatemala's revolution of 1944 was a stunning rejection of U.S. support for Jorge Ubico's reinforcement of an agricultural export economy during the 1920s and 1930s when Mexico had already rejected that model (Torres Rivas 1991, 22). After Ubico was forced to resign during a general strike of students and workers in 1944, Juan José Arévalo emerged as the overwhelming winner of the elections that followed.

The opening to democracy in Guatemala allowed urban, commercial-agricultural plantations employing more than five thousand workers and railroad workers to organize. While Arévalo concentrated on programs in education, medical care, and housing, his successor to the presidency, Jacobo Arbenz, moved ahead with agrarian-reform land distribution and major development projects that alarmed the national bourgeoisie. His aggressive administration of the new land-reform legislation ignited further opposition from the United States. During the Eisenhower presidency when the United States turned its attention from the European theater of war and postwar reconstruction, Secretary of State John Foster Dulles, and his brother Allan, who was head of the CIA, were major shareholders in the United Fruit Company and promoted the coup because of the fear of land takeovers (Hersh 1992). John Dulles advised Castillo Armas when he took office in July 1954 that "Communists should be considered [a] class additional to common criminals not entitled [to] asylum," and demanded they should be "convicted of having been covert Moscow agents" (Hersh 1992, 353). The coup represented the first major undercover operation to overthrow an elected president in the Western hemisphere, marking a change in U.S. operations in Latin America from gunboat diplomacy to more pervasive intervention.

In Mexico the Revolution of 1910–1917 had broken with the stratified hierarchy of Spanish and Indians as the *mestizaje*—mixed races—institutionalized the new revolutionary codes. These were defined by an *indigenista* ideology that extolled the past glories of indigenous civilizations, but assumed that the future must necessarily be defined in Western terms. Lázaro Cárdenas confirmed this pattern when he became president (1934–1940), introducing the institutional base for revolutionary victories such as land reform and universal education. The benefits of the revolution came late to Chiapas where overt racism delayed application of the new rights ethnic minorities had gained in the 1917 Constitution. The colonial pattern of large landowners and governing caudillos retained domination of the centers of power until the generation of Indians educated in boarding schools introduced during Cárdenas's presidency in the 1930s began to occupy town offices of mayor and secretary formerly filled by ladinos. During my first field stay in Chiapas in 1957 I saw the blossoming of indigenous participation at the local level. This new relation had not yet become distorted by *caciquismo*—bossism marked by the Party of the Institutional Revolution (PRI) that began to corrupt and divide local leaders as more funds were channeled to them after the mid-1960s.

Following the 1954 coup in Guatemala the destinies of Mayas on each side of the border diverged even more than during the first half of the twentieth century. Whereas the Mexican mestizo elites who directed the course of change after their revolution and up until the 1960s tried to co-opt indigenous groups into their national project, the military leaders who seized power after the Guatemalan coup pursued a militarization project instigated by the United States. The nationalistic project in Mexico promoted integration of Indians in accord with a uniform ethnic model, leading to ethnocidal suppression of indigenous languages, customs, and law. In contrast the export-oriented production dominated by Eurocentric elites in Guatemala and governed by military leaders promoted genocidal conflict.

Both ethnocide and genocide are rooted in structural violence, or the everyday deprivation of the basic needs of survival. When structural violence against a subordinate group erupts into a direct attempt to eradicate the cultural characteristics and communal expression of difference, this becomes ethnocide; when in turn this escalates into physical extermination it becomes genocide. Both expressions are condemned by United Nations covenants, but it is extremely difficult to pin the label of genocide on any group. Hundreds of thousands of Tutsis were killed in Rwanda before the United Nations interceded, and rampant killing of whole communities in Darfur proceeded for decades before the term "genocide" was even mentioned in United Nations circles. The delay is related to the imperatives for action implied by the term incumbent upon a world community that lacks the mechanism for immediate response. By comparing the course of military repression and democratic opposition in Mexico and Guatemala, I hope to clarify the conditions that conduce to ethnocide or genocide.

MEXICO AND THE INDIGENISTA POLICIES OF INTEGRATION

At the most general level the turn to ethnocide or genocide can be traced to the level of development of civil society. Mexico had developed civil society networks that linked pueblos drawn into wider circuits promoted by the postrevolutionary project of forging a nation. Yet the *indigenista* ideology underlying the PRI undercut the basis for an authentic indigenous society while extolling the Indian past. As Miguel Bartolomé (1994, 73) demonstrates in his analysis of three cultures coexisting in the state of Oaxaca, the state maintains a pluralistic discourse at the formal level, but an internalization of ethnic inequality in practice. This also characterizes the de facto ethnocidal practices in Chiapas policies of integration. But while civilian leaders guided the popular mandates of indigenous and mestizo populations in Mexico, Guatemala was ruled directly, and with only brief civilian interludes indirectly, by the military in communication with U.S. special forces in four decades following the 1954 coup. There the penetration of the military into all branches of government and the economy undermined democracy (Schirmer 1998, 24–25). The genocidal policies pursued by the army under Rios Montt in the 1980s resulted in estimates of 75 thousand to 200 thousand killed and hundreds of thousands of indigenous people forced into exile in the thirty-six-year war (Jonas 1991).

Mexico's civilian rule since the consolidation of the revolution of 1910–1917 with Lázaro Cárdenas in 1934 has maintained order with less recourse to military intervention. Yet it was far from representing a quintessential democracy: one-party rule and the co-optation of *caciques*—indigenous leaders who carried out the will of party bosses for payoffs—were flagrant abuses both of electoral democracy and of indigenous notions of consensual democracy. Following the 1968 Olympic massacre in Mexico City, Mexican civil society attempted to extricate the many organized corporate groups from the control of the PRI. Increasingly, members of campesino organizations, women's cooperatives, and community-based initiatives in Chiapas organized as indigenous people. By the 1990s many campesinos had broken from the PRI-controlled National Confederation of Campesinos, and, along with newly formed women's artisan cooperatives, were forming independent organizations as they sought a new relationship with the state. Some of these organizations turned to radical democratic forms of organization in Christian Base Communities while others chose armed rebellion with the emergent Zapatista Army of National Liberation (EZLN).[4]

GUATEMALA AND THE ERUPTION OF GENOCIDE

Following the 1954 coup, the Guatemalan military leaders chose, or were pressed into adopting, military strategies to eliminate every form of participatory activity, from factory workers' unions such as those in Cantel, to rural campesino producers' and sellers' organizations. Civil society had coalesced in the decade of liberty offered by the democratic governments of Arévalo and Arbenz. The Guatemalan General Confederation of Workers had ninety thousand members, the Guatemalan National Confederation of Peasants was expanding branches in the countryside, and political parties were developing new positions (AVANCSO 1994, 23). Arbenz's promotion of agrarian reform provoked a reaction that resounded from the banana plantation of United Fruit to its headquarters in Boston, and to the Dulles brothers in Washington, D.C. (AVANCSO 1994, 28–29). When Arbenz realized that the army would not fight the invaders and that there were insufficient arms for the volunteers from the Guatemalan confederations of workers and peasants to enter into battle, he renounced his post on the evening of June 27, 1954 (AVANCSO 1994, 105–7).

Shortly thereafter Col. Castillo Armas, the leader of the rebellion, was seated as president, and the makeshift government succeeded in bringing about the reversal of the democratic process. The racism of the ruling elites fueled by the anticommunist agenda of the U.S. State Department grew with each attack on the indigenous populations. Castillo Armas proceeded with his project of liquidating the revolution by forcibly dislocating one hundred thousand peasants from the land they legally owned and worked in the first two months of the regime change (Torres Rivas 1991, 8). Uncounted numbers died from starvation when the former owners of the lands that had been donated during the revolution drove their cattle into the fields that the peasants had planted. Castillo Armas was not only responsible for commanding this operation, but also of commandeering the corn imported at low prices from Mexico and selling it for personal profit in the market. The military uprising against Ydigoras Fuentes in 1960 resulted in the retreat of dissidents to the mountains and the formation of guerrilla insurgency in 1962.

The United States took advantage of violent shifts of power in postcoup years to intensify military interventions in Guatemala. The Green Berets who had fought in Vietnam helped direct and finance counterinsurgency campaigns led by Col. Carlos Arana Osorio from 1966 to 1968. Labor unrest of striking workers in 1975 at the Coca-Cola factory and in the mines in 1977 marked the increase in protest and rebellion that culminated with the formation of the Committee of Peasant Unity (CUC), a community action organization of indigenes and mestizos, in 1978. The government retaliated ever more forcefully, violating international accords with the 1980 attack on Maya peasant organizations that occupied the Spanish Embassy to denounce military massacres (Green 1999).

The colonizers of both the Lacandón Rain Forest in Mexico and of the Ixcán Rain Forest in Guatemala, which face each other across the border, took a stand against forced movements of populations when the promises to the lands they colonized were revoked. This happened first in Guatemala in 1974 when oil was discovered and the oil companies— Getty Oil, Texaco, Amoco, and Shenandoah Oil—extended their drilling into settled areas of Ixcán. The terror began in 1978 with the Panzos massacre located on the northern border of the Ixil triangle. This was not an area of guerrilla activity, such as the plantation area to the east where former plantation owners were dislocating Indians who had received land grants under the Arbenz government. The highly publicized massacre occurred when settlers tried to defend their lands against the oil companies that were extending their drilling into the settled areas of Ixcán. The army and paramilitary forces backed up the companies against the settlers who objected to the takeover of the lands they had cleared and settled (Falla 1994; Sinclair 1995, 85). It came to be called the "Zone of the Generals" since General Lucas and other army generals were grabbing land in areas where transnational oil explorers had discovered oil (Jonas 1991, 128; Jonas 2004; Sinclair 1995, 85).

The peak of armed hostilities occurred from 1982 to 1985 when Gen. Rios Montt carried out a reign of terror leading to the destruction of over four hundred Guatemalan villages in which over two hundred thousand Mayas were killed and over one hundred thousand were forced into exile. In the subsequent militarization of the entire society, indigenous youths were forced to join patrols in search of dissidents. Their complicity, out of fear for their own lives, reinforced the militarization of the society. Some resisted by joining the CUC, others joined the Guerrilla Army of the Poor (EGP), especially after the massacre in Rio Negro in 1982 when the Guatemalan Army killed over half the villagers because they opposed the damming of a river for an international hydroelectric company (Alecio 1995, 26). The unleashing of state terror failed to eradicate their identity as indigenous people (Green 1999). The notorious "beans and bullets" civil-military development of the Guatemala Army in the 1980s focused 30 percent of the effort toward killing and 70 percent toward providing food and shelter (Schirmer 1998, 35–36).

Following the decades of war in which Guatemalan Mayas were entangled as combatants or victims, Mayan organizations emerged during the peace process in the mid-1980s. Human rights groups, beginning with the *Grupo de Apoyo Mutuo,* or Mutual Support Groups, CONAVIGUA, the widows' groups, and peace groups initiated by the Catholic Church, joined civil society groups that provided accompaniment for returned exiles to

Figure 5.1.   The militarization of Central America that began with the Guatemalan coup in 1954 recruited youths as young as 14 and 15 years of age. I photographed these youths in El Salvador in 1982 when the Cold War extended militarization throughout the region.

Quiché and Alta Verapaz, and laid the basis for a Mayan movement for revitalization (Calder 2004, 118). Indigenous leaders that rose in this period of ethnic revitalization called for control over educational programs, the official use of Mayan languages, participation in election debates, and greater autonomy in local and regional politics (Fischer and Brown 1996, 15; Warren 1998). The growing demand for control of their lands among Mayas in both nations set off broader demands for territorial autonomy discussed below. These are not separatist movements since Mayas on both sides of the border seek a place with the nations of which they are a part, albeit one that is defined by their own values and culture.

Guatemalan anthropologists have made their discipline the foremost armor in the struggle to overcome military terrorism and state corruption. In 1990 Myrna Mack, an anthropologist who was doing research on military atrocities at a time when few dared even to mention the deeds, was killed outside the office of the Association for the Advance of the Social Sciences (AVANCSO, *Asociación para el Avance de las Ciencias Sociales en Guatemala*), the organization that she had founded. I learned a great deal about the potential for scholarly intervention when I joined a delegation of the Latin American Studies Association that attended the court judgment against one of the three officers charged with the crime. The 2002 trial marked the first conviction of a high military leader for violations committed during the country's undeclared war (*Washington Post,* October 4, 2002). AVANCSO worked along with two forensic teams, the Center of Forensic Anthropology and Applied Sciences (CAFCA) and the Guatemalan Foundation of Forensic Anthropology (FFAG), coordinating the data drawn from the remains of massacres in the killing fields of indigenous villages and from the narratives of survivors. Their investigations were aided by and, in turn, reinforced the attempts by representatives of the Guatemalan National Coalition of Human Rights (CNDHG) and the National Coalition of Campesino Organizations (CNOC) to reveal the truth about the terror let loose in the country.

During our week of intensive interviewing we learned to appreciate both the danger regarding the threats to the fledgling democracy posed by the clandestine paramilitary organizations still operating in the country, and the extraordinary courage exhibited by anthropologists and other social scientists who worked despite severe pressure to end the investigations, including death threats. Ever since the trial had begun in August 2002, threats were reported by the social anthropology team working with survivors to restore the historical memory of those who witnessed the massacres, and by the forensic teams trying to retrieve the history of the massacres from exhumed remains of the victims. Yet when they discovered that the indigenous informants turned away when they saw national guards sent by the police in response to reported threats, they decided to work without protection. Some paid the penalty: on September 6, just two days before our arrival in Guatemala, the body of one of the assistants to the forensic anthropologists was found with his eyes gouged out, his tongue wrenched from his throat, and his ears ripped off. We were physically overwhelmed with the horror of past events when we stepped through the courtyard of the FFAG and saw it filled with child-size coffins that served as containers for the remains exhumed from the burial site. Yet these activist scholars continue their work filling in the gaps in the historical record caused by the repression and violence exercised against indigenous people over the past thirty-six years.

Announcements of their findings often resulted in further threats to the forensic teams. This happened in Chimaltenango, when the FFAG reported to the public prosecutors. The director, Dr. Suasnavar, commented, "Although they [the justices] did not directly threaten us, they attempted to depreciate our work." They were again threatened in February 2002 when the work had increased and they had about fifty people working on the exhumations. "There is greater support for our work than at first," Dr. Suasnavar continued. "Originally when we started work in 1992 it was a project of the Holland Embassy, and they finished work in December. The

Dutch are no longer here." FFAG receives money from U.S. AID, and, since the U.S. Embassy reports their information in a variety of media with each breakthrough they make, more threatening calls came to them. "We were forced to leave our fieldwork two months this spring, and that cost us a great deal." We asked whether our report would engender more threats and danger to the work of the FFAG, and Dr. Suasnavar replied, "It will put pressure on the state. We have to isolate the *grupos parallelos* [paramilitary or clandestine groups] with pressure. Whenever we publish something, other threats come in, but also information."

When we spoke with Dr. Clara Arena at the offices of AVANCSO, she recounted the threats and assaults endured by members of the cultural anthropology research team as they carried out fieldwork in highland indigenous communities affected by the military terror in the 1980s. Dr. Matilda Gonzalez, who was working with a team of AVANCSO researchers eliciting memories of the terror, was followed and accosted in January 2002, and the research center was burglarized. When the police were notified, they sent a bodyguard, but when he went on vacation, there was no substitute. "We have to break the authoritarian culture," Dr. Arena asserted. She and other members of the team saw their task as investigators informing society how the hegemonic base of the military and state operated at the grass roots, inculcating its authoritarian practices in village society through civilian patrols so as to disintegrate the social fabric. The very success of their work in analyzing the military tentacles in this social context appeared to be the reason for the mounting threats in 2002.

The creation of a Presidential Commission for Human Rights (*Comisión Presidencial de Derechos Humanos* or COPREDE) indicates some progress, but the lack of financing to investigate and address violations in court indicates more a desire to conform to the dictates but not the spirit of human rights. The vacillation in the Alfonso Portillo presidency from its own avowed agenda of instituting the legal base for social justice is amply illustrated by the administrative branch he put in place. With the appointment of former president Rios Montt and other such appointments in his cabinet, President Portillo did not inspire confidence in his reconciliation program. In the process of our investigations as to what the attorney general's office and the human rights office were doing about the threats to researchers, our own insistence on the need for greater security for the researchers seemed absurd. Our very presence in the country on this mission might well have garnered more danger for our colleagues and the government officials working against such insurmountable odds. And we would not be there to take the same risks of retaliation they bore from the still active *guardias blancas*—white guards, or paramilitaries. But as I watched the proceedings of the trial of the officers in a courtroom where some of the survivors of the massacres they triggered were in the audience, I was overwhelmed with the need for this performance. The recourse to judicial processes may fall into the trap of being rejected as neoliberal cant, but it can evoke consciousness of human rights and the movement rejecting their violations.[5]

In October 2002 civil society groups of Guatemala, in coordination with the United Nations, drew up a statement calling for a full investigation of violations of human rights of indigenous people. In 2004 the newly elected president, Oscar Berger Pedomo, appointed a cabinet that included indigenous rights activists such as Rigoberta Menchú as ethnic relations adviser and Victor Montejo as secretary of peace. Berger had the support of civil society to introduce the first international initiative against genocide in Latin America, and thereby launch a new era in multicultural coexistence. Yet he has lost that opportunity and the confidence of the civil society supporters who have risked their lives and careers to promote these ends. At the moment when Victor Montejo announced his intention to leave a post that lacked funding and personnel to implement his responsibilities in his keynote address to the conference "Springtime of Democracy and Transition" at the University of Illinois in April 2005, he received word that he had been discharged.

In the wake of the decades of genocide, the Guatemalan elites have succeeded in implanting an export-oriented economy. The recorded increases in gross national product benefit only a narrow foreign investment sector with few gains for an increasingly impoverished working class. Yet there are many signs of a revitalized civil society and alternative development projects. I learned of some of these projects during my next and most recent trip in March 2005 to review development processes since the 1950s. When I visited Cantel the town offices were bustling with people. The town clerk referred me to an ecologist, Ramon Riqucheq, who was in charge of environmental conservation. Riqucheq quickly sketched in the major changes: Each pueblo has control of water and wood resources. Few agriculturalists remain where once even the factory workers planted the two hectares lent to them by the owners. Employment is down, with over 3,500 jobs eliminated a few years ago when Japanese and Asian competition forced the textile factory nearly into bankruptcy. The only active factory is a small artisan shop employing forty-nine workers blowing glass sold in a world market. Women who are *viudas* (widows), either because their husbands died or have migrated to the United States or Canada to work, weave shawls with material supplied by a cooperative started by a German woman. There are also systems of garment assembly done by women in their own homes if they have machines, or in other houses where they are employed at less than the minimum wage. There are no *maquilas*, or export-oriented assembly plants, in town.

Ramon Riqucheq saw as the major problem the growth of an illegal economy with corruption in high offices in the government. Unemployment, he said, stems from the overpopulation: People continue to have many children, although there are family-planning clinics assisted by a German funding agent. There are fifty-four midwives and two health stations. Where there was no fire or ambulance service in our day, the town now has both these amenities. President Berger is more effective in bringing municipal services such as the environmental conservation service, of which he is in charge.

Although I did not bring up the question of the war years, Riqucheq volunteered the information that Cantel suffered many attacks on its people when Lucas Garcia and Rios Montt were in the presidency. He felt that Cantel was targeted as a *Zona Roja*, "red zone," to which defense patrols were assigned because of the union, commenting that *Escuadrones de Muerte* (Death Squads) killed many without reason. "But now we have co-ordinated programs with three Peace Corps volunteers from the United States working with the women's group, another with environmental education, and another with agriculture developing solid waste compost."

In contrast with the readily volunteered information from the conservation agent, I learned little in my interview with the manager of the Cantel factory. A graduate in economics at the University of San Carlos, he commented on the scarcity of opportunities for many graduates from colleges and universities in Guatemala. He claimed that the factory was still producing at the same level of production with 350 employees as they had with ten times that number before the recent purchase of high-efficiency German machines. It was hard for me to reconcile that claim with what some municipal officers said about the factory being close to bankruptcy. The wage averaged "a little above the minimum," he said, and when I asked what that was, he denied knowledge of the figure. I later learned from people in the town center that the minimum wage is forty *quetzales* (about six dollars) a day and that unemployment is high. Many families in Cantel must send their young people to the United States or Canada, relying on reimbursements from them. Juan Quiem now has eight of his grandchildren working in New York and the southeastern United States. All are illegal immigrants, and live in fear of being expelled.

Despite the fact that the town suffers the trauma of years of militarization, there were signs of progress. Joaquin Pablo Salas, who came to Cantel in 1995, is director of the health clinic he built in 2000 with money and land donated by the town. The town has an ambulance that connects patients with the Quetzaltenango post. Salas was very forthcoming about the deficiencies as well as the advances that have come forth. His specialty is preventive medicine, promoting educational programs to improve sanitation, nutrition, and water treatment that are disseminated by radio and seminars held in town as well as volunteers who visit rural hamlets. He spoke freely about the violence that continues, although it is not as extreme as in 1982. Much of it is internalized violence, and he enumerated suicides, domestic abuse, and alcoholism. *Maras* and *pandillas*— youth gangs—still generate public violence, defiling pubic properties and carrying out assassinations.

The structural violence resulting from poverty shows up in sicknesses resulting from lack of hygiene and contaminated environments. Tuberculosis is not as common as it was, but AIDS has come to Cantel, and childhood developmental problems, related to poorer nutrition since people no longer have land on which to grow food crops, are beginning to show up. Prepared foods, and especially soft drinks, use scarce income with no benefit for the children. Even more disturbing are fetal disabilities that midwives are reporting to the clinic. Salas has seen fetuses that have no more formation than "a bunch of grapes" born to women in Pasac, an *aldea* where midwives have also delivered babies with holes in their spine. "We are administering folic acid to overcome poor maternal diet," Salas said, "but that is not always effective," he added, attributing some of these developmental problems to contamination of the environment. He deplores the use of pesticides in surrounding towns such as Almolonga and Salcaja, which are engaged in vegetable and fruit production. The water irrigating these commercial crops drains into the Samalá River, which carries the pesticides and fertilizer downstream.

On the day we left Guatemala to return to Chiapas we were struck by the enormity of the problems faced by the revitalized civil society leaders. We read in the morning paper of the indigenous protest against the Glamis Gold Marlin Mining project in San Miguel Ixtahuacán. Mam and Sipakapense leaders say they were tricked into signing a contract for development with Marlin that yielded property rights for operating a mine on land they considered inalienable. Massive demonstrations protesting the operation of the mine had already resulted in one death in March 2005 (Henderson 2005). We were held up for an hour at the Mexican border by campesinos protesting the imminent formalization of the Central American Free Trade Agreement (CAFTA). Both the protest and the rally at the border were premonitions of what is now developing in Guatemala and Central America with the signing of CAFTA.

CONFLICT AND THE BROADENING
OF DEMOCRACY IN MEXICO

In Mexico the break from PRI hegemony over indigenous municipalities began with the mobilization for the 1974 National Indigenous Congress and peaked with the 1992 celebration of five hundred years of resistance. This prepared civil society for the greater struggle for indigenous autonomy. In 1990 I brought the first group of students to the summer field session in San Cristóbal. We felt the first stirrings of rebellion and repression that summer in Chiapas. A contingent of some one hundred men, women, and children marched from the Lacandón Rain Forest to Palenque to object to the government over the illicit sales by police of the wood they had cut to cultivate their fields. They were stopped at Palenque, where the women and children were jailed, and the men were sent on to the state prison in Tuxtla Gutierrez. Their demands were specifically related to injustice in federal disposition of lumber resources. The Center for Human Rights (Fray Bartolomé de las Casas) became a fount of information for students in almost all the projects that were chosen.

Salinas's policies of neoliberal development allowing privatization of the *ejido*—communal lands distributed by the agrarian reform—with the 1992 "reform" of the Agrarian Reform Law and the signing of the North American Free Trade Agreement (NAFTA) touched off the New Year's Eve 1994 rebellion of the Zapatista Army for National Liberation (EZLN). This force of several thousand men and women had been training for ten years prior to the 1994 uprising, and though the government was aware of their actions, Salinas reputedly wanted to have an excuse for militarizing the *selva* (rain forest).

The contest for control of the Lacandón area that began with the EZLN on New Year's morning of 1994 intensified after what some called "an ocean of oil" (*El Financiero* February 28, 1995) was discovered beneath the forest cover, the same ocean that flowed beyond the border into Guatemala. Clearly President Zedillo was responding to this when he ordered the invasion of the Lacandón Rain Forest on February 9, 1995, since the EZLN had not violated the conditions of the ceasefire agreement signed twelve days after the uprising. The invasion enabled him to increase the troop buildup from twelve thousand during the twelve-day war after the uprising to sixty thousand soldiers. Yet he referred to the invasion simply as the capture of Subcomandante Marcos and other "terrorists" identified as guerrillas of the 1968 insurrection. In the ensuing protests against military occupation, Mayan colonizers of the jungle are putting into practice the autonomy they seek.

Negotiations between the government and the Zapatistas resulted in the San Andrés Agreement signed by the Zedillo government and the high command of the EZLN. For the Zapatistas and their supporters, the agreement was a reassertion of collective rights to self-determination as a necessary condition for the exercise of individual rights as indigenous people (cf. Miguel Concha Malo 1994, cited in Valle Esquivel 1994, 51). This commitment to the collectivity marks the crucial difference between indigenous and Western conceptions of human rights. In the past, neglect by the state had permitted indigenous communities to exercise autonomy at the local level. The increasing intrusion of the national government in the state of Chiapas, through development projects such as hydroelectric dams and lumbering and oil exploration, threatened not only control over resources but also of their way of life. But the very intrusion of alien forms of government has forced indigenous pueblos to voice the subliminal demands that have inspired retention of their customs and traditions in the five hundred years of colonization and independence under mestizo domination.

Despite the agreement, Zedillo denied the intent of the accord, maintaining an armed force of at least forty thousand soldiers. In what some have called the "War of the Peace" in the decade following the Zapatista uprising of January 1, 1994, the active intervention of civil society and transnational NGOs prevented the military confrontation from degenerating into a genocidal attack on the whole population, as in Guatemala. Immediately after the invasion of the Lacandón settlements by the Federal Army on February 9, 1995, over a hundred thousand Mexican demonstrators filled the central plaza in Mexico City, calling for justice and reacting against the invasion (*La Jornada* February 12, 1995). There were outbreaks of indiscriminate killing, as in the Acteal Massacre of December 22, 1997, carried out by coresidents of the township of Chenalhó incited by the Institutional Revolutionary Party (PRI) government, and the killing of eight campesinos while federal forces in El Bosque detained them the following year. News of these events was disseminated nationally and even worldwide in the case of the Acteal massacre in which forty-five indigenes, mostly women and children, were killed. Investigation of the massacre led to the imprisonment of local officials and army personnel charged with the attack.

What we find in the Lacandón is a low profile but continuous counterinsurgency campaign by federal forces estimated at forty thousand soldiers and augmented by paramilitary operations such as that which carried out the Acteal massacre. Since the invasion, the army has set up barracks near the settlements and taken over schoolhouses for regimental offices, violating a constitutional requirement that the army cannot reside within four hundred meters of a settlement. Although President Vicente Fox withdrew some of these barracks when he took office in 2000, the military presence is still widely manifested. Soldiers bathe in the streams that supply drinking water to the populations. Rapes are more frequent than those reported indicate. A newly born infant that appeared in the refuse of a Zapatista village I visited in 2004 attests to the unaccounted abuses of women in this hostile setting.

Since the uprising women of the Lacandón area have deplored the impact of the federal troops on communities. I was a witness to some of this

Figure 5.2. Peace activists from throughout Central America join Mexicans to protest militarization as they seek justice in Chiapas, 1995.

in May 1995, when I stayed in one of the "peace huts" organized by civil society to house observers after the February 9, 1995, invasion of the Lacandón by federal troops, presumably in an army sweep to discover Subcomandante Marcos. Helicopters buzzed overhead daily, and humvees carrying soldiers heavily armed with automatic rifles sped through the settlements, scattering children and chickens from their path. I saw a busload of women disembark at the barracks in Patihuitz where I was staying with other observers (Nash 2003a).

Women in the Lacandón villages protested these acts in a letter to the president (*La Jornada* March 13, 1995), deploring the importing of prostitutes. At the state convention of the indigenous organization Xi' Nich, held shortly after the invasion, women constituted a Committee of Defense of Indigenous Liberty "to resolve our problems and those of the Union of Communities of the Chiapas Selva." In their declaration, the women linked the presence of the army with the rise of domestic violence and control by men within their families. The participants signed a declaration that identified the war with "the most brutal expression of a patriarchal regime characterized by hierarchy, authoritarianism, discrimination and repression which exists in our country, whose consequences affect the entire Mexican pueblo." The declaration, which was disseminated in a leaflet at the convention, goes on to say that "women, historically dis-criminated against, have seen how our vulnerability has increased, with the sexual aggression and violations that the army and the White Guards [paramilitaries] have committed against women since they ordered the militarization of Chiapas."

Zedillo's plan to dismantle the Zapatista fighting force estimated at four thousand remained an objective of the army with Fox as the supreme commander (Center for Human Rights "Fray Bartolomé de Las Casas" 2005). The Center for Human Rights "Fray Bartolomé de las Casas" esti-mates that approximately ten thousand people have been displaced from their homes since 1995 and most remain so. Disappearances and assassi-nations are rarely investigated, and the failure of the justice system to ad-dress violations is flagrant. Although massacres such as Acteal were com-mitted primarily because they were identified with the Word of God Catholics opposed to the PRI and supporters of the EZLN, the dead num-ber in dozens not thousands as in Guatemala.

Since the eve of the uprising, women have been part of the military and civil society activities of the Zapatistas. Their declaration of rights challenging the domination of the state over ethnic groups and that of men over women was read in the first week of the uprising. This has sub-jected them to violence on two fronts. The Federal Army intercepts their activities with demands for services, including laundry and cooking services and forced sexual compliance. These violations are rarely re-ported to authorities because of shame and the awareness that they would not, in any case, be attended to. The second front is that of para-military troops where the lines of battle are drawn between kinship and neighborhood connections, as troops are recruited from among members of the same communities. This was the case of the December 1997 Acteal massacre. Investigations disclosed that the majority of the two hundred men belonging to the Red Masks that attacked the community included youths of fourteen and fifteen years of age who carried machine guns, which were restricted in use to army personnel. The Center for Human Rights "Fray Bartolomé de Las Casas" indicated that before the attack the assailants had taken narcotics and were prepared for their inhuman orgy with pornographic films shown as part of their training by a sergeant of the armed forces on temporary leave.

Human rights advocates have denounced the violations committed by soldiers in international arenas (Global Exchange Press Report 1995; *El Fi-nanciero* March 13, 1995, March 17, 1995). As the protest against the mili-tary presence rose, the army carried out what they called a program of "social integration" following a tactic used by the Guatemalan army in the Ixcán. They returned twenty-six thousand colonizers who had volun-tarily left their homes in the rain forest shortly after the uprising, locating them in the homes of those who had been routed by the army during the invasion. This divide-and-conquer strategy often turned indigenous people against each other, ensuring the continuation of the conflict (*La Jornada* February 28, 1995; Rojas 1995, 8).

Investigating the militarization of the Lacandón, Onésamo Hidalgo estimates that there are now 490 army positions, about 213 being Federal Army units and the rest immigration checkpoints, federal investigation units, Federal Preventive Police, and public security agencies. Parallel operations are carried out by "PRIistas," the former ruling party activists, who have been accused of distributing drugs, alcohol, and stolen cars. They are responsible for stirring up intracommunity conflicts related to water, lumber, land, religion, and trafficking of prostitutes (*La Jornada* March 21, 2004).

Why does the government of Mexico, aided by a putative antidrug program of the United States, concentrate such a massive military and paramilitary presence in a state that was completely abandoned until the 1970s? The easy answer is the discovery of oil, which only became public news in 1995 when *El Financiero*, the Mexican counterpart to the *Wall Street Journal*, announced February 26, 1995, that there was "an ocean of oil beneath the Lacandón forest." A more complex answer would include the megaprojects projected in Plan Puebla Panamá such as dams to expand hydroelectric power, assembly operations for export, and the exploration of genetic biodiversity resources. The Fox government has already prepared the infrastructure for these ventures with highways crisscrossing the Lacandón Rain Forest and high power transmission lines. The secretary of Environment and Natural Resources (SEMARNAT) opened the market for legal sale to private foreign investors of genetic resources and biodiversity prospecting in Chiapas in March 2005, signing an agreement with the governor of Wisconsin and Chiapas. The agreement prompted the resignation of two leading scientists on the SEMARNAT staff (*La Jornada* March 8, 2005).

The warfare waged against indigenous pueblos of the rain forest is directed at destroying the social reproductive base of the settlers. The tactics are laid out in the Mexican army's *Manual of Irregular War: Counterguerrilla Operations or Restoration of Order* (SEDENA 1995, cited in Center for Human Rights "Fray Bartolomé de Las Casas" 1997). Behind the military front is that of the military institutions and their civilian auxiliaries, whose objectives are defined as recruiting civilian support for counterinsurgency measures and managing the public image of the army. In perfecting their own model of low-intensity warfare, the Mexican army has developed elite forces, special commando operations, and rapid deployment units. Complementing the armed operation is the increase in civilian forces that act outside of the law in the state strategy of controlling and creating factions in the communities in rebellion. In contrast to the paramilitary forces that have always operated as the private armed force of the ranchers and large landowners, the armed bands are now recruited from within the communities where they operate. Unlike mercenaries, they are extensions of federal control forces, and often receive their arms directly from army supplies (*La Jornada* October 29, 1997). By staging what appeared to be armed civilian patrols that attacked squatters, burning houses and threatening campesinos in contested regions of the state, the "parallel military force" disrupted the cultivation cycle in the conflict area in 1998.

In the tenth anniversary celebrations of the uprising in 2004, women took the lead in protesting the presence of the army. The anthropologist Mercedes Olivera, who began her studies on the coastal plantations in the 1970s, reported during the 2004 Chiapas Encounter Against Neoliberalism on how the undeclared war continues to affect the poor indigenous populations of the rain forest. Incidents of sexual violence are so prevalent as often not to be reported, and their husbands and others often blame the women themselves. Prostitution is not just an external intrusion but involves an international net of prostitution in charge of the military, the migration agents, and the proprietors of the houses. The women are now organized in the Frente Chiapaneco Contra las Represas, uniting *mestiza* and indigenous women against such intrusions (*La Jornada* March 20, 2004).

Human rights violations have increased with the low-intensity warfare as the line between the home front and the battlefront is undermined. The militarization of the internal life of communities in continuous contact with the army erodes civilian authorities as officials abandon their functions to military personnel. The presence of NGOs that have maintained surveillance in the conflict areas has contained the scale and number of aggressions against the population, but militarization remains an ever-present threat. After September 11, 2001, the government of George W. Bush requested that the Mexican government establish a security operation be put in place on the southern frontier to prevent narcotrafficking and terrorist activities. This brought in another twelve checkpoints with another three thousand soldiers.

THE COMPARATIVE NEXUS

The movements for ethnic vindication on each side of the southern border of Mexico with Guatemala differ in the processes set in motion and the directions Mayas are pursuing. Yet these movements share a common goal in overcoming centuries of racial oppression expressed in genocidal and ethnocidal outbreaks. In Guatemala, Mayan intellectuals are exploring cultural resources as they try to integrate them in the educational system of the country. The movement is tied to transnational NGOs inspired by United Nations declarations, especially the 1983 Elimination of All Forms of Racial Discrimination and the 1989 Declaration of Rights. Although the movement is energized by grassroots organizations deriving from five hundred years of resistance to assimilation, Guatemalan pan-Mayanism is clearly dedicated to the production of cultural distinctiveness (Warren 1998, 13).

In Mexico, the movement for autonomy is more strongly rooted in grassroots activism relating to producer and distribution cooperatives, land struggles, and social services. Women have, from the early days of the uprising, asserted distinctive demands, not only vis-à-vis the society at large but within the movement, rejecting the physical abuse and social restrictions that often characterize "traditional" communities. The Zapatista Army of National Liberation resorted to armed force to back up their demands for autonomy they are now putting into practice in the colonized area of the Lacandón Rain Forest and the Christian Base Communities in highland Chiapas.[6] Mexican intellectuals have played an important role in integrating local discourses with national and international currents, but with few exceptions, they are not of Mayan descent. Yet Mexican intellectuals such as Pablo Gonzalez Casanova, Aracely Burguete Cal y Mayor, Margarito Ruíz Hernandez, Rudolfo Stavenhagen, and Hector Diaz-Polanco have rejected earlier formulations of indigenous people's subordination to the state in the ideology of indigenism in favor of autonomy and self-rule in the regions where they constitute a majority. Along with religious leaders such as Bishop Samuel Ruiz they have promoted civil society demonstrations calling for the withdrawal of the army from the Lacandón and to negotiate a settlement. Their direct involvement with Bishop Ruiz in the dialogues that led to the San Andrés Agreement in February 1996 promises a future in which the right to cultural distinction within a pluricultural state might be realized.[7]

Indigenous people bring to the mediations over human rights a sense of collective rights that is basic to their conception of human rights. This is most evident in the colonizing communities of the Lacandón Rain Forest where communities are responding to the teachings of indigenous deacons actively proselytizing the faith in the language of the people. Bishop Ruiz discovered that the revelation of the reign of God resonated with indigenous peoples who often equated it with the return of Quetzalcoatl (Ruiz Garcia 2000, 33). He learned to appreciate how "the distinct cultures . . . permit us to know more in depth the human nature and open new roads for the truth." The presence of what he calls the "ethical and contemplative seeds in ancient cultures and in the character and idiosyncrasies of each pueblo" opens up the theological task from a missionary imposition of the West to a discovery of multiple dimensions of faith (2000, 33).

A second striking dimension of indigenous perspectives on human rights is captured by Christine Kovic's (2005) study of a Word of God Catholic exile community in San Cristóbal de Las Casas. She shows how indigenous people always link their rights in a community to reciprocal obligations, as men and women take on the ceremonial and civil duties of community membership. This has profound implications for their assertion of rights in the wider society that would deepen the mutual commitment of people in indigenous and international society as they seek justice in tribunals related to massive violations of collective rights in genocidal and ethnocidal attacks. Thus far these events have eluded the mediations of courts since legal judgments are focused on individuals.

In the course of working in countries devastated by these rogue actions, anthropologists have become more conscious of the role we play in analyzing, ignoring, or denying the conditions that lead to the destruction of democracy and the imposition of military regimes in the areas we study. In answer to the questions I posed at the beginning of the chapter—Who is going to benefit by what we do or fail to publish, and who might be compromised by our interpretations? What role can we play as activists, both to reveal what we learned about past errors and to try to bring about a change in direction?—are precisely the moral issues raised by activist anthropology that allow us to understand social processes and interpret them more clearly.

A comparison of the Maya ethnic resurgence on the Mexico-Guatemala border provides a context for assessing changing approaches in the anthropological study of state and local relations. Mayas on both sides share a common substratum of culture and economy. They are among indigenous people defined by the United Nations as those who have historical continuity with preconquest societies that have developed in their territories, and who consider themselves distinct entities. Furthermore, they are defined as having an economic base in small-plot cultivation and adaptations to market forces that allow them to remain the same. Like many such societies throughout the world, Mayas now face greater threats since they have become more integrated in global communication and economic circuits. With the invasion of oil explorers, hydroelectric energy dams, maquiladora operations, biogenetic prospectors, and resource extraction these populations compete for a shrinking land base exacerbated by an unparalleled population explosion.

Forensic anthropology provides a powerful tool reinforcing narratives of terror as these are chipped away by skeptics trying to undermine the veracity of accounts by participants in violent episodes. Combining the evidence from both sources among indigenous people who endured genocidal attacks of the Guatemalan army in the decades of violence, the forensic teams operating in Guatemala cooperate with the social anthropology teams to provide legally defensible tracts to gain court convictions against the violators of human rights. This dual approach combining conventional eliciting procedures with the material evidence provided by traumatized bones and the sheer numbers of skeletal remains can provide a strong legitimizing tool in the growing field of activist anthropology.[8] Human rights groups may be discouraged that the Constitutional Court has rejected their attempt to gain judicial processes against the sixteen military officers accused of assassinating three hundred people in the Petén in 1982 (*La Jornada* February 13, 2005) and that the Berger government refuses to pay indemnity to the victims of military aggression (*La Jornada* February 13, 2005), but their struggle continues. It is now directed against the *cuerpos clandestinos* (secret gangs), often composed of retired soldiers as well as government troops (Comisión para la Investigación de Cuerpos Ilegales y Aparatos Clandestinos de Seguridad [CICIACS]) (*La Jornada* February 13, 2005).

We can no longer pretend the naïveté that characterized our fieldwork fifty years ago. We went into field situations innocent of these plots spawned in the emergent globalization and the role that we might unconsciously play. Now too much is known about the undercover plots of secret agents—first in Iran in 1953 when the precursors of the CIA engineered the overthrow of Prime Minister Mossadegh and then with the overthrow of Jacobo Arbenz in Guatemala in 1954—to ignore or deny U.S. intervention in the field sites we choose. On September 11, 1973, Chile lost another experiment in democracy when Kissinger engineered the plot to overthrow President Salvador Allende, and in 1987 Oliver North took the blame for payoffs to Honduran Contras to destabilize the Sandinistas in Nicaragua.

We have to ask ourselves what role we play in setting the conditions that lead to military regimes and the destruction of democracy in the areas we study. Who is going to benefit by what we publish and who might be compromised by our interpretations? What role can we play as activists, both to reveal what we learned about past errors and to try to bring about a change in direction? We can no longer pretend to be the anthropologist as hero, as Lévi-Strauss once called the anthropologist embarking on adventures into the unknown. We are on the other side of the looking glass, where the dark side of the image we cast is reflected in the eyes of those who observe us. In this new role we can only find acceptance as collaborators with those we study, as we share with them knowledge of our culture as we discover theirs. Indigenous people are fortifying themselves against co-optation by dominant sectors within their societies and by external manipulation. Zapatistas and the Christian Base Communities of Highland Chiapas are leaders in this consciousness-raising project. Guatemalan communities that once found their youth conscripted in military patrols are promoting judicial procedures against criminal acts of the past and present and to revive collective cultural practices to strengthen their society. They have learned that only a strong, informed civil society will overcome the transformation to more extreme forms of human rights violations. Working with these people as they unearth the past, anthropologists are overcoming the naïveté that once bound their profession as they discover the everyday expressions of structural violence and ethnocidal practices that precede and often conduce toward genocide. This is now on the global agenda. It is perforce a core issue in anthropological research wherever we go and whatever we intend to study.

NOTES

This paper was prepared for the Conference on Fifty Years after the Guatemalan Coup, at the University of Illinois, Champaign-Urbana, April 9–11, 2005.

1. When Gluckman later published his anthology *Closed Systems and Open Minds: The Limits of Naiveté in Social Anthropology* (1967, first published in 1964), he was concerned more with the naive application of other disciplinary findings in the field of anthropology than with the naïveté of the observer for the wider political context (Kapferer 1997).

2. John Perkins (2004) reveals in his book, *Confessions of an Economic Hit Man*, the strategies by which the United States has achieved dominance over countries through indebtedness manipulated by the International Monetary Fund (IMF).

3. I have borrowed the title of Paule Marshall's book, *The Chosen Place, the Timeless People*, which captures the naïveté of anthropologists of the 1960s in her native island Barbados.

4. See especially essays collected in Eber and Kovic 2003; and in Rus, Matiace, and Hernandez 2004 recording these developments.

5. Shannon Speed (n.d.) has summarized the arguments of scholars who are studying human rights defenders, showing how the specious use of the discourse of human rights may undermine the process of achieving the rights. The exercise of caution should not deter legal intervention in order to arrest human rights violations while they are happening. The accumulation of forensic and narrative evidence that becomes public in such court cases as that which we witnessed in Guatemala cultivates the awareness of the magnitude of the crimes that were often kept secret or even denied by those who were aware of their having happened. We need to relate the old forms of civil society intervention with new international agencies at every stage in the process of redressing such crimes against humanity.

6. Maria Eugenia Santana (1997) has described the daily exercise of egalitarian gender relations in Flor del Rio in the Lacandón forest. This is supported by Duncan Earle and Jeanne Simonelli's (2005) study of settlers in Lacandón.

7. Other indigenous groups of Mexico express a similar commitment. Valle Esquivel (1994, 70) quotes Totonac leaders as follows: "We indigenous Totonacs constitute ourselves in this organization so that as a pueblo we want free self-

determination of our destiny to which we have the right. We recognize ourselves as Totonacs, children of these lands. We live for the land. We have an origin and a history of our own, from this comes our blood and our language; our organization, our offices and services in favor of the pueblo; principles and thoughts of our own; traditions, customs, dances and clothes; music and our fiestas." At the heart of this world are Kimpuchinakan and Kinpaxcatsikan who are the creators of their life and lords of their history and destiny.

8. See Victoria Sanford (2003), Beatriz Manz (2004), and the reports of AVANCSO.

III

ENGAGEMENT IN SOCIAL MOVEMENTS TODAY

6

Social Movements
in Global Circuits

Globalization processes related to the expansion and integration of capital investments, production, and markets in new areas generate social movements of people mobilizing to protect their lands, their cultural identities, and their autonomy. At the same time, improved communication systems and the development of global civil society acting through grassroots movements, the United Nations, and nongovernmental organizations (NGOs) promote awareness of inequities in the distribution of wealth and misfortune related to human rights violations. News of political imprisonment and of impoverishment is disseminated in global circuits along with promotions of consumer goods and luxury products. These emerging processes pose a challenge to anthropological methods and practices. Anthropologists have traditionally studied the populations that feel most threatened by these changes—indigenous people, and those who are impoverished and marginalized. The scope of our problems expands as we respond to the social movements of those seeking retribution or reintegration in new global alignments. There is a resurgence of fundamentalist religious groups that seek redemption by militant actions against what they see as godlessness. Summit meetings of the global financial and commercial institutions are accompanied by protest demonstrations staged by a motley array of groups from all over the world. In the wake of these movements, we find countermovements designed to repress protests in the interest of ensuring the power of global elites. The diffusion of armaments worldwide through transnational networks by paramilitary and terrorist groups adds an increasingly lethal dimension to global processes. These movements recruit youths who are alienated from their communities and families, unable to find employment or to claim the prerogatives of males in a world where production is carried out by an increasingly feminized workforce. In this chapter I consider the manifold expressions of resistance and protest to the process set in motion by global integration. These processes and the responses they may trigger are summarized as: (1) the fragmentation and recomposition of society, (2) secularization and fundamentalist reactions, (3) deterritorialization and the politics of space, and (4) privatization and global cosmopolitanism. The anthropological response is to broaden the horizons of the field inquiry, to engage in multisited research, and to be ever more vigilant in examining our paradigms.

Social movements in a global ecumene[1] take on a great diversity of cultural manifestations as new social actors invent novel expressions for their causes. They necessarily develop "transnational activist networks" (Edelman 2001) that cast the goals of movements in ever more universal terms. Issues of social justice are more frequently voiced in global arenas today than in decades preceding global integration. In the 1970s major development institutions such as the World Bank and the International Monetary Fund (IMF) were in denial about the impact of global trade and direct foreign investment (DFI) abroad. The World Bank still failed to respond to the negative effects of their policies even when massive protests against "deindustrialization" and double digit unemployment of core industrial regions rose in the 1980s and later when the IMF conditions for debt payments forced whole nations into bankruptcy in the 1990s.

But after the 1997–1998 crisis in financial markets this changed. George Stiglitz, former president of the World Bank, introduced his millennial report with the statement, "The experience of the past year has underscored how financial volatility can increase poverty significantly in the short to medium term," and concluded that "in order to maximize the positive effects of growth that can come with openness, the international community must find ways to reduce the frequency and severity of economic crises" (Stiglitz 2000). The burden imposed by recurrent crises is borne by working people, who are often required to work harder, migrate to find jobs in distant sites, abandoning family and community, accept wage cuts, and/or learn new skills. This is the "flexibility" of labor markets in developing countries that Stiglitz, summarizing the lessons to be learned from the 1997–1998 crisis in Thailand, Indonesia, and Malaysia, (2000, xi) indicated had helped absorb the shocks. The turn away from neoliberal rhetoric advocating free and untrammeled markets can also be seen in the Noble prize selection in 2002 of Amartya Sen, an economist known for his work on the moral implications of global development (see especially Sen 1984).

As yet, regulation of global capital investment practices is lacking, and the "openness" (the World Bank's code word for neoliberal free markets) in commodity markets required of developing countries is not imposed on Western powers. The conditions set for "recovery" by the IMF that precipitated political crises in Southeast Asia in 1997–1998 devastated Argentina at the turn of the millennium, although the country was considered the best pupil of the IMF. Yet the lesson of each crisis that recovery cannot be achieved internally so long as anti-inflationary financial policies and "openness" are the unique goals did not lead to changes in the policies of global institutions. The United States and European countries are able to flout free trade and debt limits without penalties. The fact that their governments persist in dumping their subsidized crops in Third World countries, underselling crops raised by subsistence farmers, precipitated the end of negotiations at the 2003 Cancún World Trade Organization summit meeting. Two years later, President George W. Bush was forced to end his tour of Argentina, Brazil, and Chile without any agreement on free trade in South America.

Those who advocate a "moral economy" will only succeed with the massive mobilizations of the people who now suffer from unconditional free trade policies. These are the workers and peasants, indigenous people, small-scale entrepreneurs, and professionals who are forced to bear the "external shocks" of a global system in crisis. They embody the breakdown in education and health services, both as clients and providers of diminished public welfare provisions; the generation they produce has dim prospects for survival or status in a world that requires high technical and communication skills. Even as their visions of a better future within the global system as it is now structured recede, they are the ones who signal, "Enough!"

Within the past half century, notions of human rights, environmental conservation, and pluricultural autonomy developed along with and in response to the changes brought about by global integration. Anthropologists have been documenting the impact of global integration and subsistence insecurity for decades (Nash 1981, 1993). The difference in the third millennium lies in the tripling of global population in the past half century and the depletion of unutilized territories and resources. The "flexibility" that Stiglitz refers to is based on the reverse flow of workers from urban to the rural areas and from formal to informal employment when urban and industrial employment collapsed in 1997–1998.[2]

The locus of class struggle in the workplace that emerged with industrial capitalism in the eighteenth century now takes place in other sites as well. Shopping mall boycotts, protests against neoliberal policies of the World Trade Organization (WTO) at summit meeting headquarters, and highway blockades by small-scale commodity producers of third world countries have become symbolic grounds for protests by the dispossessed and impoverished. Just as global production and distribution sites demand maximum flexibility in their organizational charts, so do the social movements that respond to them require flexibility in their strategies and agendas. Antonio Gramsci and Rosa Luxemburg, who looked beyond the vanguard of industrial workers favored by Karl Marx or Frederick Engels, are more important reference points in current social movements. Luxemburg's revival came with feminist scholarship and the recognition of the subsistence sector or "noncapitalist sector" in providing a reserve market for exporting surplus value generated in the industrialized sector (Bennholdt-Thomsen 1981). Bakunin's (1873; reprint 1972) advocacy of multiethnic rights that caused him to break with rank-and-file Communists in the nineteenth century draws praise from activists in antiglobal protests today. Indeed, just as the dissidents led by these advocates of grassroots and ethnically discriminated groups in earlier revolts were branded as anarchists, so are these new cohorts of resistance, protest, and transformative change. With the acceleration of capitalist penetration in today's global markets and the growing threat to the survival of the subsistence sector, we can appreciate other contributions of the noncapitalist sector that were taken for granted. These are the reproduction of the labor force made available at low wages to the capitalist sector and the care for the aging populations once addressed with social security provisions of nation-states and now rejected by neoliberal regimes (Nash 1990, 1993).[3]

In Mexico, Zapatistas who rebelled against the North American Free Trade Agreement on New Year's Eve 1994 tapped the new energy erupting in the countryside of the states of Oaxaca, Chiapas, and Guerrero during and after the celebration of Five Hundred Years of Resistance (Quinientos Años de Resistencia). I learned this when I participated in the national and international conventions called after the 1994 uprising. Italian and French socialists, anarchists, and would-be revolutionaries rubbed shoulders with indigenous peoples from Canada, South America, and the United States in the Lacandón Rain Forest. Basques, who are still engaged in their opposition to the Spanish state, were helping the Zapatista support groups to organize peace brigades to the Lacandón Rain Forest throughout the years of counterinsurgency warfare in the years following the military invasion of the Lacandón.

Zapatistas also understood the futility of old style guerrilla action. Rather than yield to the cohort of student activists who joined them in the Lacandón Rain Forest in the 1980s, they persisted in using indigenous strategies that had maintained resistance to assimilation for over five hundred years. In their 1994 New Year's Eve uprising some carried wooden rifles along with their comrades who had acquired high-powered automatic rifles from narcotic "control" forces operating at the southern border of

Mexico. Whenever their "army" went on display during national and international demonstrations, women and children carried hand-fashioned wooden rifles that dramatized their determination to hold their place in Chiapas despite heavily armed government troops that occupied their communities.

In their departure from the typical behaviors of the revolutionary left, Zapatistas symbolized the changed global environment. For them, weapons were accessories, not the means, to gain power. Their symbolic armaments underlined the weakness of their arms at the same time that it showed the strength of their determination. The goals of their struggle also differed from traditional rebellions; they did not seek to take over power, but to ensure democratic participation for all in self-governance. The enthusiasm with which this message was received by large sectors of Mexican civil society and people from all over the globe resonates with a formative global civil society.

I shall try to document through case studies of social movements their ongoing task of putting in place the institutional networks needed to transform policies required to ensure social justice in the process of globalization. Activists in this agenda are recruited from discontented, but not disconnected, feminists, indigenes, cultivators, working class, and petty entrepreneurs. Intellectuals and creative artists who are generating a new vocabulary for engaging with, documenting, and analyzing such movements provide their armaments. Avoiding political parties considered to be co-opted, they find common ground in civil society mobilizations of morally committed pacifists, political leftists, and religious groups. These central values are phrased as human rights, environmental conservation, public as well as personal autonomy, and justice. The meanings assigned to these values are spelled out in universalizing terms related to local contexts explored below.

Human Rights.   When the United Nations first promoted the Human Rights Declaration in 1948, the American Anthropological Association rejected the document on the score that this violated the principle of cultural relativity since it lacked inputs from member nations that would address distinct understandings as to what was universally acceptable as a code of human rights. Since then the civil rights movement in the United States has begun to establish certain inalienable rights of race and gender groups that were excluded from civil society. For the second time in human history, the world court in Brussels is seeking to determine whether a leader of a nation, Slobodan Milošević, committed acts of genocide against Muslims of Bosnia and Kosovo. Another historic advance took place on February 8, 2003, when the African Women's Congress resolved to end genital mutilation in the many nations of Africa where it is still practiced, and the U.S. Immigration Service is now trying to determine whether girls seeking asylum from countries with such practices are indeed victims of human rights violations. The decisions made in these contexts will provide a matrix of precedents with which to define justice and rights in a global context.

Anthropological case studies on multicultural understandings of human rights are beginning to expand the meanings associated with the Western concept. Kay Warren (1993a, 1993b) and Carole Nagengast (1994) are among those who examined the increasing incidence of violence and terror in cross-cultural contexts during the 1980s and 1990s. These studies attune us to cultural and historical differences in the manipulation of state force and how it is countered by those engaged in civil wars. We can see this in the case of Mayan populations engaged in a civil war to change their relations with the Guatemalan and Mexican states in which they reside. While the Guatemalan army has killed over two hundred thousand Indians in their thirty-year war, those killed in Mexico number in the thousands. Structural differences related to the demographic balance of Indians to the ladino, or non-Indian, population in each country affect the degree of racism expressed in intercultural relations. Ladinos' fear of Indians in Guatemala, where they constitute a majority, heightens the tendency to genocidal attacks when there is a threat to the status quo. The degree to which racial violence is expressed is also related to the greater democracy in Mexico and the more effective mobilization of civil society in defense of indigenous people (Nash 2004).

The notion of human rights includes more than formal political rights in the scope of the activities that human rights workers address throughout the globe. It is now extended to the right to adequate nutrition, health care, the protection of the living environment, and the exercise of cultural prerogatives of distinct ethnic groups. Those whose rights are under attack may have a distinct conception of what the premises for human rights consist in from that of the West, as Christine Kovic's study (2005) of a Chiapas Mayan indigenous community in exile reveals. Unlike the Western perspective, they see rights as reciprocal obligations that must be fulfilled on each side (Kovic 2005). Human rights movements acquire broadened and enriched understandings as diverse populations become activated.

Environmental Conservation.   At the turn of the third millennium, the green movements in the United States and European countries have promoted strong advocacy groups for sustainable development programs that measure progress in relation to advances in human welfare. Indigenous peoples of the Americas are becoming recognized as important protagonists of conservation. Their mobilizations during the 1992 celebration of 500 Years of Resistance promoted an awareness of their commitment to the earth. Indigenous peoples played a prominent role in the global forum in 1992 in Rio de Janeiro along with supporters of their programs for sustainable practices of cultivation and extraction. Their distinctive voices are remarkable for the poetry of their expression and the message it conveys of the need for balance in the cosmos and at home. In their two decades of intensive activism culminating in the Colombian constitution of 1991, indigenous people developed a public voice that captured a new image of what it was to be modern. Gow and Rappaport (2002, 57–58) capture the multiple idioms in which the indigenous people relate a cosmovision of the ancestors as guides and to gaining harmony with nature. Indigenous women have emerged in the 1990s as central protagonists defining the values of their people in national and hemispheric congresses. At the Beijing Women's Tribunal in 1995 indigenous women from throughout the world defined their relation to global change in these terms:

> The Earth is our Mother. From her we get our life, and our ability to live. It is our responsibility to care for our Mother and in caring for our Mother, we care for ourselves. Women, all females, are manifestations of Mother Earth in human form. (cited in Vinding 1998)

Comparative studies of the tropical rain forests bring out remarkably similar trends in development programs and their critics in widely separated regions. Ronald Nigh and Nemesio Rodriguez (1995) show the power of comparative analysis of rain forests in the Lacandón in Chiapas and the Amazon in Brazil and Colombia. In both areas, development projects based on planning from above that did not take the concerns of indigenous communities into account have contributed to, rather than alleviated, the devastation of the environment. Programs claiming to restore the forests often resulted in clear-cutting huge areas of variegated tropical forests, replacing them with fast-growing varieties that use quantities of groundwater and destroying precious medicinal trees in the process.

Since post–World War II years when the United States promoted development overseas, anthropologists have critiqued the premises of these projects.[4] State violence and paramilitary attacks often accompany the imposition of large-scale projects. This was particularly marked after the 1960s in Brazil with the intrusion of miners and in the following decade the construction of a highway. Subsequent invasions of cattle ranchers led to the forced movement of indigenous communities and burning of large areas of the rain forest. Oil explorers, gold miners, and forestry enterprises that caused widespread mortality from diseases and lured men into wage work followed them. Indigenous people have organized in federations to save their lands and to seek educational, health, and development projects in which they participate as planners. In communities devastated by the out-migration of men, women organized collective projects to maintain their families. In 1991, a Venezuelan presidential decree established an 83,000 square kilometer Upper Orinoco-Casiquiare Biospere Reserve for Yanomami on the Venezuelan and Brazilian border. The constitutions of both Brazil and Venezuela claim respect for indigenous territorial rights but as the history of the area shows, these formal rights are often ignored by local and national officials (Colchester 1994). The present government of Luis Inacio Lula da Silva in Brazil promises to maintain a direct dialogue with indigenous leaders on development programs that measure progress in terms of the welfare of human populations as well as the fauna and flora.[5]

Along with the invasions of predators seeking gold, biogenetic, and other resources into the rain forest are military and paramilitary forces bent on quelling the protests of settled populations. In the Colombian rain forests, indigenous leaders declared that "the guerrillas, military, and paramilitaries are killing all of us" in 1996 (Jackson n.d.). As a result of the growing unity among indigenous communities, the government signed two decrees, one establishing a human rights commission and the other a national commission of lands established on August 8, 1996. But while government agencies speak the language of pluralistic national identity, their practice remains vague and generalized (Jackson 2002).

When indigenous people participate in environmental movements, they change the discourse from homocentric utilitarianism to nature-centered universalism. Jackson (2002) illustrates the shift by quoting the spiritual leader of the Colombian rain forest, Kancha Vavinquma, who hails from a sacred site in Sierra Nevada:

> Oil explorations tap the lifeblood of the land. Mother Earth is given by the Eternal Father. Thus oil explorations and exploitation would ruin U'wa's land and identity. Our law . . . is not to take more than one needs, like the land which gives food to every living being, but to not eat too much, because then everything will be finished; to take care of our environment and not maltreat it. For us it is forbidden to kill with a knife, machete, or bullet; our arms are thought and words, our power is wisdom; we prefer death before seeing our sacred elders profaned.

Indigenous people of Colombia, who are turning to their traditional leaders as they reject government agents, raise new questions as to who are the legitimate leaders and who has the rights to the land (Jackson 2002).

Autonomy. The desire for autonomy, or self-governance in accord with their own cultural values, has been central to indigenous societies throughout the colonial and independence periods. The increase in violence attendant upon the invasion of capitalist enterprises in new territories heightens the awareness among many indigenous populations of the need for control over their lives and territories for their very survival. As women enter into struggles to dismantle the structures of domination, they become acutely aware of their own experience of discrimination as women within their communities and families. Their drive for autonomy often takes the course of gaining control over the body in reproductive issues and sexuality, and gaining mobility and representation in public spheres. As women gain awareness of the way in which their history, creativity, and mental and physical aspirations are suppressed or co-opted in patriarchal society, they are forging the networks whereby they could regain a status as independent adults. Women are seeking autonomy not only in their community and region, but also in the home, where they seek relief from patriarchal oppression. This is the demand of the Namibian women as they confront the AIDS plague (Susser 2004), and it is a recurring theme among women of Mexico (Stephen 2004).

A similar vision of development is occurring among distinct indigenous people as they assert the right to live their own lives in accord with their culturally constituted values. In the past indigenous people were able to retain some control over their lives by the remoteness of their retreat zones from the centers of modernity. The desire for the oil, precious metals, and biogenetic DNA of people, plants, and animals in their territories threatens whatever resource base they retained that allowed them to exercise autonomy. In their present quest for autonomy within the nations in which they reside they reject that limited to local community that was part of the colonial accommodation, and call for regional self-government in areas where they constitute a majority with direct representation in national arenas. This is seen as a means to subvert the corruption of native intermediaries called *caciques* and retain self-rule through consensual governance.

Justice.   Justice ensures the trinity of moral values embraced by revolutionaries of the eighteenth and nineteenth century and referred to as liberty, equality, and fraternity. The class struggle that once embodied these aspirations has not, as some postmodernist observers claim, been abandoned as an arena of conflict and mobilization for change, so much as it has become encapsulated in multistranded institutions that are indirectly related to the accumulation of and power over capital. Feminists, conservationists, and activists for human rights address issues once subsumed in the class struggle.

Feminists address the injustices institutionalized in patriarchal social systems both in and beyond the workplace. The invisibility of women's labor in the domestic arena that enabled men to enter public life properly clothed, fed, and sexually maintained in earlier decades (Smith 1987) now becomes part of global assembly lines where women produce and dispense at extremely low prices the goods and services that circulate in international circuits. Their precarious niche in the labor market was, until recently, hardly recognized by trade unions. Lacking entry into national power circuits that male union leaders curried until recently, women's wage demands and strikes were largely ignored or reinserted as paternalistic benefits responding to the dependency status of women in family units (Lim 1983). Some breakthroughs have occurred, as in the case of South Korean factory women who achieved labor victories not only for themselves, but also for workers throughout the country in the late 1980s (Kim 1997), and in Nicaragua, where women in assembly garment factories sustained a strike in their shops for several weeks.

The encapsulation of labor's struggles in multistranded institutions has diverted attention from the fact that the central conflict between the producers of surplus value created in production and those who expropriate and determine its function in society still exists. As a result of labor struggles in the first half of the nineteenth century, employees at every level in the labor hierarchy gained entitlements through government intervention in health and retirement provisions. These publicly based welfare provisions are now threatened by neoliberal policies that dominate global markets, threatening even well-established social democracies of Europe. If capitalist class interests prevail in world markets, there may well be a return to the direct confrontations that characterized labor struggles until the early decades of the twentieth century.

Among the new forms of labor struggles are those seeking fair market practices in both regional and global markets. The movement for fair trade includes justice on both sides: producers are committed to allowing inspections and certification guaranteeing an organic product of quality with the added value that it takes into account environmentally sound practices. Consumers for their part are responsible for paying a just price as "citizens of conscience." The movement includes five million people integrated in agricultural cooperatives in eighteen countries with 64 billion Euros of sales a year.[6] The discourse of these movements echoes that of the moral economy exponents in the nineteenth and early twentieth century.

The marketplace has itself become the site for labor demonstrations, with student and middle-class protests against sweatshop labor at the malls and the sales outlets for Gap, Nikon, and other internationally known brands. College students and community activists join the movement promoted by progressive unions such as UNITE and AFL/CIO textile workers union. By capturing an audience of potential consumers at the very moment when they are about to express their power of consumption, UNITE has been able to succeed in major strikes for organizing shops in the United States (Nash 1998).

These steps toward developing a moral and juridical framework for global society through human rights commissions, environmental conservation, personal and political autonomy, fair labor, and trade associations are fostered in the context of social movements. The institutional bases for human rights, for a sustainable economy, and for the exercise of autonomy are developing within the framework of the United Nations and in the daily practice of a regenerated civil society. The labor movement may be losing its parochial and gender-biased base with the waning of national state commitments to fair labor laws, but it is gaining strength in these extended networks. Some of the most vigorous labor action occurred among the Asian tigers—the newly industrialized countries of the Asian economy when workers in export-oriented production demanded fair wage and working conditions in the 1980s. Labor organizers in third world countries, especially those of Central America where brutal repression exists, often turn to human rights and United Nations organizations such as the International Labor Organization for legal and advisory support (see chapter 3 on Nicaraguan assembly workers, this volume).

The construction of the spaces for representation changes with each cohort of claimants. Some of these movements were initiated in advanced industrialized countries, such as the women's movement and the civil rights movements of the 1960s, ultimately spreading throughout Latin America and Asia where they acquired new directions among unexpected cohorts. The civil rights movement addressing ethnic and racial discrimination undoubtedly grew out of anticolonial movements inspired by Gandhi in India and influenced a new generation of nonviolent protest. The reverberations in the U.S. South have lent support for long-delayed reforms throughout the North, eventually igniting movements to overcome segregation in Africa and other formerly colonized states. Civil society mobilizations against corruption in despotic Asian societies such as Indonesia and the Philippines expanded the range and variety of people's mobilizations. Inequities in the labor scene are now addressed in free trade associations as well as in the revitalized trade union movement. Labor unions seek covenants affirming human rights and democratic negotiations in regional trade pacts such as the North American Free Trade Agreement, the European Community, as well as in bilateral agreements such as between the United States and China. Small businesses seek entry into trade negotiations along with producer cooperatives that object to unilateral control exercised by multinational corporations. Religious sodalities are becoming increasingly involved in economic discussions as they witness the growing gap correlated with globalization.

THEORY AND PRACTICE IN SOCIAL MOVEMENTS

Theoretical models for the study of social movements derived from nineteenth- and twentieth-century political economists are being modified in response to new directions in global processes. The focus on exclusively economic issues in specific sites of labor is diverted with the emergence of civil rights, feminist, and "postindustrialist" identities. Identity-focused and multisited case studies responding to the volatile political and economic activism in the decades of the 1960s and 1970s demonstrated the need for multiplex analyses of contemporary movements.

Sociological theorists, such as Alain Touraine (1988), Ernesto Laclau and Chantal Mouffe (1985), and Alberto Melucci (1989), began to address these "new" social movements and incorporated cultural issues as central to the motivating logic of society.[7] Their rejection of the Marxist base/superstructure dichotomy was presaged in the challenge made by feminist scholars who rejected Cartesian dichotomies of nature/culture and female/male that precluded agency and intellect in the feminine spheres, and by cultural studies spearheaded by Raymond Williams. By drawing attention to the ethnic, gender, and racial composition of movements that were suppressed by those that privileged class position, new social movements theorists opened the stage of history to many new actors. The faceless masses and the suppression of difference in the interest of promoting unity were no longer viable strategies. The new leaders embodied the muted demands of diverse groups as women, ethnic, and religious groups contested repressive conditions. In the course of their struggles, they expanded the cultural potential for symbolizing their objectives and embodying their concerns.[8]

The advances made by proponents of what is sometimes associated with postmodernist theory tapped the bodily and psychic energies of the people as they were affected by change. However, the tendency to emphasize the individual as actor and protagonist of social change in "new" social movements theory often minimized the collective base that inspires many such movements. The resurgence of ethnic identification among populations marginalized in the course of conquest challenged the indigenist ideologies shaped by dominant elites of mixed origins and brought to the fore collective practices and aspirations that had long been buried.

Indigenism is the ideological ground in which ethnic elites set the parameters for interethnic discourse. Mexican anthropologists engaged in a critical view of the prevalent indigenist ideology as a unilineal lens that extolled the past glories of indigenous civilizations while denying them a position in the contemporary society (Warman, Batalla, and Armas 1970). As Brazilian anthropologist Alcida Rita Ramos (1998, 6) defines it, indigenism is the mirror by which the *mestizos* (mixed-bloods) of the Western hemisphere see themselves in relation to the Indian, just as orientalism serves the Western European observer. It is a distortion for both ethnic groups, one that exaggerates an essential core of elements while disregarding other characteristics. The claims for autonomy and the right to

Figure 6.1. Globalization processes cultivate the seeds of protest, but also the communication channels that generate social movements. Civil society from throughout the region joins indigenous people in Chiapas as this civil group urges Mexican government support for indigenous demands.

cultural diversity pose the ultimate challenge to nations that conceptualize their populations as homogeneous, or at least en route toward expunging difference. The governments of both Mexico and Brazil promoted indigenist ideologies that praised cultural diversity even as they promoted policies that contributed to the extinction of cultural difference.

Kay Warren's study (1998) of the Guatemalan pan-Mayan movement is unusual in placing the cultural vindication of Mayan traditions in the context of an intellectual formation. This challenges the tendency to relate ethnicity to subordination and marginalization, repeating the transgressions of the conquerors that destroyed manifestations of the high civilizations they invaded and sought to conquer. We are also reminded of these still-vital cultural expressions in the recuperation of a literature carried in the memories and sometimes transcribed by early Catholic missionaries (Tedlock 1984, 1993). These resources for social mobilizations are a storehouse for future generations.

Feminist anthropologists and sociologists have explored the conjugated bases for social movements deriving from race, gender, and ethnicity. Transformative change in society must combat the barriers based on race, class, and gender in order to achieve success precisely because of the reinforcement of hierarchy that occurs in each category (Mullings 1997).

This conjugation is clarified in the global arena when the distractions of parochial cultural elements are removed and repression prevails in its crudest forms.

The tendency toward using reductionist categories in caricaturing other people is often countered by the subordinate group uniting under one banner bearing what was the term of opprobrium. I have heard indigenous people of Guatemala argue that the term *Indio,* or Indian, should be accepted as their own designation since it reflects their history of opposition to the dominant ladino. Women have often found common cause with others related to their role as mothers.[9] Ironically, postmodern deconstructive critiques tend to denounce as "essentialist" this kind of discourse whether used by dominant sectors in denigrating the ethnic sectors they wish to exploit or by activists seeking to unite with other indigenous peoples in self-defense. Yet essentializing is an aspect of all intellectual processes. Michael Herzfeld (1997, 36, cited in Ramos 1998) recognizes how essentializing gives shape "to ideas and impressions as they collide with skepticism." It is particularly prevalent among new cohorts of activists in the early stages of mobilization as they use what some consider to be essentializing language to unite distinct groups around common elements of group consciousness. These constructed emblems of identity enable them to counter negative stereotypes used to denigrate the excluded groups as they seek dignity and respect in the world from which they feel excluded. Lynn Stephen (2004) addresses these concerns about the *Comadres,* exiled women who found common cause during the thirty-year civil war in Guatemala, and the Zapatista women who combine their commitment to the rebellion against public subordination with patriarchal domination at home.

Touraine (1988) demonstrated the emergence of ever present but unsuspected premises for political expression in his study of the May 1968 riots in Paris and the Polish solidarity movement. His analysis obviously impressed "Marcos," the *subcomandante* of the Zapatista rebellion, who invited him to the 1996 International Convention Against Neoliberalism and for Humanity in the Lacandón Rain Forest. In an interview with a reporter for *La Jornada* (August 10, 1996, 11) after the event, Touraine summed up what he saw as the global process in the making:

> Now it is a question of going from revolutionary to something that does not have a name yet, but that ties democracy to the defense of cultural rights, the capacity of communication to the defense of diversity. The union of identity is that of specificity with the universal. I believe that international opinion appreciates a great deal of what Indian communities of Chiapas are, as a people located in a particular space, a time, a culture, who speak a universal language. In some way, the ski masks signify "we are you," the universality. I

am at the same time a member of my community but with the voice of my mountain I speak with the phrase *I am you*, that, along with the phrase, *to command while obeying* is one of the greatest definitions of what is democracy. (emphasis in original, translated from Spanish by author)

Not all scholars of global processes share Touraine's sense of the potential for universalizing the message of pluricultural coexistence in a global setting. Hardt and Negri (2000) reject the "new forms of struggle" such as the uprising in Chiapas, along with the Tiananmen Square events of 1989, the Intifada against Israeli authority, the May 1992 revolt in Los Angeles, the strikes in France in December 1995, and those in South Korea in 1996, as failed struggles "because the desires and needs they expressed could not be translated into different contexts." Yet, those who have studied the preexisting and subsequent conditions of these movements have pointed out, and as current news emanating from the Middle East confirms, momentous changes are ongoing in these areas. Korean capitalism has entered a new phase of state-supported enterprise in which the workers have attained rights that exceed those of the export-processing zones of other Asian and Latin American countries. In Mexico, indigenous peoples have gained many supporters for their San Andrés Agreement on autonomy, and though it has not yet been implemented by Congress, the indigenous peoples have gained ground in civil society. Although China redrew the line against political freedom in Tiananmen Square, the site remains a signpost for resistance to tyranny in the global arena. As for the other social movements in Los Angeles and Paris, these truly local struggles that do not rank with the other world struggles have had incremental improvements through a process of mimesis. Indigenous movements are consistently underestimated except by a few anthropologists and political scientists[10] who are studying them. Yet some believe that they provide one of the few alternative visions of a future in which multicultural coexistence challenges the hierarchies of sovereign nations and empires.[11]

GLOBALIZATION PROCESSES AND THEIR OPPONENTS

In this chapter, I have taken the frequently reiterated themes in anthropological literature that characterize globalization and grouped the movements that respond to them in order to show how social movements are engendered to oppose what people perceive as threats to central values enunciated above. These processes and the responses they may trigger include (1) the fragmentation and recomposition of society, (2) secularization and fundamentalist reactions, (3) deterritorialization and the politics of space, and (4) privatization and global cosmopolitanism. The assumption that global integration would lead to a faceless, borderless, homogenized, and universalized world that exists only to consume the products that are endlessly reproduced in a global assembly line is not realized in ethnographic case studies. What careful study reveals is that social movements often subvert or transform the thrust of these processes in accord with central values related to human rights, environmental conservation, autonomy, and social justice that I refer to above. These values provide an ever-changing frame of reference that animate social movements and serve to validate the changes they institute or the revitalization of an imagined past without conflict.

The conjugation of differences in race, religion, and gender brought together in spaces where they were never before seen is generally considered as divisive. Yet it may promote a recomposition of civil society transmitted through nongovernmental organizations (NGOs) and other transnational networks to a global society.[12] Those who are subjected to the processes designated by analysts of globalization contest the assumption that they are inevitable concomitants of the new world order. Their reactions may have the power to subvert even the most formidable military force.

I have avoided the tendency to organize social movements according to specific populations—women, indigenous peoples, etc.—or to focused issues that preoccupy social movements. Feminism is a movement against sexism that has expanded to include men and gays as well as women. The goals of many feminist groups are the liberation of society from behaviors that constrict the humanity of any one group. The same is true for indigenous movements that, in seeking the right to express their own cultural values, may also work for the liberation of all people from other arbitrarily imposed behaviors.

By addressing issues in relation to tensions created by globalization processes the reader can perceive and compare how the populations affected by them reenvision their positions as they respond to global tendencies in culturally and historically distinct ways recounted in the cases analyzed in each chapter. Civil society movements that unite diverse actors around values enumerated above counter the fragmentation of family and community. Secularization is opposed in fundamentalist religions as well as New Age spirituality. Deterritorialization and forced migrations are the basis for indigenous protests against neoliberal invasions of their lands and expropriation of their resources. Union movements and civil society actions that expand their base oppose privatization and the decimation of the social welfare state. For activists in global civil society engaged in these many sites for protest and vindication, democracy is no longer limited to electoral politics imposed by foreign superpowers but is, rather, a participatory practice in the governance of everyday decisions.

Fragmentation and the Recomposition of Civil Society

Fragmentation of society has been characterized by the breaking up of communities and the institutional premises of traditional ways of life with deindustrialization, the forced migration of people to new production sites, or the intrusion of Western beliefs and institutions into native territories. Exclusionary factors that limit the ability of certain members of society to gain access to health services, political power, and economic opportunities often become precipitating causes for class, gender, and ethnic mobilizations directed toward removing the barriers.

In order to emphasize the ephemeral quality of social groupings in a global setting, some of the analysts in this volume have followed the trend visible in social movements to relate to civil society and networks rather than party politics or revolutionary cadres. Organized parties are often criticized as a site for co-optation and social movements, and guerrilla operations seem destined to escalate militarism without addressing the social needs they espouse. Hence we find that many social movements find a new ground for uniting in civil society networks. Mark Edelman (2001) cautions readers to recognize both the multiple usages and interpretations of the terms "civil society" and "networks" by transnational NGOs and national interest groups. Networks linking associations in several countries may fail to overcome the turmoil that they generate, but in the process they launch many leaders that voice *campesino* issues in transnational arenas.

Not all civil society movements are salutary. Nazism, the fundamentalist Christian movement in the United States, and the militia that bombed the Oklahoma federal building mobilize energies for often antisocial acts (Castells 1997). The government may even instigate such movements to support a repressive state apparatus, as Katherine Bowie (2004) found in 1970 when the right-wing Thai government sponsored a scout movement in which young males became a distinct embodiment of nationalism and right-wing militaristic surveillance squads at work. The guerrilla movements of many Latin American countries have sometimes devolved into paramilitary operations as they become linked with cattle ranchers or counter-narcotics-trafficking operations. Thus we must recognize that civil society is not just a cohort of fair-minded citizens seeking justice, but may also include those who align themselves with powerful military and statist interests to achieve control over the citizenry.

Women's increasing emergence in public roles adds a volatile dimension in societies where men have dominated civil society. Lynn Stephen (2004) shows how Latin American women extend their identities as mothers through the nomenclature of their organizations. Specifically she addresses this issue in the case of El Salvador's CO-MADRES (Godmothers), who follow the lead of the Mothers of the Plaza de Mayo in Argentina, who were instrumental in bringing down the military regime that killed many of their children. Identification with maternal roles has a strategic as well as spiritual value since it evokes the most revered social sentiments in society and endows the nurturing quality that is at the heart of the relationship with enhanced value. The same spirit imbues Zapatista women who as mothers oppose the military in Chiapas by shaming young soldiers for their war against their own people. In countering the charge of "essentializing" their status as women as they try to gain positions in the public arenas from which they have been excluded, it is important to recognize that only through self-realization is it possible to overcome their own distancing from public life.

The once unifying basis of class relations that coalesced in industrial society when a workforce united as a mass of exploited workers confronting industrial capitalists has diminished as many different forms of labor compete in the global assembly line. The trend away from business unionism in U.S. industry and toward more fluid categories of work such as "co-partnership" or "quality circles" that denied class boundaries was on the increase in the 1980s. In the class versus culture warfare unwinding in studies of the workplace in the new global assembly lines some analysts such as Paul Durrenberger (2002) attempt to show the enduring tension re-created daily on the shop floor; others such as Sharryn Kasmir (2004) analyze how management attempts to subvert cohesion by expanding management categories. In her article, "Activism and Class Identity: The Saturn Auto Factory Case," Kasmir finds the resurgence of trade union consciousness among Saturn automobile factory workers when they realized that their immersion in the details of production in quality work circles left them out of policy making regarding issues that fundamentally affected their work lives, such as wages and hours. By 1999 workers expressed their disaffection from the touted "partnership" to vote in favor of the United Auto Workers (UAW) as their bargaining agent.

The multistranded nature of social relations serves to reconstitute social relations that become fragmented in the many settings I have reviewed here. During extreme instances of social breakdown, society tends to resort to extreme role models such as the nationalistic scout movement in Thailand or the Mothers of the Plaza de Mayo in confronting the generals of Argentina. Essentialized forms of such appeals in periods of extreme stress evoke primordial sentiments that may have both positive and negative outcomes depending on how the energy they release is directed. Often reviled because of their association with chauvinistic or romanticized sentiments and behaviors, these essentialized categories are nonetheless powerful reminders of our atavistic responses to social breakdown and the attempts to reconstitute society.

Secularization and Fundamentalist Reactions

The alienation from spiritual communities of faith, incipient in eighteenth- and nineteenth-century society, is magnified incrementally with global commoditized exchanges in more and more domains of life. Within the past twenty years we find that health services, which were once controlled by religious and public institutions, are now rendered only on payment for higher and higher fees in privatized, for-profit hospitals. Biotechnological strategies for achieving reproduction reduce the affective basis for heterosexual and homosexual mating. Just as the Christian world has seen fundamentalist sects reasserting some of the verities that seem threatened by the breakup of established social relations, so has the Muslim world found new and often more militant expressions of Islamic faith. Privatization of what were once publicly available services and goods, combined with secularization of institutions that were based on charity, reduce the basis for renewing communal life.

Islamic resurgence in the face of traumatic political and economic events was furthered by the development of print media that helped diffuse the political ideology of radical Islamic ideology in Afghanistan, as David Edwards (2002) shows in his study of the impact of print Islam. Just as national newspapers helped form a sense of the nation in other countries of the West, spurring revolution in Russia, so did various forms of the media allow the diffusion of new ideologies in Islamic countries. The media, which were rarely even quoted in scholarly work, have gained prominence in global studies as a force in themselves for social change.

The encounter of oppositional religious and cultural groups in an increasingly integrated world more often leads to hostilities than to acceptance of the common human denominator. This requires anthropologists to analyze the dialogic encounters that overcome the impasse of antagonistic opponents.

Deterritorialization and the Politics of Place

The worldwide deployment of capital demands flexibility in the disbursements of wages and other costs of production. Labor is the principal component of flexibility in the production system. The "deterritorialization" of people, communities, and industries is taken to be axiomatic in global flows (Appadurai 1996; Gupta and Ferguson 1997). But in the postmodern vein of inquiry, the terms of discourse—deterritorialization, creolization, hybridization, or fragmentation—often become reified as processes. This naturalizing of the phenomenon may result in the underestimation of the social movements born in the resistance of local populations to disperse.

This process of resistance to deterritorialization is forcefully illustrated by the Zapatista reaction to the privatization of land in Chiapas. When President Carlos Salinas's administration forced the passage of the "reform" of the Agrarian Reform Act in 1992, and followed this with the North American Free Trade Agreement eliminating tariffs on agricultural goods that competed with their cash crops, the Zapatistas chose New Year's morning of 1994 as the advent of their uprising to signalize their distress. With these two acts, the indigenous people, who migrated to the Lacandón jungle with the promise of gaining title to national territories, were effectively disinherited, and the markets for their commercial crops were lost to competition from the United States. They found support for their mobilization against the neoliberal programs of the Mexican government in Christian Base Communities in highland villages. The fusion of ethnic resurgence and religious faith that reinforces their demand for autonomy to pursue collective forms of life is now directing their opposition to the government program for change called the Plan Puebla Panamá (Nash 2001b).

This development scheme to integrate communication, production sites, and markets in the southern states of Chiapas with the Central American countries is shaking the solidarity of Mayan communities mobilized in the Zapatista uprising. In the early spring of 2003 each day brought news of confrontations in the Lacandón Rain Forest as those who remained loyal to the Zapatistas opposed the megaprojects such as the building of hydroelectric power dams and tourist facilities. But many of the people living in the autonomous communities had begun to accept government dispensations of medicines and to send their children to public schools.

Whether the Mexican Maya's claims to the land as indigenous peoples with title to collective lands will supersede their affinities with landless peasants is an open question. As yet they have not joined forces with Maya across the Guatemala border where the indigenous people constitute a majority of the population. If such an alliance should occur, the nightmare of Guatemalan ladinos that has driven the government to massive violations of human rights would be realized. The geopolitical reality of autonomy within Mexico cannot be realized without the strong and continued support of Mexican civil society. But the expansion of an economic zone created by Plan Puebla Panamá might provide the associations among Maya beyond the artificial borders drawn by independence governments in the nineteenth century to create a new class and ethnically based opposition to capitalist invasion.

The indigenous people of Oaxaca are also seeking alternative development enterprises to those of the assembly plants and exploitation of energy sources proposed by the Plan Puebla Panamá for the Isthmus of

Tehuantepec. As Molly Doane (2001) shows, indigenous people of Chimalapas, Oaxaca, turned to international ecological teams to bolster their attempt to define their spaces for autonomy in the area of the Oaxaca rain forest when transportation projected by the Plan Puebla Panamá threatened to remove them from the territories they have colonized.

There are also parallels in Max Kirsch's review (2004) of the effort on the part of community-based organizations to engage Florida Everglades residents in the legislative policies. Their concerns about the environment they live in provoke a distinct solution to that of technocrats and bureaucrats. Anthropological inquiry into the mix of government agents, NGOs, and local inhabitants provides a comparative basis for analyzing the points of conflict and coordination. Hopefully this will become integrated at a level where local interests can successfully challenge the top-down approach to planning that still characterizes global environmental planning.

The question of identity becomes a crucial issue in state relations with indigenous peoples at a time when indigenous rights to traditional territories are contested. Renée Sylvain (2004) discusses how the Omaheke San of South Africa negotiate their identity in the current dilemma of diminished hunting and gathering territories and encroachment on their lands. This identity is, the author maintains, shaped by assumptions of apartheid racist premises. In order to convince a still-racist government of the authenticity of their claims they conform to identity expectations forced on them by the state and the international donor community. Whether the San can escape the reductionist position of promoting a stereotypical primordial identity based on an archaic lifestyle will depend on their ability to make alliances with other marginalized and oppressed classes.

The San seem to encompass the full trajectory of human life as isolated bands "living a stone-age culture"—as the media depicts them—to becoming a part of global circuits. For some analysts, like Richard Lee (1979), the San exemplify a cultural survival of a way of life that is "communally based, that speaks of spirituality, non-capitalist values . . . harmony with nature" and with a strong "sense of place." Sylvain rejects this characterization, which she claims emerged only after independence allowed them the opportunity to make land claims. She envisions a future that would restrict them to playacting a traditional foraging life for eco-tourists seeking the thrills of a true-life safari if they choose the route of cultural survival. Yet if they choose to rethink their ethnicity in all of its "reciprocal accommodations of culture to class oppression" as they live it, they may achieve a cosmopolitan opposition to globalization processes.

In a setting of tribal people's encirclement by invasive agents of global enterprises, women's embodiment of the needs and spirit of the people they represent can become an impressive assertion of their value as citizens. Ligia Simonian (2004), who has worked with the Amazonian indigenous women of Brazil during their most difficult years in the 1980s and 1990s, shows a similar development to that of Namibian women when they emerged as political figures. Their situation as indigenous peoples, often abandoned when their husbands were forced to seek wage work in the gold mines and elsewhere, merits attention since their role as primary food providers and as mothers reinforced their leadership role in their communities. Among their greatest problems are the alcoholism of the men and the subsequent abuse they suffer from them. They must therefore fight a battle on two fronts, at home and in public against predatory invaders of their jungle habitat. They have, through their own initiatives and the assistance of NGOs, been able to extend their networks in wide regions occupied not only by their tribes' people but also by other language groups. Despite the opposition they face at home, where their husbands object to their political activities, but also in the wider world where white invaders see them as objects of rape and forced servitude, they are achieving some success in their struggles for land, credit, and markets. With the help of NGO promoters, they have extended the range of income-earning potential with their jungle products—body oils, medicines, and handicrafts.

In their struggles to secure their place in national and international settings, Zapatista cultivators of the Lacandón Rain Forest, indigenous peoples of Chimalapas, Mexico, settlers of the Florida Everglades, women of the Amazonian forest, and the San of South Africa are all asserting their place in their home environment. Max Kirsch's account of the contested conservation of the Florida wetlands can be seen in tandem with Renée Sylvain's concerns with the San's attempt to retain a presence in the Kalahari desert terrain where they once hunted and gathered wild grains. Or either paper can be illuminated by Ligia Simonian's (2004) portrayal of Amazonian women as they attempt to ensure their survival in habitats that are being invaded by gold miners, ranchers, and biodiversity DNA poachers as they engage in community-based political action. Molly Doane's analysis (2001) of the defense of Chimalapas's smallholder campesinos against highway development is linked to Nash's (2001) discussion of the Zapatista uprising triggered by the North American Free Trade Agreement. Indigenous groups in both areas are now protesting the same megaprojects sponsored by the Plan Puebla Panamá. By embodying the many forms of consciousness and practice in specific cultural contexts, the authors elucidate the processes in formation throughout the world.

The current trend toward privatizing the most basic rights to water, land, and the resources by which they ensure their survival heightens the struggle to retain rights that were once taken for granted by virtue of being there. This "environmentalism of the poor" (Guha 1997), which encompasses the protests by hill villagers against logging companies, by forest tribals against dam builders, and by fisherfolk against multinational corporations deploying trawlers, can mobilize massive protests, and often brings about transformative change without guerrilla actions. The recourse to cultural politics of social protests often brings local leaders to the forefront. In the following section, we shall examine how people are reasserting moral issues in exchange through a global cosmopolitanism that achieves links without the loss of local identity, and reasserts the moral component of national and international trade in the marketplace.

Privatization, Commoditization, and Global Cosmopolitanism

Privatization and the individualization of human responsibilities, duties, and claims on society are aspects of modernity that are intensified with globalization. From the perspective of global capitalist enterprises, the private rights to control property and resources are the *sine qua non* of expansion and growth, without which the motivation of profits vanishes. The freeing up of social relations through money exchange, referred to in political economy as the commoditization of all social relation, was seen as a threat to humanistic values. This was particularly marked in the nineteenth century when monetary exchange accelerated in all sectors of life. Marx discusses it in the *Grunderisse* written between 1857 and 1858, suggesting that as cash exchanges increasingly enter into and mediate social relations, they become emptied of institutional and affective content. (1973, 156–58). He envisioned a future in which commoditization progressively would come to dominate all social exchanges, negating their social relational content. As Marx comments (1973, 157), "as money expands . . . the social character of the relationship diminishes." This understanding provided the basis for his thesis on commodity fetishism, which is often misunderstood as excessive consumption rather than the loss of social connections between producer and consumer.

The common characteristic of those living in global metropolises is the growing privatization and individualization of activities that were once the domain of publicly funded welfare or charitable institutions. Money exchange becomes a substitute for reciprocity and redistributive traditions. Capitalist expansion does not occur without the assurance that private property rights will be respected. Migration of peasants and tribal people from rural and forest areas necessitates a transformation in personal self-presentation as migrants attempt to mask their rustic origins or tribal membership. When the people of the Amazon appear in capital cities wearing feathers (as they did when protesting the burning of the forests by cattle ranchers) or when settlers of the Lacandón appear carrying bows and arrows (as they did in the Celebration of Five Hundred Years of Resistance), they are usually there on a political mission.

For others, the isolation effect—or alienation of individuals in society as Marxists called it—is considered rooted in monetary exchange as the products of human labor become commodities. Money not only stands for the value of the product, as Marx pointed out, but releases the seller and the buyer from further obligation. In the *Grunderisse* Marx (1973, 59) explores how money takes on a "material existence, apart from the product" that also denies the moral relation between the producer and the consumer. This is dramatically illustrated in the case of prostitution, but lingers in the medical profession in some countries that are not completely commoditized.

Fair trade organizations provide a counterpoint to the privatization and individualization of global exchanges, introducing a strong moral component that challenges the alienation implied by commoditization. Driven by the desire to render fair prices for the producers, products produced in environmentally sustainable production cooperatives are now an important part of global trade, as Kimberly Grimes and B. Lynn Milgram (2000) show. For over a decade, student movements have used the boycott to penalize rogue nations for human rights abuses. This moral component in market exchange is expanding as the inequities in global trade become ever more apparent.

Secular institutions are beginning to intervene in the politics of commoditized food markets in the form of fair trade associations. Mark Ritchie, president of the Institute for Agriculture and Trade Policy (IATP) based in Minneapolis, Minnesota, warns that the United States is promoting the dumping of subsidized crops at below-market prices. Mexico has been afflicted by these policies, especially since NAFTA forced an opening for U.S. crops in Mexico. The World Organization of Commerce is fighting the policies of dumping goods because of the destruction of the subsistence production sector. Resources such as water and air are now threatened with commoditization.

Robert Albro's (2004) discussion of a social movement triggered by the privatization of water by a multinational corporation is central to understanding the consequences, and subsequent protests, against privatizing resources considered to be "the gifts of nature." Albro shows how one such water privatization plan put into operation in Bolivia mobilized massive protests by cultivators led by Oscar Olivera, a labor union leader and urban activist in the Bolivian state of Cochabamba who has become a world-renowned figure in environmental circles. The "Water War" began when the government allowed a multinational corporation to control and sell water to campesinos and urban residents of the region, and the people rose up in protest. This extraordinary violation of what are considered the most basic resources of the people became a celebrated international issue caught up in antiglobalization activism. Albro's analysis of the discourse and the cultural symbols utilized by local protest movements can, with the help of NGO strategists, mobilize global support.

Communicable diseases are the most cosmopolitan of world problems, transgressing class, race, and geographical boundaries, and linking the local and personal to global processes. Ida Susser (2004) addresses the local definitions of HIV as Africans categorize the patient population and allocate resources for treating it in accord with local priorities. The women's movement in Namibia challenged these priorities, which excluded women from scarce medical treatment just at the moment they were becoming the majority of the population affected by HIV. The inequity in the disbursements by male-dominated institutions is so persistent that women's grassroots organizations are proliferating to contest the failure to address women's as well as their children's health problems. Susser's work with Richard Lee in assessing the success of the female condom in limiting the spread of the disease in Namibia is a tribute to the successful cooperation of international agencies and grassroots organizations of Namibian women. It also galvanized women to address other aspects of discrimination in the groups that they formed to combat the threat of HIV.

Women in India have embraced feminist cosmopolitanism in their attempt to escape some of the most extreme forms of gender subordination. As the country became enmeshed in global processes of change, women began to perceive their condition from external perspectives. Yet as women became engaged in local civil liberties activism they went beyond the gender-based injustices that were part of global feminism to mount a critique of state involvement in such practices as gang rape by police custodians and dowry killings. In Deepa Reddy's review (2004) of the history of the feminist movement in India, women simultaneously forged a public place from which they had been excluded in both national and international society as they strove to reform corrupt state politics. Gender oppression, they reasoned, was not just an outcome of traditional practice, but also a product of patriarchal exercise of power to maintain class, gender, and ethnic hierarchies. The broad scope of women's activism allowed them to challenge oppression in all of its manifestations as they engaged in fundamental social change.

These movements for fair trade, the right to utilize freely the basic resources of the community, and to engage in public life without restrictions based on gender are reactions to the increasing individuation. Michel-Rolph Trouillot refers to the cosmopolitan transfers of human rights and other homogenizing value systems carried in global circuits as "the isolation effect" of globalization (2001, 126, 132). This carries two dimensions. For some, the antidote to the spiritual malaise brought about by isolation with the decline of public life is a global cosmopolitanism evoking "a unifying vision for democracy and governance in a world dominated by globalizing capitalism" (Harvey 2001, 271). Harvey rejects such specious conceptions of cosmopolitan unity that ignore historical-geographical processes of community construction. The effect on society of this increasing individuation brings about a sense of isolation that was once referred to in Marxist scholarship as alienation.

CONCLUSIONS

Anthropologists are retrieving the macropolitical and macroeconomic context that was often obscured by the emphasis on identity or single-issue social movements. The holistic analysis of social movements that is the hallmark of anthropological studies reveals the interlinked effect of gender-class-race-ethnicity in the context of growing wealth gaps and concentration of political power. The inclusion of cases dealing with universal issues confronting diverse societies as they respond to the impact of globalization processes reestablishes the basis for comparative studies that can assist policy makers and international NGO activists. Anthropologists who once ignored the intrusion of national and international in their field sites are now among the principal observers of social movements, particularly those of indigenous people, women, and the disinherited as they seek a new relationship with the states in which they are included. Although the potential of these movements is often underestimated, it is in these circuits once considered marginal to global processes that the major transforming changes are occurring. Because of their cultivated peripheral vision, anthropologists are in a position to assess new directions.

The globalization processes that cultivators and fisherfolk, former hunters, artisans, wageworkers, and pastoralists confront relate to the predatory advance of capitalist enterprises in areas that once provided reserves for subsistence-oriented producers. They signal the retreat from old industrial areas where the return on capital has diminished. These areas have become the brownfields or museums of a past era. The rising demand for energy sources brings about increasing integration of people throughout the world at the same time that it exacerbates the contest for control over these assets. Competition for the most basic resources of water, air, and land raises the price for these increasingly privatized necessities, adding to the precarious conditions of marginalized populations in the global economy. Collective sharing of resources in conditions of scarcity becomes the bitterly contested redistribution for the sectors impoverished by capitalist advances.

If there is a single theme that unites the many social movements in the world, it is the growing autonomy sought by the participants. Women, ethnic minorities, semi-subsistence producers, wageworkers, and immigrants are in one way or another seeking a voice and a space of their own. If the predominant goal in the twentieth century was to achieve a unifying model for mass action in a world polarized by class, the demand running through social movements of the twenty-first century is the right of participants to be themselves. If this is achieved, it will enhance the plasticity of human responses to our social and physical environment, which was our unique advantage over other species at the dawn of civilization. This remains our best option for survival in a world of diminishing resources where humanity has become its own worst enemy.

NOTES

This chapter is a revision of the introduction to the anthology edited by June Nash, *Social Movements: A Reader*, Blackwell Press, 2004.

1. Ulf Hannerz (1996) defines the global ecumene as the "interconnectedness of the world by way of interaction, exchanges, and related development, affecting not least the organization of culture." I have found it useful in analyzing ethnic resurgence to relate the ecumene in which interaction and exchanges unfold to the concept of habitus. This links "the space through which we learn who or what we are in society" (Bourdieu and Wacquant 2002, 126–27) with the expanded significance given it by David Harvey (1989, 2–21 219–21) as the site for relative "generative principles of regulated improvisations" to practices that "reproduce the objective conditions which produce the generative principles" (Nash 2001a, 32–33, 220–21). The novel sites in which these interactions and communications occur vary from concrete geographically situated communities to cyberspace.

2. Those countries that respond to the impending crises by addressing the needs of people are better able to negotiate the transition without political breakdown. The king of Thailand was able to reinforce the constitutional monarchy by urging a restructuring of capital, setting aside one-third of land and investments to restore subsistence production. In contrast the failure of Prime Minister Suharto to respond to the crisis by addressing the needs of the Indonesian people led to his downfall (*New York Times* May 24, 1999).

3. Veronika Bennholdt-Thomsen, Nicholas Faraclas, and Claudia Von Werlhof (2001) have brought together case studies asserting the importance of retaining subsistence economies as alternatives to the global integration. I address some of these protests against global control in Nash (1993).

4. Arturo Escobar (1995) has exposed the assumptions of international development policies and the role of anthropologists. I have addressed anthropological critiques in my article "Indigenous Development Alternatives" (Nash 2003a).

5. In an extraordinary conference organized by Dr. Ligia Simonian at the University of Para in Belem in May 2002, research in the Amazonian area of Brazil, French Guiana, Colombia, Venezuela, and Bolivia demonstrated the importance

of collaborative research with a strong participatory and practical application of knowledge. Papers on the AIDS epidemic, violence against women, drug addiction, and other prevalent health and behavioral problems showed the similarities in problems faced by culturally differentiated groups that share a common environment.

6. Nico and Francisco Vanderhoff, who founded the Union of Indigenous Communities of the Isthmus Region of Oaxaca, have written a book called *The Adventure of Just Commerce: An Alternative to Globalization* (Vanderhoff 2002) that adds to the growing literature on organic farming traded in just circuits.

7. Cf. LaClau and Mouffe 1985; Melucci, Keane, and Mur 1989; Touraine 1971 and 1988.

8. Escobar and Alvarez (1992), and Alvarez, Dagnino, and Escobar (1998) critique the literature on social movements.

9. The ruling junta could not suppress the social movement by mothers and grandmothers in their silent vigil in the Plaza de Mayo of Buenos Aires as they protested their children's disappearances. The universality of their appeal as mothers evoked widespread support and embarrassed the military, leading to their demise. President George W. Bush faced a similar indomitable opponent in Cindy Sheehan protesting the lies he used to gain support of his war in Iraq.

10. The few studies emerging in the 1990s such as Collier and Quaratiello (1994), Gray (1997), and Warren (1998) were followed by a flood of anthologies published after the third millennium (see Nash 2006).

11. Andrew Gray (1997) makes a strong case for indigenous autonomy movements as alternative coexisting paths of development, and I have argued the case for Mayas of Chiapas (Nash 2001b, 2006).

12. Arjun Appadurai (1996), Jean Comaroff and John Comaroff (2001), and Ahkil Gupta and James Ferguson (1997) have characterized the devastating impact of global processes in their essays and anthologies as a loss of place or deterritorialization.

7

Interpreting
Social Movements

*Bolivian Resistance to Economic
Conditions Imposed by the IMF*

It took me over a decade to realize that my fieldwork in Bolivia that began with a two-month survey of mining communities in July 1967 and
ended in August 1986 also marked a shift in U.S. policies in Latin America from support and sometimes instigation of military coups to control
through debt servitude. I arrived in Bolivia soon after René Barrientos,
who seized power in 1964 with a military coup, had ordered the massacre
of miners in Siglo XX on the eve of San Juan, December 24, 1967. My presence in the mining community of Oruro was an anomaly since all the
Americans had left after a break-in at the United States Information
Agency library when many of the books were burned. When I returned to
carry out a year-long study in 1970 I was tolerated only because, I was
later told, the Dirección de Investigaciones Criminales, the equivalent of
the U.S. FBI, had, under orders from the CIA, investigated me. I returned
in 1985 to extend the autobiography of a miner (Rojas and Nash 1976)
with the inclusion of chapters for his children who were now grown up.
Paz Estenssoro, who had served as president of the first revolutionary
government in 1952, had returned to power and was proceeding to undo
the revolutionary legislation he had implemented in the 1950s. With the
help of Jeffrey Sachs, an IMF agent, he drafted the New Economic Policy,
an initiative that included privatization of the mines, revoking land reform, and taxing the peasants. I returned in August 1986 to present the
draft of the new biography (Nash 1992) at the moment that mining communities initiated a march from Oruro to La Paz to present their plea that
President Paz Estenssoro keep the mines open. Bolivia had become the

testing ground for the paradigm shift to bloodless coups resorting to financial manipulation of indebted countries through the International Monetary Fund (IMF) and simultaneously the crucible for protest and rebellion. The five-billion-dollar debt run up by Hugo Banzer, the colonel chosen to carry out the U.S.-instigated military coup in 1971, provided the basis for IMF intervention. The conditions imposed by the IMF forced President Victor Paz Estenssoro, reelected for a second term in 1985, to reverse the populist programs of nationalizing the mines and land reform that he had introduced in 1952 as leader of the National Revolutionary Movement (MNR). In July 1986, I arrived in Bolivia to witness the March for Life and Peace when over ten thousand members of Bolivian mining communities and civil society supporters mobilized to protest a series of austerity decrees and the New Economic Policies imposed by Paz Estenssoro, in response to the IMF's conditions for emerging out of the debt crisis. Although the marchers failed to reach the capital because they were halted by four military regiments outside of La Paz, the march provided a model for the 2000 indigenous march that set off the movement that brought Evo Morales to power in 2006.

Figure 7.1.   Interpretations of fieldwork should include a participant's own assessments as they change over time. The author sits in on a meeting of the miners' union, discussing the March for Life and Peace, Bolivia, 1985.

In analyzing the movement, I tried to retain the range of variation in the interpretations that actors made of the events, along with those of the media and spokespeople as contesting groups. This exercise demonstrated to me that interpretive anthropology taken as a goal in itself, that is, precluding the concrete, historically situated analyses that are the core of ethnographic studies, tends to subvert a processual analysis of cause-and-effect relations. At the time of my writing the article shortly after returning from the field in 1987, I called for a reassertion of the anthropological task of analyzing social interaction in everyday life. Specifically, I argued that traditional ethnographic participant observation can be enhanced by paying attention to discrete units of action and discourse in the different moments in which a social movement is unfolding. Only then can we attend to cause-and-effect relations in a social process.

*   *   *

BOLIVIAN RESISTANCE TO CONDITIONS IMPOSED BY THE IMF

Anthropologists are moving from an ostensibly objective and uniform portrayal of cultures to a reflexive and simultaneously multivocalic one. In the 1970s, the contributors to the anthology *Reinventing Anthropology* (Hymes 1974) called for recognition of the political economic framework in which anthropologists work. In the 1980s anthropology tended toward involution. The authors of *Writing Culture* (Clifford and Marcus 1986), for example, urged ethnographers to focus on texts in order to discover the systems of meaning inherent in the subjects of our discourse. Yet in the ever more refined analysis of texts, anthropologists eclipsed the conditions imposed by macroeconomic and political structures addressed in earlier ethnographies. Moreover, the emphasis on rediscovering meaning in past texts often sidelined the discovery of knowledge about what is happening in the world.

In this article I try to extend the interpretive analysis of culture from eyewinks, cockfights, and canonized texts within anthropology and literature to a social movement in which I became involved. In analyzing the protest movement against IMF conditions, I shall be concerned with the variety of interpretations and reinterpretations the actors made of the events in which they participated. The contrasts among the interpretations of the leaders and followers within the movement with those of the government and the media provide the matrix from which my own interpretations will be drawn. I use the plural form "interpretations" since I was constantly reformulating my views as the movement developed.

What I shall present here is a provisional analysis of an ongoing process, a segment of which I observed in two summer field trips to Bolivia in 1985 and 1986. Bolivia was caught in a debt crisis that one analyst

(Goslin 1985) had called "terminal breakdown." I witnessed a movement of thousands of peasants, miners, teachers, and civic leaders from mine centers threatened with extinction in the restructuring of the economy to meet debt payments. Balancing a latent mistrust of Yankee intruders with the hope of getting their message to the American people, the protestors chose to put me in the role of interlocutor.

THE DIMENSIONS OF THE DEBT CRISIS

In Bolivia the debt crisis brought about a more profound restructuring of the economy than in any other Latin American country. Although the country's debt of almost $5 billion may seem insignificant in comparison with those of Brazil and Mexico, which surpass $100 billion, it requires 60 percent of Bolivia's dwindling exports to service the interest and amortization annually. In a country where the average annual income is $288, the debt amounts to $552 per capita (Strengers 1985).

The debt accumulated during a decade of military rule that began in 1971, when Col. Hugo Banzer seized power in a coup, and was followed by a series of military dictators who seized power after he was ousted by a popular uprising in 1978. In 1981, Bolivia became the first Latin American nation to fail to pay the servicing of its debt. The renegotiation of the debt during Gen. Garcia Meza's term of office, from July 1980 to August 1981, set disastrous conditions on the interest rates and term for repayment. The economy was in disarray in 1982 when President Siles Suazo was finally installed as president on the basis of elections he had won in 1978. The government failed to meet payments for servicing the debt in 1981, but it was not until 1984 that the country was denied international credit, thus bringing about the complete collapse of the Bolivian currency. The official rate of exchange during Siles Suazo's term of office, from October 1982 to July 1985, rose to 67,000 *bolivianos* (Bolivian dollars) per U.S. dollar, but the unofficial or "parallel" rate rose from 350,000 bolivianos to one U.S. dollar in June 1985 to 1 million bolivianos to one U.S. dollar just before the presidential elections in July. No sector of the population (except those involved in the drug trade, which had become a $4 billion industry) could endure the rampant inflation that exceeded 100 percent per month. Following the election of President Paz Estenssoro, the national currency was allowed to "float" on the exchange market, reaching 1.9 million bolivianos per U.S. dollar. The impact of these dramatic fluctuations in the exchange rate and cost of living varied considerably from one place and economic sector to another. The "dollarization" of the economy, that is, the pegging of domestic currency to the U.S. dollar, occurred most rapidly in the major market centers of La Paz, Santa Cruz, and Cochabamba.

So long as the mining centers received subsidized food through the commissaries they were insulated from the most adverse effects of the cost of living increases. But because of rising deficits in the industry, by March 1985 very little was being supplied to the mines. The miners protested in a march on La Paz that had little impact on a government beleaguered with inflation and a stagnating economy. Semisubsistence peasants were less adversely affected than wageworkers, but their discontent with the control exerted by Siles Suazo's government over the prices of commodities they produced and sold resulted in blockades in Santa Cruz and Cochabamba in June 1985. The agro-industrial area of Santa Cruz had grown rapidly during the 1970s, but the resulting extreme unevenness in wealth meant that subsistence peasants in the colonizing areas were being driven off their lands and reduced to wage work. While adult male workers were drawn into coca production where wages were up to $150 and $200 a month, children as young as six and seven, unaccompanied by their parents, were being bused down to Santa Cruz where they worked harvesting cotton and cane crops, usually for little more than tea and corn kernels.

Shortly after President Paz Estenssoro won the election of July 1985, he introduced New Economic Policies, which incorporated the neoliberal philosophy of an IMF adviser from Harvard, Jeffrey Sachs. Among the provisions to hasten payment of the debt was Decree No. 21060, calling for the closing of marginal mines, the transfer to cooperatives of others, and the sale of more profitable mines to private companies. The mines had been losing money in the 1980s, and the deficit had more than doubled between 1980 and 1984, going from $34 million to $83 million; a sharp drop in the price of tin on the world market in October 1985 increased the deficit. Throughout 1985 there was a sharp attrition in the mines, with more than eight thousand miners laid off. Many of these men have now gone to the lowlands in the southeastern department of Santa Cruz where land was promised to colonizers, who sometimes left behind their wives and children. Others have joined the thousands of unemployed living in shantytowns around Cochabamba and El Alto, a growing suburb of La Paz. Countless numbers of discouraged workers migrated to the colonization centers of Beni, Chapari, and the Yungas where cocaine production is the only viable crop.

POPULAR MOBILIZATION
AGAINST IMF IMPOSED CONDITIONS

When I returned to the mining centers in August 1986, a year after Paz Estenssoro was installed in office, production in the mines had come to a standstill. In April and May, the miners had attempted to demonstrate the possibility of increasing productivity, but the lack of materials and technology doomed any such effort. The Federation of Mine Workers' Unions of Bolivia (FSTMB) declared an indefinite strike until the administration would provide the needed supplies. An investment of $50 million, they projected, would significantly increase the returns from complex minerals often ignored in tin mining operations. Opposing the government's decree to close the Mining Corporation of Bolivia (COMIBOL) that had sustained the economy of a population ten times that of the workforce of seventeen thousand still employed in the mines, they drew up an emergency plan calling for rehabilitation of the mines, which had suffered from the failure to invest in exploration and technology during the military regimes. They argued that the mine centers had the best infrastructure in the country, with power lines, roads, railways, communication networks, schools, and markets highly developed since the turn of the century, and that new sources of income should be generated there.

Paz Estenssoro was adamant in carrying through the New Economic Policies despite the unified opposition of the Center of Bolivian Workers (COB), civic committees of the departments of cities Oruro and Potosí—committees that involved a wide spectrum of commercial and professional people—and the Catholic Church. His 1986 budget clearly indicated the priorities of his government: 36.5 percent of the expenditures allocated to the foreign debt, 22.3 percent to defense, 11 percent to education, 1.9 percent to health, and the remaining 28.3 percent to miscellaneous items (CEDOIN 1986b, 1).

The resistance of the mining communities peaked at the 21st National Congress of Miners on May 12 and 13, 1986. At that time Congress petitioned the president and Parliament to keep the mines open and to veto a proposed tax reform on farmers. But the government did not respond to these petitions. Instead, it invited U.S. troops to come to Bolivia, purportedly in order to monitor the drug traffic in Beni. Leaders of the COB, the FSTMB, and student groups interpreted this invitation as a threat to curb the rising discontent in the country. On July 4, civic committees in the departments of Potosí and Oruro united with unions and university students and professors to protest the government plan to "decentralize" mining operations. They were aware that the crisis in the mines would also affect them since the entire society was dependent upon activities in the mining sector. They supported the FSTMB plan calling for rehabilitation of the mines, and they opposed the denationalization of the economy, particularly the destruction of the mining centers, which had served as the backbone of the export economy.

Peasants joined in the protest against the New Economic Policies because of a new tax to be imposed on all sales and on real property that was part of the New Economic Policies. The protest against taxes on those groups with incomes that did not meet minimal food requirements culminated at a meeting called by the COB, of the National Committee of the Popular Council, on July 17 just three days after the arrival of U.S. troops. Among the acts of the council was the approval of a move to delay payment of the debt until the country had recovered economically. The council reacted strongly to what was called the "armed intervention of the army of the United States" (CEDOIN 1986a).

UNITY DURING THE MARCH FOR LIFE

When the government ignored the petitions of broad sectors of the population to keep the mines open, civic committees and workers from the mining centers organized a March for Life. Thousands of miners, housewives, peasants, schoolteachers, and students congregated in Oruro to begin their march. Several people were wounded in a demonstration protesting the government's New Economic Policies when the armed forces threw tear-gas bombs and fired rubber bullets.

Despite this early indication of the government's willingness to use violence against the march, the protestors set out on August 22, planning to arrive in La Paz a week later. On Tuesday, August 26, they reached the halfway point of Patacamaya, where tanks and troops met them. After some discussion between leaders of the march and representatives of the government, it was agreed that the marchers would be allowed to continue to La Paz without military intervention.

On Thursday I drove with my Bolivian colleagues Rosario León and Cecelia Salazar to meet the marchers before their descent into La Paz. There was a great show of camaraderie and optimism as we greeted advance groups of marchers, passing out bread, oranges, and cigarettes. We drove slowly along the edge of the highway to avoid crowding the thousands of marchers walking five to ten abreast.

All that day, marchers arrived in the sun-baked farming village of Calamarca, carrying the Bolivian flag, their union banners, bedrolls, water flasks, and coca leaves. Some women carried babies. Reports in *Presencia*, the newspaper identified with the Catholic diocese, compared the waves of weary travelers to the biblical exodus from Egypt, and the streams of dust-covered travelers did indeed evoke the great pilgrimages in human history. Some limped on feet bandaged to protect blisters, and many had sun-swollen lips. As I watched the marchers entering the plaza, I was reminded of Brooke Larson's (1983) description of whole villages of highland Indians trekking to the mines to fulfill their labor tribute during the colonial period.

University students, Red Cross workers, and nuns from the Catholic parishes of the mining centers cleaned the blistered feet and massaged the aching leg muscles of the marchers as they arrived in towns. As Turner has so eloquently said of pilgrimages, "social structure becomes simplified and homogenized as the spontaneously generated relationship between leveled and equal, total and individuated human beings comes to the surface." The pilgrim "becomes himself a symbol" as the pilgrimage "liberates the individual from the obligatory everyday constraints of status and role, and defines him as an integral human being with a capacity for free choice" (1974:201).

Bolivia was in the most profound crisis that I had ever witnessed in the twenty years since I had begun work in mining communities, and people in the march were direct in their appraisal of it. Though the many different contingents of marchers had specific concerns, they all saw the march as a means of communicating with the government at a time when the crisis had reached a critical point. The people had lost faith in political parties and in formal channels of communication. They felt that it was urgent to bring their message to the president, to involve him immediately in their distress.

We spoke first with a group of women from the mining centers of Santa Fé and Siglo XX as they were peeling potatoes and readying a brushwood fire in order to prepare a meal for the marchers. Their message was basic. When I asked them what demands they had, one woman replied, "There is no food in the commissary, and the government is not giving us any help. Life in the mines is unbearable. Our children are poorly fed and poorly clothed. This generation will be lost." A miner standing nearby added,

> The most important point is that they should not close the doors of COMI-BOL. We want the government to give help to our comrades who have already been laid off. They have already laid off 8,000, and the problem is that there are no other sources of work. And now that the government intends to close the mines, it is the same as throwing us into the street. There is nothing wrong with the mines. The problem is that they are poorly managed, and our technicians have not given good advice. We have great metal reserves, but the government is not aware of this. Our Federation has made a plan for the mines' rehabilitation, demonstrating that the government lies in many respects. Our advisers have posed a plan to save the mines. But the government doesn't want to respond, although we have a great deal of reason.

When we asked what would happen if the mines were closed, their answers revealed the depth of their despair in taking to the road. A miner told us:

> Well, you can see that we are from the highlands, and the government proposes to send us to the east. We could not endure it there, we are not accus-

tomed to the heat. Some have also proposed that we go looking for gold, but in reality we know only how to mine tin and not other metals. We do not know where we can go with our families. They just want to throw us into the street after we have worked all our lives. My father was a miner and he died young because of poor nutrition. . . . What they are doing is inhuman.

Given their faith in the future productivity of the mines, the miners concluded that the government wanted to close the mines because it wanted to destroy the economic base of the most highly organized sector of the workforce. One of the marchers said:

Siglo XX has the best tin of all Bolivia. . . . But we do not have good tools or supplies. There is enough mineral in the shafts, but the administrators do not go down there. The government wants to close the mines because we are the best organized sector of the proletariat class and we demand just salaries. That is why they want to close the doors.

His companion added:

Well, as he said, we have put all our strength into trying to raise production in the mines, and we are going to continue trying. But we do not have tools. Despite this, we are determined that Siglo XX will never die, because if Siglo XX dies, all the working class will be done for. This is where the unions are organized, these are the bases.

When I asked if he thought the government's object was to counter the opposition of the working class, he answered, "Yes, that is their means of eliminating the bases."

Other speakers asserted that the march was definitely a movement by the rank and file, not one imposed by the leaders of the unions. One man claimed:

We are the base, and just now we have risen up for this we are marching. I believe that this march is going to be known nationally and internationally, because what the government is doing is contrary to humanity, you could say. No?

Many underscored the moral implications of the march.

We are fighting for a just case. With a salary of two million bolivianos [about one U.S. dollar] a day, we cannot live. It isn't enough to survive. That is why we are here.

The language of class struggle and exploitation that I had become familiar with in my earlier study of the mines (Nash 1979) was translated here into the moral issue of the right to live. Religious leaders are more familiar with moral than with economic issues, and they showed this in their participation in the march. The bishops of Oruro and Potosí were fully supportive of the march, and many representatives of the Church were among the participants. A nun who came with provisions to feed the marchers told us, "God is on our side!"

The peasants to whom we spoke identified their interests with those of the miners, but their main concern was the new tax law. As one stated:

> Our complaint to the government is that we cannot pay the tax. The marchers, the great ones that have considerable resources, can turn our money over and make a fortune. They can pay the tax, and all of us are going to be exploited. That is the reason. Even when we have a good year, we can't pay the tax. They say that every year it is going to increase 50, 100, 200 percent and more. Where are we going to be? That is the reason we are rising up.

None of the workers with whom we spoke professed to be a member of a political party. The unity in the movement derived from organized labor and peasant unions grouped under the COB. The only people we interviewed who professed a political ideology were students who were involved in university political organizations, the Communist Party of Bolivia, or the Workers' Revolutionary Party.

As evening drew on, people lined up at the improvised soup kitchens to eat. Commensality was another powerful symbol of the unity and equality of the mass of humanity. Through the extraordinary organization of the mine centers' Housewives Committee (Comites de Amas de Casas) and women in the schoolteachers' federation, aided by students, thousands were able to eat hot soup in the town of Calamarca. Some entered the church to find shelter from the cold winds that buffet the hill towns in these winter months, and others bedded down in the houses and courtyards of the farmers who lived in the town.

The morning news was ominous. In a move that contradicted the permit allowing the march to proceed, President Paz Estenssoro declared a state of siege and sent out four regiments to surround the marchers as they were sleeping in Calamarca. I got a ride with press representatives from La Paz to Calamarca in the open truck of a businessman who was delivering mattresses to Oruro. We were warned at the tollgate that the marchers had set up a blockade on the highway at Calamarca, but we decided to proceed.

When we arrived at the edge of town we found thousands of soldiers posted at one-meter intervals, three lines deep stretching from the highway to the plaza about a half-kilometer away. We were stopped on the highway by a sergeant who said that no one was allowed to pass. The soldiers had already detained a Red Cross truck and newspaper reporters.

Troops were digging trenches on the side of the road opposite the town. I joined some women who were carrying food up to the village. We had to skirt the soldiers, many of whom were sleeping in the morning sun, until we arrived at the plaza. Where there had been gaiety and singing the night before, in the cold morning light people looked serious and stunned.

One man asked me, "Are you from the press?" When I replied that I was an anthropologist from the United States, he noted, "It's that we cannot make declarations to just anyone. It seems that they have placed people here, government agents, looking for our leaders. But . . . you must have seen what the government has submitted us to, no?" I said, "Yes," and he added, "We want the press to know what is happening and to report it." They had found a role for me as a witness who could attest to any of the crimes that might be committed. And they had done so without my presenting any credentials except an oral statement that I had done an anthropological study of a mining community in 1970. But their need was great, and I was glad to find a functional role in what had become a disquieting scene.

I walked down to the highway, where dense lines of soldiers holding machine guns in readiness hemmed in a huge crowd. At the northern exit of the town a group of about a dozen women were seated at the edge of a Bolivian flag spread across the highway, separating themselves from the mouth of a cannon and the lines of soldiers. Behind the women was a mass of young people singing revolutionary songs. A meter away, standing at the other edge of the flag with their guns pointed at the seated women, were several rows of soldiers. Later, a woman who was in the front line facing the soldiers told me that at two or three in the morning paramilitary troops had driven them out of the church. (She was from Oruro and had become my "godchild" in 1970 when I supported her bid to sponsor a saint's day celebration.) These men, dressed as peasants (a ruse frequently used to turn miners against peasants during the military regime of Gen. René Barrientos in the 1970s), were the infamous *leopardos* who had been trained as antinarcotics agents by U.S. military advisers. The marchers who had been driven out of the village had slept on the highway all night with the snow falling on them. The army had ordered the peasants not to give them shelter or even a crust of bread. The marchers had awakened to the music of guitars and the singing of students. It was clear to me the danger that they (and I) were in with the barrels of M-1 rifles pointed directly at us.

Deciding that this was the limit of my participant observation, I went up to a soldier to tell him that I was going to the other side of the line. He said that was impossible. I argued that I had to rejoin my friends who were waiting for me, sitting patiently near the pile of foam mattresses they were delivering. He replied, "No one can pass. This is a field of battle." Until that moment I had not defined it as such. The military presence is ubiquitous in Bolivia, and one becomes used to ignoring the potential danger of soldiers who walk armed with guns that fire rubber pellets and with tear-gas canisters.

I thought I would take advantage of the detention to interview some of the Federation leaders, but when I asked where I could find them, people just stared at me blankly. It occurred to me that the leaders were in hiding and that my presence was probably endangering them and others. I walked back to the village plaza, trying without success to get past the soldiers at each side street. When I arrived at the outermost guard post, I was finally allowed to pass, perhaps because the sergeant on duty did not have a walkie-talkie and had not received orders from below. I was thankful for this lapse in preparation of the troops, who were remarkably well outfitted for soldiers in a country faced with severe financial crisis. I walked down to the highway, feeling somewhat safer behind the rows of soldiers as they directed their machine guns in the opposite direction.

Having outflanked the army, I returned to my friends on the highway. There we witnessed the arrival of a van filled with congressional representatives. They approached the soldiers, who ordered them not to pass. The National Democratic Action Party (AND, identified with Hugo Banzer) representative turned on his heel to go back to the van, looking relieved that he did not have to follow through with this, but the Socialist Party representative scoffed at him, saying, "You can't let yourself be turned back just by a sergeant! Let's ask for a pass from the general." They sent a note behind the lines to the general, but the answer was no, no one passes. Two fighter planes started to buzz the crowd diving within a few meters of the road where we stood. Six tanks pulled up and parked nearby.

We decided to return to La Paz. In the next town, San Antonio, we stopped to talk with people who had gone ahead the previous night. As a huge crowd gathered around our van, a man told us, "We were intending to stay in Calamarca last night, but as we did not have any shelter, we came here to San Antonio." When I commented on the state of siege declared by the president, he said, "Look, I believe that we are not living in a democratic epoch, but rather in one of repression. For the armed forces that we have are supposed to defend the country's borders, not repress the workers."

Another man stated, "The worst thing is that the armed forces of the nation here in Bolivia are trained to repress workers—the miners and factory workers." A third continued:

> Now, if we were to analyze the government, we can see that it is not governing. These decrees are the imposition of Senor Sachs of the United States. We

know that the New Economic Policies are his work and the fruit of his advice. We don't want to have anything to do with them. It isn't as though we
were forcing anything. We want a national country. This just causes cynicism,
doesn't it! Let's make this our country. These people don't understand that
having the Yankees here in Bolivia is a condemnation of the Bolivian army!
And we know that they are not here for the narco-traffic problem. It isn't for
that that they lent us $100 million U.S. dollars [the loan received by the pres-
ident had just been announced the previous day], it is to repress the workers.
But we are not going to die, ever. We know that the reserves of tin that the
United States holds are from the Bolivians and that we supported the United
States in the Second World War.

This man told us that he came from the Bolivar mine that had been shut
down, and that he had been vice president of the strike committee. He
took advantage of the fact that media representatives were filming the interviews to say, "What I want to say is that it is essential that the media
tell what is happening. We know that this government says that we are
subversives. Well, any social situation is in fact political."
When I asked him what hope he now had for the march, he said,

In the last union meeting, we decided that this march was for life, for the survival of the people, for the survival of Oruro and Potosí, because the miners
fight not only for miners, but for all the people. And we have support you
know that all the pueblo of Oruro and Potosí support us, just as do those in
other districts, no? And we have to carry on our fight to the end. The government, with the decree it has imposed, wants to cause our Federation and
the COB to disappear, but we will defend ourselves, no? And this government should not forget that the nationalization of the mines is the fruit of the
workers' struggles. How can the government deny us now? But we are going to continue our fight until the final battle. We know that some generals
are not in agreement with the government, because there are some patriotic
military! We are going to break out and go on to La Paz. . . . The press should
not fail us. They should say what has happened.

I asked a man standing nearby, "Do you want to say anything about the
march and the objectives of the workers?" By this time, many of the
marchers were coming up to offer their words. He readily responded:

Well, the most important thing is that they not close the mines. And that the
government be sensitive because we brought it to power. And now it wants
to wipe us out with the decree. That is not possible, is it? In what century are
we living? On the other hand, the North American government ought to understand our situation, no? The government of the United States ought to indicate to the Bolivian government that it cannot treat us in this way, us workers because this government is killing us with hunger. Never has this
happened, in no other part of the world. If we could get work elsewhere, we

would not be hanging out in the mines, but this country has always been a mining area.

I asked him what he thought of the political parties and whether he felt any of them had a solution for the country. He responded in the same way as all the others whom I had questioned: "None of the politicians have presented a plan. None are preoccupied with preserving the mines. They have always avoided the issue, or tried to take advantage of it." Another man added, without prompting:

This is a country that is rich in every way, but has never done anything. And now the government wants to send us to the colonizing areas, where there are not even roads. They are places where you can't do anything. A miner is not acclimated to this. Some of us are sick and we can't bear the lower altitudes.

A companion of his broke in:

What is happening is that all the aid that the United States offers us is taken advantage of only by the high society, not for the poor there is nothing. Yet the North American government continues giving aid. For that reason, we think that someday we will have to restructure this country to change things.

As my companions trained video cameras on the huge mass of people that had gathered around our van, a man began to speak extemporaneously:

Yesterday, about 5:30, we arrived in this locality from San Antonio with approximately five thousand workers. And the inhabitants of this town have, out of their good will, cooperated with us in all that is necessary. We understand the sacrifice of the campesino workers, who are surely also facing a difficult situation. They have taken bread out of the mouths of their children in order to share it with their mining comrades. All of us workers in the nationalized mines, and the rest that are in the march, remain profoundly thankful for this favor that they have done us, and at some later time they will be recognized and heartily thanked by the whole working class movement. Unfortunately, we remain here, without any guidance from our leaders, but we hope to continue with the march.

Our march does not have any partisan tinge. We only want to show the government what we want—what we need—and to save our sources of work. We are not bearing any arms! Nor are we going to overthrow any government. We thank the reporters who are with us and who have come to us daily, who see how the government is treating us.

It is a pity that the government has no understanding of our problems, especially those of the women who have come from Oruro on foot with their children. There is no sensitivity! We hope that the Bolivian people will hear our declaration so that they will know how the government has treated their comrades in the mines, those who have sacrificed themselves, leaving their lungs in the mines, and who today are being kicked out into the streets.

As he spoke, the fighter planes swooped overhead, punctuating his speech in a way that dramatized his points. His rejection of political party alignment was typical of the responses of many with whom we spoke; he, like the others, seemed to fear any co-optation of a grassroots movement by political leaders seeking popular support.

In the rhetoric of these impromptu leaders—the famous "masses" addressed in the left-wing parties—the government's charge of subversion was turned against it for deploying the troops against the demonstrators. The women's use of the Bolivian flag as a symbolic weapon reminded army officials of their identification with the nation as citizens. Spread out on the highway, the flag served as a boundary between the women and the army that confronted them with massive force. The march was, in its broadest unifying sense, an appeal to all Bolivians to recognize the subversive nature of the government, to recognize that the government was bent on destroying a way of life that had sustained the country in the centuries when mining was the principal means of supporting an export-oriented economy. Some felt that the message might even reach U.S. advisers.

What struck me as remarkable about this rhetoric was the relatively calm projection of determination and conviction. The discourse was notably formal, with few incomplete sentences or interjections. Even more impressive was the fact that there were no interruptions or catcalls from the crowds standing around the speakers. No one lamented that they had been misled, nor was there any sign of discord among the marchers. It was clear that they were personally committed to the march and that it had not been imposed from above. I began to think that the unity demonstrated by the disparate groups that had joined in the march, and the cooperation of the farmers in provisioning and finding places for the marchers to sleep, were the reason that had prompted the government to prevent the march from reaching La Paz. Such an impressive show of unity had the potential to trigger a fall of the government, as had occurred in 1978.

I was also struck by the marchers' determination to remain pacific in their words and manner although they were threatened by guns, tanks, and aircraft. As I was interviewing them later during their hunger strike, some of the women in the front line told me they did not fear the soldiers facing them. "They are children of the pueblo," they said. One woman even expressed sympathy for the soldiers, since their officers kept them awake all night, counting out their posts. It was only the paramilitary, she said, the outcasts who served in the leopardos unit as antidrug agents, who inspired fear. The moral force of a community in action counterbalanced the sense of fear.

All day the people were held hostage in the town of Calamarca. The army sent in trucks to take them back to their districts, but the women of Siglo XX resisted, saying that the soldiers might carry them off to kill them. Clearly, the people were ambivalent about the army, on the one hand recognizing the soldiers were "children of the pueblo," but on the other hand, knowing that military orders often prevailed—behind each contingent of foot soldiers stood lieutenants ready to kill any soldier who refused to fire when the order was given. Some women recalled the rumors that military buses had carried civilians detained during the battle against Banzer to their death. Finally, the government sent in the nationally owned buses and the marchers returned to their districts.

MEDIA INTERPRETATION

On the following day, immobilized by the state of siege and unwilling to endanger people by interviewing them about the crisis, Rosario León and I collected all the newspaper reports about the march and wrote a commentary (Nash and León 1986) in which we summed up the myths it had evoked, some of them identified as official government statements issued to the press, and others reported to us as truth:

1. The march was a political act, directed from above by extremist political groups. This argument, made by many official figures, was formulated most clearly by Angel Gomez Garcia, prefect of the Department of La Paz, and printed in *Ultima Hora* on August 28, 1986. Right-wing papers such as *El Diario* reported the insurrectional character of the march as fact; *Presencia* and *Ultima Hora* reported it as an assertion made by government agents.

2. The marchers wanted to overthrow the government and destroy the peace and security of the pueblo. This myth had various versions: one blaming the union leaders and others the left-wing parties. Fernando Barthelemy, an official in the Ministry of the Interior, reported as the source of this notion, commented: "the object of the march is to focus the attention of the country and the world." (*Presencia* August 26, 1986.)

3. The marchers were linked to striking workers in the electrical energy company and were aiding them in violent and illegal acts. Various acts occurring throughout the country were blamed on the strikers in an attempt to foster hysteria among the *Pacenos* (people of La Paz).

Herman Antelo, Minister of Information, added his cries to those of Fernando Barthelemy (*Presencia* August 29, 1986).

4. The marchers were confused and mistaken in their objectives. One reporter claimed the mineworkers were "unwittingly serving, once more, as the lance for subversive extremists" (*Ultima Hora* August 26, 1986).

5. The attitude of the miners was unpatriotic. President Paz Estenssoro made this assertion in a televised message to the nation on August 30, 1986.

In the first days of the march, newspaper editors seemed to accept some of the government's versions more readily than they would do later, when their reporters actually witnessed and began to describe the march. As early as August 25, the editors of *Presencia* commented, "The object of the march is to focus the attention of the country and the world on the problems of metal miners and to press the government to adopt a plan for rehabilitating COMIBOL that will not mean closing the mines and laying off workers." The editors of *Hoy* added, "The Orureños [citizens of Oruro] will offer their lives to avoid the closing of the mines" (August 27). *Presencia* stated in an editorial, "the crisis ought to be shared by all sectors of the population, and not only by the humble" (August 27, 1986).

Editorial comments in three of the daily newspapers, *Presencia, Hoy,* and *Ultima Hora,* became progressively more positive, some even emphasizing the solidarity of the various sectors participating in the march. The newspapers began to quote various civic and community leaders who had organized the march. *Presencia* quoted the bishop of the Catholic diocese of Oruro, who saw in the march a replica of the biblical exodus in search of the Promised Land. The stories, accompanied by impressive pictures showing the masses of participants, contradicted the statements of the government, and over the five-day course of the march the newspaper reports increasingly diverged from the official versions, the only exception was *El Diario,* which limited its reports to news bulletins from the Ministry of the Interior. Representatives of the political parties opposed to the government supported the miners, as did the FSTMB and many of the other unions.

In summing up the observations of the event, we emphasized the movement's unity, broad base, and solidarity of purpose, in contrast to the media, which reported the opinions of leaders and not of the working people who participated in the march. Where the newspapers emphasized the decision making by leaders of the group that backed its publication—the "official" press (*Diario, Ultima Hora*) stressing government leaders and the Catholic press (*Presencia*) emphasizing the bishop's initiatives—we saw a people moving in response to forces far more persuasive than words or published articles. We concluded by questioning the extent to which the government of Paz Estenssoro could be called democratic if he found it necessary to mobilize the army to threaten unarmed civilians.[1]

THE EMERGENCE OF NEW DISCOURSES

Frustrated in their attempt to gain an audience with the president through the march, the protesters adopted two new forms of communication. The miners began a hunger strike, first in their districts and a week later in La Paz. At the same time, the leaders of the FSTMB entered into a dialogue with government ministers initiated and mediated by the archbishop of the Catholic diocese. However the two forms of discourse precipitated a breach between the leaders and the masses: the hunger strike was an action designed to foster public empathy for the miners, a direct and unequivocal statement that people of the mining community were prepared to die rather than leave the mines; the dialogue was predicated on compromise, on mediation between the overwhelming needs of the mining communities and the exigencies of the national economy as directed by the IMF and U.S. Aid for International Development (AID). The anthropological task of interpretation took on an added dimension: Not only did it involve relating symbolic action and messages to the social behavior of politically mobilized masses, but it also required that one see this communication in relation to the dialectical interaction of leaders and led in two distinct arenas, the dialogue and the hunger strike.

Dialogue of Government and Federation Leaders

Initiated by the archbishop of the Episcopal diocese of the Catholic Church on September 2, several days after the military intervention in the March for Life, the dialogue between the government and the Federation involved Minister of the Interior Guillermo Bedregal, along with other functionaries of the government, and three FSTMB leaders, Simon Reyes, Filemón Escobar, and Victor Lopez. The press and other visitors, such as myself, were excluded from the actual meetings in the archbishop's quarters; reports were limited to the comments that the participants uttered as they entered or left the meetings and to general statements on the agenda. The first stage of the dialogue covered the plan to create a cooperative of the mines, while the second was devoted to social welfare issues concerning the miners (*Presencia* September 10, 1986). The COB called for an opening up of the dialogue to include rank-and-file members of the FSTMB, and a few were admitted. But throughout the dialogue, communication between the leaders of the Federation and the vast majority of the rank-and-file was virtually nil. In the state of siege declared when the march was halted, many leaders were imprisoned, and even those who were participating in the dialogue were subject to seizure each day as they emerged from the archbishop's quarters.[2] Except for the period when they were in the archbishop's chambers, they were nearly in hiding. Whereas communication between the constituents and the leaders of the Federation was almost nonexistent, the government's representatives were in continuous communication with the president, members of the cabinet, and legislators. This imbalance in the degree of communication had a profound impact on the ability of each party to affect political behavior in the ensuing weeks, as I hope to show below.

After the first session of the dialogue, I asked one of the leaders of the FSTMB, Filemón Escobar, secretary general of the Siglo XX–Cataví mineworkers' union, what he thought of the plan to organize the mines that had been part of COMIBOL as co-operative mines. He replied:

> The philosophy of the government, the essence of its political economy, is that the state ought to privatize the economy. The development of the economy will depend on the free enterprise of private firms. Everything will pass into the free market. This explains the pact of Paz with Banzer, the presence of the U.S. armed forces on Bolivian lands, and the relationship between the private firms and the government. All three—the United States, the Bolivian government, and the private sector—agree on the need to return to free enterprise. When Paz arrived in power, he adopted the philosophy of free enterprise rather than of state enterprise. This is the change with which we are living.

Escobar was preoccupied with the survival of the nationalized mines, COMIBOL, which he equated with the survival of the FSTMB:

> The government of Paz Estenssoro represents a new political economy of the private firms. . . . The lowering of the prices of minerals, the increase in the deficit in the mines, are arguments to justify their program. The moment has come when the government intends to liquidate COMIBOL in order to liquidate the working class and in particular the Federation, because these are the major obstacles to the government's plans for privatization. We have worker control. The managers of free enterprise, especially the international private firms, view COMIBOL as an obstacle to gaining complete control over the working class.

I asked him why the FSTMB did not try to organize the cooperatives, and he replied patiently:

> The plan to co-opt us is to liquidate us. In Siglo XX we have co-operatives. In Potosí there are ten thousand *cooperativistas*. The *lameros* [workers engaged in

placer mining], the *locutarios* [those who rent sections of a mine to work] all
are organized in co-operatives. In the last thirty years we could never unite
them with us. They are not paid salaries; they do not receive social security.

When I asked Escobar how many supporters the Federation leaders had
upon entering the dialogue, he replied that all of the marchers supported
them.

THE HUNGER STRIKE

I was prepared to believe the assertion of the leadership that the hunger
strike was a continuation of the unified action of the groups mobilized for
the march, since it seemed a logical outcome of the unity expressed in the
march. People referred to the hunger strike in the same terms as the
march, calling it the "Hunger Strike for Life." I went to the mining center
of Oruro expecting to find the same consensus and unity that had characterized the march. My interview with the secretary general of the San José
housewives' association seemed to confirm my expectation, as she expressed the frustration that had led to the hunger strike.

> We are very angry at the surprise attack that the government made on us,
> and it is for that reason that we decided to take the final step that we have a
> right to. We had to go to ask for what we need. Sometimes here in the mines
> we have as many as twelve children, and sometimes our children don't have
> anything to eat. That is what we were asking the government for. Our hus-
> bands work for very little pay; they work almost in vain. That's why we went
> with our companions on the march. We lost one battle, but we haven't lost
> the struggle. We are going to follow this out to the ultimate consequences. We
> are going to submit ourselves to a hunger strike. We prefer to die together
> with our children but not to die slowly.

Most of the others I talked with, like this woman, rejected the government
as intransigent and untrustworthy. Opposition to the government sustained a sense of unity, as a man from Siglo XX who had been on strike
along with a dozen others for six days explained:

> In reality, the government has submitted us to hunger and misery, ever
> since it decreed 21060[3] ordered by Yankee imperialism that is always be-
> hind it. With this decree it hopes to eliminate all the mines and the towns
> that circle the mine centers. The people don't know that this decree is
> throwing us into the street, not only miners but the town in general. Be-
> cause the United States has set a low quota on tin, the government has a
> pretext to liquidate the miners, just as during Barrientos's time. Where can
> we go? The people of Oruro and Potosí walk in hunger and misery. Whole

families have gone to Cochabamba and Beni, where we are going to be fighting among the unoccupied. We are fighting for a just cause here. With a salary of two million bolivianos[4] daily we cannot live. It is not enough for our household subsistence. That is why we are submitting ourselves to a hunger strike. Because of the decree, it seems to me that the government is fascist. It wants us to pay the debt that Banzer and Garcia Meza raised, and we refuse this completely. It wants to impose a tax reform on us, and we refuse because we are already subject to hunger and misery.

When I asked what they hoped would come of the hunger strike, he replied, "Our hunger strike should touch the heart of the government." But when I inquired whether he thought the government had a heart, he said:

> No, I do not believe that this government will come up with a solution, for it has confronted our marching comrades with the armed forces of our country and with North American forces. Therefore I say that this government is just a puppet. I and my companions are against the government and its ministers. We know that the governing parliament is for the bourgeoisie that is dominating us now with the alliance of the MNR [National Revolutionary Movement, the party of Paz Estenssoro] and the AND [Acción Nacional Democratica, the party of Hugo Banzer]. They have frozen our wages, taken away our supplies, eliminated our bonuses, and thus submitted us to misery. I have no hope of anything from this government. At any moment, the pueblo is going to make that point.

I assumed from these rather stereotyped replies to my questions, often contradicted by the speakers themselves when I asked more probing questions about the same point (as the above speaker reveals), that the strikers were acting in unison and adding weight to the position of the leaders engaged in dialogue with the government. It gradually became clear to me that no organized leadership controlled the strikers. All the participants I questioned assured me that the strike was an action of the rank-and-file, and even leaders of the Federation in the mining camps reiterated this point. It was, I realized, autonomy exercised within a collective framework of action.

As I began to hear some of the dissonant voices, the meanings of the hunger strike became clear. The strike was not, as I had at first imagined, an affirmation of the dialogue between the government and the Federation, but rather a collective act to reinforce the base's determination to resist any compromise solution. As an action by many distinct sectors in the mining communities and the student populations that professed to support them, the hunger strike contained many distinct meanings. While there was some agreement in the opposition to the government, there were significant differences among those in the hunger strike as to the degree of militancy in the rhetoric and as to notions of who was speaking for "the masses." With this in mind, I tried to get to as many pickets as possible in four days, as I traveled by bus to the mining encampments of Siglo XX–Catavi, Machacamarca, and Oruro and back to La Paz, where I and Cecelia Salazar, a student who joined me for the trip, visited all the pickets in the offices of *Presencia*, the University of San Marcos auditorium, and the archbishop's diocese.

All of the people with whom we spoke in the pickets in the mining communities rejected both the decentralization of the mines and the colonization program in the southeast. One man said:

> For us to go to the east is to go to hell. Every government promises and promises, and does not fulfill anything. In the case of Corocoro, for example, sixty families went to work in the east because the government had offered them lands. And all of them went to hell! Their children died without any medical help. Merely to enter the region is to die. Once the lungs cannot support air, a miner cannot work any more. The life of a miner may be sad, but we in Siglo XX are proud to be miners. And we have to make our country respect us. A district like this is the base of the working class. It is a force that the government wants to destroy. But that is not going to happen.

Yet like many others whom I questioned, he did not have any hopes for the dialogue between the leaders and the government. I saw many men who had descended five days before into the mine shafts of Siglo XX, where the lack of ventilation had resulted in a buildup of toxic gases, lying bundled together as if waiting for death. I also joined the students attending their first year of classes in the college of Siglo XX–Catavi. They reflected the optimism of youths who had, in the organization of the college, realized one of the dreams of the mining community to expand the opportunities for the children of miners.

A young miner who had joined the "key" group of the 21st Congress of the FSTMB and who criticized what he saw as the growing distance of the leadership from the rank and file had joined the San José picket two days before my interview. In responding to my question on his motives for participating in the hunger strike, he outlined the strike's most basic premises:

> The government has not established the minimal conditions for worthwhile survival. Thus, our concern with the survival of the mining centers reflects more than just a love for the mines. We are posing the question: How are we going to live? What will be the basis for our survival? The government leaves it up to us to seek forms of survival, and because there are few alternatives, the unemployed have in desperation sought employment in drug traffic, in the illegal mining of gold, or in the selling of contraband merchandise. The

government has not undertaken its role, as it should, of guaranteeing work or legal means of making a living. It has left it up to the unemployed to seek jobs that are illegal and corrupt.

The "key" group that he represented opposed the dialogue with the government. They wanted no compromise in a movement they hoped would lead to the overthrow of the government. This position was increasingly clarified in subsequent weeks, as national Federation leaders were criticized for their participation in the dialogue.

Housewives had recently organized on a national level and had their first authorized delegation at the 21st Congress of the FSTMB. The development of a collective consciousness, something that I had observed in germinal stages when I worked in the mining communities in 1970 (Nash 1979) had really taken hold. When I joined the women on hunger strike in the office of the newspaper *Presencia* in La Paz, these housewives articulated the broader aims of the movement. One responded without hesitation when I asked her what her motives for participating in the hunger strike were:

We are defending the national sovereignty against Yankee imperialism. The MNR and the AND are servants of Yankee imperialism and have accepted U.S. armed forces in order to repress the people.

Another added:

In proposing the decree that the mines be closed, the government is fascistic. It is submitting us to hunger and misery. Each of the governments, from the Banzer coup to García Meza, has submitted to Yankee imperialism. They have increased the debt and now it is time to pay for it. It is for that reason that the present government wants to impose tax reform.

A housewife from Huanuni who was with a picket of mining community women in the university theater made an even more elaborate statement. She stunned me with her response when I asked her what her goal was in joining the hunger strike:

We have joined the fight to preserve the mines as property of the state and to deepen the nationalization process. Our parliament is composed of people linked to the great international oligarchy of the IMF. They are not carrying out the aims of the people. We live in constant dependency on the great firms of South American Placer, Shell, and others, which set the prices of our national resources. They are trying to dismantle the nationalized sectors of the economy and thrust us into the informal sector. We will not have any of the rights we have gained from years of struggle.

The articulateness of this woman reflected the collective communication that had inspired it. Most of the workers have little more than five or six years of education. However, with the help of leadership classes sponsored by the unions often with invited university professors, many have educated themselves in a discourse of empowerment, thereby overcoming the alienation of class presumptions based on education. Women are participating in the discourse at national levels in greater numbers than ever before. The discourse of all the people we interviewed was strikingly different from that of the American working class, one in which the links of people's individual circumstances with global issues are rarely mentioned. Bolivians in the mining communities use those links as a reference point to assess their position in almost every context. The woman's analysis drew upon this heritage of class struggle and preempted my own strategy of relating the protest to economic policies, drafted in response to global restructuring, that would relegate the organized working class to the informal sector. I felt that my role as "authoritative interpreter" had been usurped.

Along with this picket of women from the mining centers was a group of university students who were supporting them in the hunger strike. Although the students said they had been on a liquid diet for five days like the others, they seemed to be more energetic than the women from the mining communities. After having interviewed people in many stages of food deprivation, I had gained a sense of how many days they had gone without nourishment. Whereas the miners of Siglo XX, who were entering their sixth day of hunger strike, were lying bundled together, unwilling to waste their ebbing strength on any excessive motion, the students were laughing, playing guitars, singing, and moving around freely. When I spoke with them, it was clear that they were the most intransigent in their demands. One of the young men who claimed to have been on strike for five days said:[5]

> The intention of the dialogue is simply to delay and to demobilize the people who are in the struggle. We do not believe in the dialogue. We are against the Federation because the leaders cut short the march. The shutting down of the march was not an act of the government but of the leaders of the union, who took a position that was ignorant and timid. They didn't want to go forward.

He went on to clarify the estrangement with the unions:

> This hunger strike is undertaken without the leadership of the Federation. We are creating pressure that has forced the COB to become involved in the hunger strike. There are bourgeois tendencies in the Federation, and there are those who do not care to join the strike as we have done. We are disposed to

enter into the struggle, but while the dialogue is on, we are unable to do so. We know that the dialogue will not modify the government decree.

I asked if he really believed that they were in a position to fight and he replied:

> We are ready to participate in the fight until we die. We are not only the few you see here; we speak for all the pueblo, who will gradually enter into the fight. Now, this hunger strike began the moment the people got into the buses and left the march. The miners must occupy the mines and fight, and the pueblo will join them. The Federation has taken a position that is not that of the majority. It should not have entered into the dialogue. The dialogue with the government has not modified the essentials of the decree, and that is what we want.

This extreme example of what my Little Lenin edition would have called "left-wing extremism" was strikingly distinct from the low-key expressions of the workers I had left behind in Siglo XX. When they expressed a willingness to die, it was done as a statement of fact of the only alternative left to them. Nor would they abandon the Federation, even when they felt most critical of it. For them, it was still the flotsam of a shipwreck that could help keep them afloat.

The number of hunger strikers increased during the two weeks of the dialogue. The strike was not under the control of anyone, and it became a multivocalic medium of communication. In the mines and among the pickets of housewives in La Paz, it was a rank-and-file movement initiated by the miners and their families. They seemed resigned to death since they felt they would otherwise slowly starve if the mines were closed. Some of the student leaders began to call for a "dry" hunger strike, right while I was visiting them in the university auditorium. Such a strike would have caused death in no more than three or four days of total deprivation. They rejected any dialogue between the government and the people, demanding that the mines be preserved as state enterprises and that the process of nationalization be extended to include some private mines; they called for freedom for those who were detained; and finally they called for the removal of the U.S. troops from Bolivia. Many of the students and miners in the "key" group of the Federation began to accuse the government of inviting in the U.S. troops to help control the popular uprising, not, as they said, to counter the drug trafficking.

During the hunger strike, the divisiveness that had marked the 21st Congress of the FSTMB became more pronounced. Various political parties, particularly the Trotskyist Workers Revolutionary party, were trying to capture the political energies arising among the workers as their frustration turned to anger and hostility toward the leaders who were trying to reach some kind of compromise. It was increasingly clear that the hunger strikers were not all in accord with the dialogue between the Federation leaders and the government.

The government, meanwhile, was consolidating its position. The state of siege order remained in effect throughout the days of the dialogue, and the parliament voted on September 11 to extend it three months. The government rounded up rectors of the universities of Potosí and Cochabamba. Over a hundred leaders of unions, student groups, and civic committees were arrested, with some sent to "Puerto Rico," a jail for political prisoners. Two of the Federation leaders who were engaged in the dialogue left each session fearing they would be picked up and jailed. The paradox of their position—they were charged by the government with subverting law and order and by the students, particularly the followers of the Workers Revolutionary party, with betraying the people— did not escape their attention.

The dialogue between Federation leaders and the government came to an end on September 13. Signed by both parties, the final agreement included provisions to keep the mines open and retain them as state property, with closing permitted after a careful study by professional geologists and economists. It approved the release of university, civic, and union leaders who had been detained, and it promised freedom of action for civic and union groups. Finally it suspended the strikes in the mines and the hunger strike.

Some of the women and men who had undertaken the hunger strike continued their action throughout the following weeks. They had no confidence in the government's compliance with the agreement, and they questioned the right of the leaders of the FSTMB to enter into an agreement without referring the issue to a vote. In the "trialogue" involving the third unit of hunger strikers at the base, the FSTMB leaders, and the government, the gap between the rank and file and the leadership of the mineworkers' union widened, while the government, with the advice and financial assistance of U.S. advisers, consolidated the attempt to close down the nationalized mines.

Throughout the crisis, the protesters made recourse to two traditions of discourse, emphasizing both the demands of an exploited working class and the rights of a moral community. The dialogue in the diocese diverged from both traditions of discourse since it dealt with issues at a technical level. The leaders of the Federation disputed how many workers should be laid off and how much of the state structure should remain in place. When the dialogue was over, mine unions in Potosí, Siglo XX, and Huanuni rejected the agreement as little more than a screen permitting the government to dismantle the nationalized mines and permit the entry of private firms. As a result, Simón Reyes resigned as secretary general of the Federation, and some of the other leaders followed suit.

Lacking leadership, the hunger strike was opened up for many factions to interpret and use according to their own lights. The powerful symbolism of the people's willingness to die when confronted with the closing of the mines became a play with death negating the assertion of the right to live that was basic to the March for Life. At an extraordinary meeting of the FSTMB in the middle of October, the eight hundred delegates attempted to restore the unity of the miners. Victor Lopez, an old leader of the Federation who was not aligned with any political party and who represented the independent mines, was elected secretary general, and he named Simón Reyes, who had recanted his part in the dialogues, second in command. Filemón Escobar refused to retract his endorsement of the compromise measures contained in the agreement. The government took advantage of the split among the leaders during the weeks after the agreement to lay off thousands of workers. By the end of October, over seventeen thousand of the twenty-seven thousand miners employed by the COMIBOL mines had been dismissed.

The miners' belief that in closing the mines the government was trying to eliminate the only centers of organized resistance was borne out in subsequent months, as thousands more workers in mine-related occupations were laid off. The termination of the March for Life marked the end of the first phase of resistance to the New Economic Policies. Designed to promote the reign of market forces without interference from the state or the Federation, the policies have in fact led to stagnation in the private sector, growing unemployment, and a decline in the standard of living for the middle class as well as for the workers. Control over wages has been more effective than control over prices, and the minimum wage of $30 monthly is insufficient for any worker, rural or urban. Plant shutdowns caused by an increase in the tariffs for all goods, including the raw materials and machinery needed for national industries, have added to the disorganization of the economy and the potential for mobilizing the working class. The regional cities in mining centers are now nearly paralyzed, as commerce has declined and government services have been withdrawn (Ramos Sanchez 1986).

The rural economy remains as hard-hit as the urban economy. Government support for agriculture is now restricted to the export-oriented commercial crops of major producers. Credit rural schools, labor laws covering agricultural workers, and other benefits of the 1952–1972 agrarian reforms have all suffered from government cutbacks. At the same time, the taxes and price controls on the commodities of small producers have curtailed production so that Bolivia has become increasingly dependent on food imports (Urioste n.d.). The only product that remains competitive in the world market is coca used in the production of cocaine, but because it is illegal, its proceeds cannot be taxed for investment in other economic ventures.

In attempting to destroy the organized working class, the government, backed by U.S. advisers and IMF financial consultants, has succeeded in destroying the economy. Yet the extreme suppression has not succeeded in preventing people from mobilizing in neighborhoods and barrios throughout the country. Former miners who have gone to the colonizing areas of the Chapare, for example, have undertaken marches protesting the suppression of coca production. And the combined reaction of the COB and the Confederación Sindical Única de Trabajadores Campesinos de Bolivia (CSUTCB) has forced the government to back down on the tax on small farmers as well as on permitting the free import of competing goods. The official announcement by the government in April 1988 on the state-controlled radio station tried to link the relaxation of policies to the support Paz Estenssoro had given campesinos in the land reform act of 1953: "Comrade farmers, Dr. Victor Paz Estenssoro gave you land in 1953 and now has proclaimed that the farmers do not have to pay the tax on land."

Despite these concessions, the government has succeeded in transforming the economy into one based on private capitalistic enterprises and in encouraging individualistic morality. Yet it has not solved the economic problems of a country that relies on external funding from the IMF and the International Bank. Without the drug traffic, which is estimated to bring in $5 million a day, the Bolivian people could not survive.

CONCLUSIONS

The meanings of the March for Life derive in large part from the political co-optation of the words and deeds of people who felt their way of life was threatened, mediated as those words and deeds were by leaders of the many different groups and presented, often in distorted form, by the media. When the union leadership was discredited during the dialogue in the archbishop's diocese, owing to a political process that went beyond its control, the interpretations of subsequent events had already become the contested territory of divergent streams within the Federation as well as the nascent leadership among student groups.

Few adherents of interpretive anthropology are willing to relate to the multivocalic interpretations of social actors who are deeply rooted in distinct class structures. Most have limited their concern to surface phenomena, ignoring the microhistorical process in which those phenomena are embedded. Eschewing a unitary theory of society—certainly a justified position given the failure of theories that have pretended to comprehend all aspects of human behavior in the past—interpretive anthropologists often deny that social phenomena can be explained by any structured theory.

The tradition of literary criticism from which the textual interpretation in social science is drawn is in danger of resulting in a sterile analysis of texts as "isolated objects," as Raymond Williams points out. "This cutting loose of readers and critics from any obligation to social connection or historical fact," Williams goes on to say, distances the work from the "socially and historically specifiable agency of its making" (1986, 18). Paradoxically, at a time when literary critics are trying to expand the range of their analyses into the world cultural context (Said 1983), many anthropologists are trying to isolate and constrict the scope of their own inquiry.

Yet "by viewing cultures as assemblages of texts, loosely and sometimes contradictorally united, and by highlighting the inventive poetics at work in all collective representations," interpretive anthropology can, as Clifford states, contribute to the "defamiliarization of ethnographic authority" (1988, 17). In order to make sense of them, we must anchor the discourse in specific actors as they respond to a changing political environment. Thus we may be able to devise ethnographic techniques to probe the complex way in which people with very disparate images of reality find a way of acting collectively.

Interpretive accounts need to be attentive to the canons of ethnographic competence developed by generations of fieldworkers trying to explain the relationships between behavior and structural conditions. Most important, they must include the actors' interpretations of the processes in which they are participating, rather than making (as many of them do) preemptive statements purporting to be the authentic, or universal, account.[6] Geertz (1973b, 9; 1973a, 9) puts the weight of responsibility for interpretation on the ethnographer. I differ from Geertz in putting greater weight than he does on the interpretations given by the actors in the scene.

As anthropologists we must also seek to capture process in our ethnographic description in periods of social transformation such as that which I witnessed in Bolivia. I have sensed that the process itself was contained in the interpretations of what was happening and that these were changing rapidly as events unfolded. These multiple perspectives should be captured over a period of time so that by relating them to the ongoing political process we can gain some control over our own interpretations. Such an analysis can highlight the turning points in a process that is larger than any single event. As yet textual interpretation restricts its view to a limited framework that denies history as well as the larger structural context.

In trying to understand social movements, we must abandon the analytic distinction between social behavior and culturally encoded symbolic form, as Wolf (1986, 327) has pointed out. In periods of crisis when institutional structures are threatened, it is easier to analyze what Wolf calls a dialectical interpenetration of two realms (1986, 327). It is then too that one can perceive the genesis of symbolic restructuring, as hidden meanings surface and find expression. People experiencing a crisis are more willing to talk; their goal is not so much the discovery of self (the obsession of most interpretive anthropologists) as it is the discovery of a collective consciousness directed toward achieving social change.

The moments of unity experienced by a group are generally ephemeral, and even in the height of a crisis may become diffused. Yet people are still able to coordinate their actions even when responding to a variety of ideological outlooks. I was impressed in my earlier fieldwork in Bolivian tin mining communities with the many levels of sophistication coexisting in a single community, even within a family, and sometimes in the same person over time. People could and did maintain several distinct and apparently mutually contradictory theories of social reality—ones as disparate as Christianity, animistic beliefs in the immanent power of the earth and hills, and Marxist, Maoist, or Trotskyist ideologies—without a sense of cognitive dissonance (Nash 1979). People throughout the world have, like the Bolivian miners, found ways to deal with the ambiguous, often contradictory, beliefs and understandings they have inherited and generated in dealing with an ever-changing reality.

As I saw how the people in the mining community were able to act in a field rife with conflicting claims to authentic interpretations, it occurred to me that they were more prepared to deal with the multivocalic complexity of human consciousness than social scientists in academic settings. The drive in the modern age for a unified dominant theory of human development has blinded us to the fact that people who are not part of the scientific community are not discomfited by the diversity of claims to truth that sprout in any social movement. Third world people were living in a postmodern world long before it was discovered by theorists, who were of the elites who could live in a world of ideas undisturbed by disparities in the real world. The greater participation of women and of indigenous peoples has increased the need for a pluridimensional approach to social problems (León 1986). If we listen attentively to the multiple strands that enter into our informants' dialogue, we can learn to take such an approach in our analyses.

At a time when other social scientists are reinventing the ethnographic method as a tool of analysis, some interpretive anthropologists are attempting to transcend the practice of field research, drawing on literature for metaphors in examining society. Yet in the social awakening we are experiencing, we need more, not less, experience in the field. When we participate in social movements with people who set them in motion, we must constantly test our interpretations against those of informants in a dialogical approach that will open up texts to future reinterpretation. We may then embrace as complex a reality as that people live with in their everyday lives.

POSTSCRIPT

Political turbulence in Bolivia continues with indigenous people taking center stage in a second March for Territory and Dignity in 1990. Guaraní from the lowland tropical jungles rose up to join highland Aymara and Quechua in a show of unity that enabled indigenous people to extract the first official recognition of indigenous territories. Shortly thereafter Bolivia became the first signatory ratifying the International Labor Organization (ILO) Convention 169 guaranteeing multicultural governance, and the Sanchez Lozada government passed the Law of Public Participation allowing greater local control over economic, political, and social practices (Van Cott 2002). With the election of their first indigenous president, we may see the new awakening that Quechua, Aymara, and Guaraní populations have awaited for so many centuries.

NOTES

An earlier version of this paper appeared in *American Ethnology* 9 (1992).

1. Susan Bourque and Kay Warren have shown the power of media analysis in their article on the Sendero Luminoso, or Shining Path, in Peru (1989).
2. I learned of some of the behind the scenes issues confronting the union leaders when I had lunch with Filemón Escobar on two occasions during the dialogue.
3. Decree 21060 was the bill ordering the closure of the nationalized mines.
4. The value of Bolivian currency had dropped in 1985, when IMF conditions were imposed, from 386,000 bolivianos to a dollar to approximately 1 million to a dollar. Money changers were standing on street corners of La Paz and Cochabamba offering to pay more than the official rate for dollars, since Bolivian currency was almost without value.
5. Questioning of the authoritative voice of the ethnographer is part of the "deconstructive" critique (Clifford 1988; Clifford and Marcus 1986). Combined with an appreciation of informants' contributions to what is often usurped by the ethnographer-observer, such questioning can yield us ever more accurate ways of capturing what goes into writing "the text" (thus making it easier for those coming later to pull the new construction apart). For obvious reasons, few of those

who get to the writing stage would want to make the production process of their texts available. Sol Tax tried for years to promote the microfilming of field notes, which are more revealing of the construction process than any edited material, but few except his students and close colleagues submitted their work.

6. As Sanjek (1990, 407) remarks in referring to the tension in relations between informants and ethnographers, the line between the ethnographer and the "other" can hardly be maintained when the latter begins writing her or his own notes.

IV

THE HOBBESIAN WORLD OF TERROR AND VIOLENCE

8

The Export of Militarization

*Counterinsurgency Warfare
in the Periphery*

Militarization is a corollary of the penetration of advanced capitalism into indigenous territories. The low insurgency warfare waged against the native populations when they try to defend their rights to land and resources involves whole populations, with women and children becoming the primary victims. As Mexico and Central America have become sites for the expansion of investments from commercial agriculture to oil drilling, medicinal drugs, genetic DNA resources, new sources of minerals, and export-oriented assembly production, the military arms of governments have expanded their operations. Paramilitary forces, often recruiting indigenous youths that no longer have a stake in their own subsistence economies, carry out operations that are banned by federal troops. Returning to field sites in Guatemala and Chiapas, where I studied peasant populations in my early research, I find increasing devastation from the "shadow wars" Carolyn Nordstrom (2004) described throughout the Third World.

I presented an earlier version of this paper while I was in residence at Smith College in 1996 as the Nielson Professor. I had just spent a year in Chiapas, Mexico, where a low-intensity counterinsurgency let loose by President Ernesto Zedillo was waged by federal and paramilitary troops against the Zapatista insurgency. The action was carried out by national and paramilitary troops against settlers of the Lacandón who supported the Zapatista rebellion, but armaments and advisory personnel in the U.S. counter-drug-trafficking program backed it up. In the following field stays I was witness to the low-level counterinsurgency I had read about in Guatemala. I was carrying out research in Guatemala in 1954 when the

U.S.-instigated coup took place and had retuned to my field site in Cantel, Quetzaltenango, to do a comparative study on the impact of neoliberalism and insurgency in the Maya areas on both sides of the Guatemalan-Mexican border. The comparison between the two areas provides a close view of indigenous-ladino (non-Indian) relations that are changing state relations with ethnic groups throughout the hemisphere. My growing interest coincides with that of a number of anthropologists such as Ricardo Falla, Lesley Gill, Katherine Lutz, Beatrice Manz, Carolyn Nordstrom, Victoria Sanford, Kay Warren, and others who have observed the growing violence and turn to militarization throughout the world.

"Militarization" applies to regimes in which the armed forces dominate politics. It is a process with a material as well as ideological dimension (Enloe 1983). In a material sense, as Enloe (1980) points out, it encompasses the gradual encroachment of military institutions into the civilian arena—the social, economic, and political institutions of a country. Ideologically, militarism identifies manhood with soldiering in a way that validates behavior of aggressive, abusive control over civilian populations, particularly women (Gill n.d.). When the military encroaches on indigenous populations, particularly when it is composed of indigenous men recruited to fight their own people, the consequences can be devastating, tearing apart the moral structures of the society. This is more evident in Guatemala, where a thirty-six-year civil war has scarred the countryside and disrupted or laid waste to whole communities. The support of a far more coherent civil society in Mexico provided support for an indigenous uprising that promised to change the racist policies of Mexico.

In these war zones a new form of governance arises with the advent of nongovernmental organizations (NGOs) that provide some of the educational and medical services no longer rendered by the state. These are part of a widening field site linking indigenous societies in a global arena. Ethnography provides a methodology for capturing the culture imposed in the shadows of war, combining the holistic strategies of teams that include forensic anthropologists assessing the evidence from the analysis of bones along with social anthropologists capturing the memories of survivors (AVANCSO 1990; Manz 2004; Nordstrom 2004; Sanford 2003; Schirmer 1998; Warren 1993b).

The roots of militarization in Latin America are at least as deep as the Spanish conquest and can be traced to primordial societies of Latin America. Aztecs mobilized all sectors of society in the flowery wars they fought to gain the hearts needed to satisfy the appetites of the sun god Huitzilopochtli. Mayas pretended to keep the celestial orbit of sun and moon in balance through contests waged in ball courts and battlefields. In the aftermath of the conquest, beliefs regarding the relationship between human populations and cosmological powers persisted but no longer in bellicose form. Military repression exercised by European elites commanding indigenous foot soldiers contained rebellions that threatened the hegemonic state achieved by the church and state.

The wars of the past five decades in Central America and for over a decade in Chiapas, Mexico, are an export of the U.S. military-industrial complex. Driven by the ideology of combating communism, controlling narcotrafficking, and more recently countering terrorism, the United States has supplied guns, ammunition, aircraft, technical guidance, and even special operatives to reinforce military and paramilitary operations in Central America, the Andean countries, Chile, and Mexico. Counterinsurgency warfare, invented in Vietnam by U.S. army intelligence and perfected in the 1980s in Central America, differs in the internalization of the conflict in which the lines between civilian and military are obliterated as the military pervades the domestic and political sphere. Paramilitary operations, often working in tandem with federal troops, provide the flexibility needed to evade international covenants regulating warfare.

Counterinsurgency as a military strategy means that the armed forces are routinely called out to deal with any group that protests government policies. It occurs in countries where the military is so imbued in the fabric of everyday life that all institutions of the society are invaded. The economy is distorted as a nonproductive military force takes over large shares of the gross national product and increases debt burdens, thereby driving up the interest costs for productive investments. By reducing welfare funds for the very population the army is dedicated to defending, counterinsurgency depletes funds for education, health services, and cultural expressions.

In the 1980s, Central America became the preferred site for militarization that affected the entire population of Guatemala, Costa Rica, and Nicaragua, as well as Honduran peasants recruited into the *contra* army of mercenaries. So ubiquitous is the military presence in Central America that the economy, the polity, and the domestic arena are being reshaped by its presence. The ever-present threat of force embodied in an army that takes up residence within communities domesticates the use of violence. By this I mean that armed men are able to assert their rights to the resources, labor, and bodies of a civilian population held hostage in their own communities. Yet at the same time that counterinsurgent armies pervade the most intimate spaces of society, they threaten the validation of armed forces as defenders of the civilian population and national security. In addition to the body count of the dead, which number in the hundred thousands, thousands of women are left widowed and hundreds of thousands of children are orphaned (Green 1999).

It is precisely in settings where the military is based within communities that the image of the military as a defender of national security is threatened. When women, the very population armies claim to be defending, increasingly become the victims of armed encounters in internecine wars,[1] it raises questions as to the distinctions between civilian and military, between legal and illegal, and between war and peace. When women protest the presence of the military living within their towns, it undermines the macho culture on which militarism is constructed. When women take up arms in guerrilla movements that oppose military repression, they further threaten the stereotypes of gender in ways that undermine patriarchal power. Viewing the military through gendered lenses provokes us to question the legitimacy of the military as defenders of national sovereignty or of civil order in the counterinsurgency warfare waged in Latin America. The questions become acute when we address the militarization process that threatens to take over all social and governmental functions in indigenous areas where threatened by predatory investors backed by military force.

In this chapter I discuss what we are learning about the nature and impact of counterinsurgency as a particular form of warfare aimed at civilian populations in the Guatemala-Mexico borderlands inhabited by Mayas. Most of the two hundred thousand victims of the thirty-six-year war in Guatemala were indigenous Mayas. Comparison with the counterinsurgency operation in the neighboring Mexican state of Chiapas following the Zapatista uprising of January 1, 1994, provides a basis for assessing the changing relations of indigenous people with the state with the onset of militarization.

Counterinsurgency warfare was introduced into Guatemala at the start of President Julio Cesar Mendez Montenegro's civilian presidency in 1966 with the advice of a U.S. military advisory mission to maintain the northeast region of Ixcán under control (Aguilera Peralta et al. 1981). A war that began in the Lacandón jungle of Mexico just north of Ixcán with the 1994 uprising of Zapatistas has continued up to the present in the form of a low-profile counterinsurgency. It is no coincidence that the deployment of troops is in two areas that share recently discovered oil deposits. These two conflict zones in the periphery of Latin America may be a harbinger of the looming resource wars in the third millennium.[2]

THE GUATEMALAN MILITARY PROJECT

The regimen of institutionalized terror that militarization cultivates consists in masking official repression in kidnappings, torture, or assassination that are carried out in sporadic, apparently arbitrary ways, as the acts of privately initiated left- and right-wing extremists (Aguilera Peralta et al. 1981). State terror began in Guatemala in the late 1960s and prevailed throughout the decades of the 1970s and 1980s, subverting all organized opposition and sending hundreds of thousands of poor farmers as well as middle-class professionals into exile within the country and abroad (Aguilera Peralta et al. 1981). The process of militarization became so embedded in the institutions of government that when civilian presidents came to power, such as Vinicio Cerezo in 1985 and Alfonso Portillo in 1998, they were forced to yield to military prerogatives (Schirmer 1998, 31). President Berger's initial promise to recognize the indigenous majority by naming Rigoberta Menchú and Victor Monteja to high posts in government has failed to produce results since budgets are not forthcoming to finance their mandates to overcome racist discrimination and to implement the peace accords.

Anthropologists began working in the colonizing areas near the northern border with Mexico in the 1970s and 1980s.[3] The people who came from land-poor villages in the highlands to colonize the jungle were guided by liberation theology priests and lay sisters in organizing cooperatives and collective enterprises with education as a key component (Manz 1988, 2004; Falla 1978). The Guatemalan army initiated the use of counterinsurgency warfare in 1976, selectively killing schoolteachers, priests, and leaders of the colonizers. This culminated in a major massacre in Panzos, a colonized area of Ixcán, in 1978 (Manz 2004, 94; Schirmer 1998, 39). Although up to that time the major guerrilla activity was concentrated in the coastal plantations, the indiscriminate killing of women, children, and men persuaded many Indians to support the Guerrilla Army of the Poor (Ejercito Guerrillero de los Pobres, EGP).

With the presidency of Rios Montt, the United States, under Ronald Reagan, reinstituted military aid that had been withheld during Jimmy Carter's presidency. In 1982 the military began to massacre and burn entire villages, and in the following year they carried out a divide-and-conquer strategy, importing people from many parts of the country to take over the lands the original colonizers had cleared and the houses they were forced to abandon. The Inter-American Commission on Human Rights summed up the results of these policies in its 1983 report: 250,000 to 1 million people displaced, with over 150,000 fleeing to Mexico; killing and torture of hundreds of thousands by the army decimating from 10 to 25 percent of the population in Indian townships of the central zone and leaving over 50,000 orphans in the departments of El Quich and San Marcos alone (Davis 1988; Smith 1990a and 1990b). United Nations reports raised the estimated dead to 200,000 after research on exhumed bodies provided more adequate data, and the numbers of displaced remained an estimated 250,000 to 1 million. Many of the 150,000 who fled to Mexico remained there.

Even after the Guatemalan army claimed to have defeated guerrilla forces by the massive massacres and institutionalized terror of 1980–1983, militarization increased in the countryside. Through a "pacification program" that masked the army's drive to exert military control over the population, over a million males between sixteen to sixty years were forced to serve unpaid in "civilian defense patrols." With the return of the exiles from Guatemala beginning in January 1993, the former colonizers were forced into intense conflict with the new residents for the land and villages (Manz 1988, 2004, especially chapter 5).

The economic restructuring brought about by the army has weakened the social and political autonomy of Indian communities throughout the western highlands beyond the militarized zone. Carol Smith (1990a and 1990b), who has for decades carried out anthropological research in the western highlands of Guatemala, demonstrates how this came about. With little land to cultivate and markets for artisan production diminished by the war, the basic economy of the region was disrupted, forcing the population into dependency on army supplies. Military bases in twenty of the twenty-two departments of the country and garrisons in almost every town were the major economic force. Each year the army recruited eight thousand new soldiers from indigenous communities for two-year stints, and in addition commandeered the labor of men and women building roads, provisioning soldiers, and caring for their laundry and other tasks without compensation.

Through their "model villages," a program in which the army resettled thousands of people in alien territories, the military perfected their control over the indigenous population. Fear and intimidation cultivated by the presence of military force enabled the army to infuse all institutions of the villages. Citing the intellectual authors of the program, Schirmer (1998, 59) states the army planned "a cultural transformation of an *Indigena* not tied to cultural tradition." In her interviews with present and retired army officers, she shows the link between "Beans and Bullets" (30 percent beans and 70 percent bullets) development policies fashioned by Guatemalan generals, often trained in U.S. centers of military formation, and with the help of USAID and counterinsurgency experts trained in Vietnam (Schirmer 1988, 33–38). Given the impoverishment of the villages, which since their settlement have lacked schools or other public services, there were few intervening agencies for the army to compete with. The population was divided by the introduction of new settlers hungry for land in 1983, and they were left to fight for their claims with settlers (Manz 2004, 155 et seq.). Thus the development program instituted by the army created a dependent population fighting among themselves for land and ready to work for low wages in export-oriented industries (Smith 1988). Smith (1990a, 33) concludes:

The severely deteriorated condition of people who were once partially self-sufficient peasants can only work to advantage of capital, even if it does not benefit most Guatemalans. The long term effect of economic restructuring in the highlands will be the creation of a large reserve army of unemployed who, for both security and development reasons, will have to be controlled by an ever-expanding state apparatus.

Beatriz Manz (2004, 156 et seq.) found a weary and dispirited population in Ixcán when she returned to her field station in the 1980s. Divided linguistically and coming from distinct areas of the country and their refugee camps in Mexico, the displaced population lived with suspicion and dread of their own neighbors.

After a quarter of a century of army control in alliance with compliant elected presidents, Guatemala is counted among the three poorest countries of the hemisphere, its economy shattered by the parasitical force of the army and its people reduced to theft, internecine violence, and despair (Schirmer 1998, 262 et seq.). Guatemala's peace agreement signed in December 1996 came at a time when there were few resources left for the army to plunder and even the propertied classes of Guatemala were beginning to object to the taxation and the continued reliance on violence. The attempts by civil society to get the army back to the barracks and restore the institutions of government are undermined by lack of resources. Unemployment remains high long after the peace agreements, and Guatemalan *campesinos* are paid so low that they risk imprisonment migrating illegally to work in Mexico for half the legal wages of two dollars a day paid in the plantations in that country.

The emergent civil society that coalesced in the peace initiatives in the 1990s objects to the sham of elected governments put in place after the violence subsided. During our visit to the industrialized department of Quetzaltenango shortly after the inauguration of President Oscar Berger in March 2005, we heard the anguish of health workers and environmentalists hired to bring order in communities still devastated by the war and its aftermath, often working in agencies that were never funded. Disenchanted by the government's appropriation of the imagery of the rule of law and of the procedures of electoral democracy, they realize that the human rights of Guatemalans are still violated with impunity. Yet protest and resistance are not ended: we read accounts of indigenous people opposing the gold mining operation in the Alta Verapaz in the *Prensa Libre* and on our return at the Guatemalan-Mexican border we were stopped for over an hour by a protest demonstration of campesinos against the Central American Free Trade Agreement (CAFTA) then being considered in Congress. Although it was passed later in the spring, and will undoubtedly provide a firmer base

for plunder by foreign firms, the spirit of resistance of the Mayan population has not been transformed in the military model.

MEXICO'S TURN TO COUNTERINSURGENT WARFARE

Despite the record of Central American militarization that has inspired
horror, contempt, and, sometimes, outright derision, President Zedillo
chose the military path after a year of stalled negotiations with Zapatista
rebels. On February 9, 1995, he ordered sixty thousand troops to invade the
boundaries of the Lacandón territory established in the truce made by Salinas twelve days after the uprising. Once settled within colonized villages,
the Mexican generals called upon Guatemalan generals as advisers in waging counterinsurgency warfare against the indigenous people of Chiapas
that spread to Guerrero and Oaxaca. In the buildup of the military force in
Chiapas we find recurrent patterns in the domestication of violence and its
consequences to those that prevailed in Guatemala. The difference lies in
the greater strength of civil society in Mexico that prevented the genocidal
consequences that prevailed for thirty-six years in Guatemala.

The difference between the Mayan experiences on each side of the border also derives from the character of the guerrilla operations on each side
of the border. The new Zapatista army, which counts women in high command, does not countenance macho controls over women within or outside the military that prevailed during the 1910–1917 revolution. Ramona,
a *comandante* in the Zapatista Army of National Liberation (EZLN), said,
"In the beginning, the EZLN was only eight or ten people." That was
when she and Ana Maria joined the group. Many more followed and at
the peak, 30 percent of the Zapatista central command were women (Marcos 1994). Zapatistas drafted the revolutionary law for women in 1993.
Their founding document circulated at the Chiapas state convention of
women in October 1994 and listed ten demands. These included the right
for women to participate in the revolutionary struggle, the right to work
and receive a just salary, the right to decide the number of children they
want to have and care for, the right to participate in the affairs of the community and hold office if they are elected in free and democratic elections,
the right to education and attention to their health and nourishment, the
right to choose their partner and not be forced into marriage, prohibition
of physical abuse either by relatives or strangers, the right to occupy positions in the governance of their villages and have military rank in the
revolution, and finally to have all the rights and obligations that the laws
and revolutionary rulings prescribe.

In their attack on male hegemonic practices, Zapatistas have attracted
even stronger supporters among women than among men in highland

indigenous communities in Chiapas (Nash 1997). Women of the colonized area, along with women of highland Indian villages who are single, divorced, or even widowed, enjoy few of the benefits of patriarchal society and are particularly energized by the new vision of femininity demonstrated by Ramona, Ana Maria, and Trini in the high command of the Zapatista EZLN. They marched in the ranks of thousands of Zapatista supporters who bore wooden rifles and masked their faces as they demonstrated their support in national conventions held in the Lacandón Rain Forest during the 1990s.

In the year following the uprising of January 1, 1994, the military increased its presence in the towns surrounding the conflict zone in the Lacandón Rain Forest from the estimated twelve-thousand-troop buildup during the twelve-day military encounter. In Altamirano, where one of the most intense armed confrontations had occurred and where Mexican militia had invaded the hospital run by sisters, the army occupied buildings throughout the center. In July 1994 when I visited Altamirano, I noticed a few women in uniform in the detachments located within the town centers. The presence of women posted in towns occupied by the national army softened the image of counterinsurgency warfare that proliferated after the armed invasion by Zedillo in February 1995.

I was living in San Cristóbal during the days of suspense in December, January, and the first week of February when we realized events

Figure 8.1. Zapatistas bring their appeal for autonomy to civil society in San Cristóbal de las Casas.

were reaching a crisis. On the eve of February 9, 1995, I was astounded to see on the evening television news broadcast a kind of show-and-tell game designed, it would seem, for children. The attorney general of the republic showed a photograph of a man with a beard that he repeatedly covered with a ski mask, pointing out to the audience the clear resemblance between the man whom they called Rafael Sebastian Guillén Vicente, to the leader of the Zapatistas, alias "Subcomandante Marcos." He announced that the attorney general's office intended to deploy agents to apprehend the "terrorists" led by Marcos, including Fernando Yanez, alias German, Jorgé Santiago Santiago, a director of a nongovernmental organization, Jorgé Javier Elorreaga, a filmmaker who had close communication with the Zapatistas, and Silvia Fernandez Hernandez, alias Elisa, who they claimed was a member of the Oaxaca contingent of 1970s revolutionaries. The attorney general proudly displayed a small arsenal of weapons, including hand grenades and assault weapons, which his agents, he claimed, had discovered in terrorist hideouts in Mexico City and Veracruz. The display, though less impressive than what most of the cattlemen and their paramilitary troops carried in their pickups, motivated President Zedillo to give the order to deploy a reported sixty thousand troops into the jungle to carry out the arrest of the four terrorists.

On the eve of the February 9, 1995, Zedillo-ordered invasion of the jungle, I listened on my shortwave radio to the voice of an Australian reporter broadcasting from Las Margaritas, the western gateway to the Lacandón Rain Forest. He exclaimed at his frustration in being cut off from the combat lines, and quoted some of the inhabitants who had escaped from the hamlets being invaded as saying that they had seen helicopters picking up dozens of bodies of civilians, presumably to avoid body counts. In the following two days, no reporters or even Red Cross vehicles were allowed in the rain forest. Helicopters circled over the city of San Cristóbal and troop movement could be seen on all the highways into the jungle.

The following day, February 10, I accompanied a U.S. delegation of Pastors for Peace[4] from the United States to discover what was happening in the jungle. We could not get beyond the guards blocking the road into the rain forest from San Andrés Larrainzar. We saw many houses in the hills on the outskirts of town flying white banners, a sign of neutrality. On February 11 the Pastors for Peace were able to get through the lines along with reporters and Red Cross agents. Their reports given at a press conference in the Center for Human Rights "Fray Bartolomé de las Casas" confirmed the stories of those who had escaped the invasion of these impoverished settlements: towns abandoned, houses burned and destroyed, food stores sprayed with pesticides, looting and vandalism, theft and destruction of tools, animals, and personal belongings. All of the international covenants regarding combat were violated: hospitals, schools, churches, and private homes were taken over by troops, potable water supplies and food stores that are specifically prohibited as military targets had been systematically violated.

Amidst accusations that President Zedillo was not commanding the troops but, rather, was covering their tracks, Zedillo appeared on television on February 9, 1995,[5] announcing, "I expressed my firm commitment to attend to the roots of rebellion. These roots are: poverty, absence of opportunities, injustice, lack of democracy." Reiterating his commitment to a negotiated settlement, one that in fact had not been actively pursued by the Salinas administration after March 1994 when the dialogue with the Zapatistas ended with the assassination of the Institutional Revolutionary Party (PRI) candidate Colossio, he denied that the Zapatistas would negotiate, despite their repeated communications from the jungle seeking a peaceful path throughout 1994 and into the first three months of his presidency. Pointing to the evidence for the link with the student rebellion of 1968, that is, the small caches of weapons said to have been discovered in Mexico City and Veracruz, he claimed that the origin, composition of the directors, and propositions of its grouping are neither popular, nor indigenous, nor Chiapanecos. "We are talking about a guerrilla group formed in 1969 in another state of the Republic called Fuerzas de Liberación Nacional, a party of the armed fight to seize political power." Deploring the threat to social peace he pledged to attend to the needs of indigenous communities in health, nutrition, living quarters, jobs, agrarian claims, human rights, and procuring justice in Chiapas. He concluded with his decision to provide the support of the Mexican army to the attorney general's office in enforcing the arrest warrants and to see that they patrol several locations in the state in order to prevent violent actions.

In response to the president's announcement of the invasion, over a hundred thousand Mexicans filled the Zócalo (central plaza) in Mexico City with demonstrators calling for justice and shouting, "We are all Marcos!"[6] Marcos, who remained in hiding in the canyons of the Lacandón Rain Forest, sent a communication to newspapers (*Cuarto Poder* February 13, 1995) announcing that the price for the heads of Zapatistas had risen. "The Zapatista uprising raised the price of Mexican Indian blood. Yesterday it was worth less than a plucked chicken, today his death is the condition for the most ignominious loan in world history [reference to the government loan of $11 billion to be paid back in crude oil]. The price of the Zapatista head is the only one that remained high in the rise and fall of financial speculation."

Despite the repeated assertions of interim governor Ruiz Fierro that there was no war in Chiapas, the experience of people in the rain forest

and in the northern territories denied his words. An estimated forty thousand troops arrived in Chiapas, augmenting the fifteen thousand to
twenty thousand already deployed in the conflict area. Some estimates
were as high as twenty-five thousand troops within the zone of conflict
and sixty thousand without.[7] The *ejidos*, communal land reform villages,
that had been invaded began to petition the president to withdraw the
army. In the petition from Ejido Perla de Acapulco, Municipio of
Ocosingo on February 20, 1995, members of the community complained
that people of the community were not able to carry out their daily tasks
in peace, especially the women who could not go out to do their work of
washing clothes. Of the 140 signatures, 90 were given as thumbprints, a
declaration in itself of the failure on the part of the government to educate
its citizens.

On February 28, 1995, human rights organizations from Mexico,
France, the United States, Spain, Italy, and Germany visited communities in the rain forest, collecting information on what had transpired
during the invasion. Villagers from San Miguel, La Garrucha, and
Lazaro Cárdenas told them that the army had destroyed property, food,
and clothing, and refused to give water to those who stayed in the village; others reported the army had tortured some of the people. *Global
Exchange* reported that the army had entered the Calvary in Ocosingo
and poisoned food, stolen machetes and hatchets, killed chickens, and
robbed everything of value.[8]

In March Gil Olmos wrote (*La Jornada* March 13, 1995a) that the whole
Ocosingo zone was militarized by land and air, with military encampments on all sides. Ruben de León described a desolate scene, "like a territory prepared by war, houses destroyed, burned animals wandering
freely through the wreckage, and fearful people with no water, food, medicines; the church and schools of Lacandón communities were burned,
and heavily armed soldiers occupied abandoned houses." Hermann
Bellinghausen (*La Jornada* March 8, 1995), whose reports from the jungle
gained him a prize from the National Press Association that he refused,
quoted a campesino who told him, "We ask for a house and they send us
planes; we ask for water pipes and they send us cannons; we ask for doctors and they send us soldiers. And this is how they help us live."[9]

Reports of increasing militarization of the conflict zone following the
invasion began to emerge. José Gil Olmos reported on March 13 that
women complained they were forced to wash clothes and make tortillas
for the soldiers. Men were harassed when they tried to go out to cultivate
the cornfields. Soldiers took over the school in Santa Elena as their barracks. They entered the huts with their weapons raised, forcing women to
kill their chickens to feed them. They bathed in the drinking water. All of
these are in direct violation of international covenants on warfare.[10]

Clearly the Secretariat of National Defense (SEDENA) had to justify the troop buildup. It aired television spots on the government controlled news channels showing the activities of teams of "social labor" carried out in dental dispensaries, food distribution, family planning, cutting hair, medical consultations, etc. Despite these public relations overtures, the people viewed the army as one of occupation according to reporters. They refused the handouts and told the soldiers to go. Miguel Badillo, reporting for *El Financiero*, observed that women of the jungle community La Realidad rejected medical attention offered by the army, and when heavily armed soldiers offered them bags with beans, rice, and sugar the young Indian girls refused them. Infuriated, one of the soldiers exclaimed, "Then they're asking for a good beating," while another took a bullet from his holster and showed it to the women, saying, "Then they want to try this." One of the young women replied, "Well if you're going to shoot us, do it at once." While she stood still in the road, the military withdrew.[11]

Soldiers in the armed patrols are very young and come from poor families: 70 percent are between seventeen and twenty years of age. Each day on patrol their masculinity along with their lives are threatened as they find themselves threatening young women, and, even worse, being threatened by them. Many of the soldiers are of indigenous origins, and they, even more than their *mestizo* (mixed-blood) comrades, experience the alienation of being despised by the indigenous people. As *El Financiero* reporter Miguel Badillo pointed out, "the frustration to the soldiers is the lack of a battlefield and of a clearly defined enemy, but at the same time they are afraid because they know that in front and on the sides and behind the battle can be initiated at any moment."[12]

Both sides were playing with time as the army persisted in the jungle, even after the order to retire the troops transmitted on Tuesday, March 15, 1995.[13] Zedillo's popularity ratings were diminishing, going to a low of 13 percent, while those of Marcos were rising. Contradictory reports abounded: While some reports stated that the army was a mere three hundred meters from the rebels,[14] the military seemed not to want to depart far from the encampments or the highways they patrolled in tanks. Marcos gave orders to his troops, which included a few thousand armed troops backed up by two hundred rebel groups throughout the countryside, to use arms only if the military continued to enter villages and to burn or steal food or animals or torture people. The *oficialista* (progovernment) *Asociación Rural de Interes Colectivo* (ARIC) claimed that five hundred Zapatistas had surrendered arms in Santa Elena, which the Zapatistas denied. Marcos quelled rumors of his death with a letter from the jungle received by *El Financiero* on March 22, 1995, which said he was listening to Stephen Still's album, *Four Way Street*, to the lyrics, "Though the cost of freedom be buried in the ground, Mother Earth will swallow you. Lay your body down," when his troops came running to tell him that the army had killed him.

> "Where? When?" I asked.
> "Today in a confrontation, but they didn't say where."
> "Ah, good," I replied, "and did I remain badly wounded or dead?"
> "*Todito muerto* [totally dead]—so the announcement said."
> I cried.
> "Why cry?" Dorito said.
> "Because I couldn't attend my funeral!"

Enraged at their inability to seize the four "terrorists" the army proceeded to destroy Aguascalientes—the site of the first National Democratic Convention—in the Lacandón Rain Forest in August 1994. The army then proceeded to turn it into a barracks. On March 30, 1995, a group of over four hundred political militants, housewives, Mexican dancers, industrial workers, intellectuals, students, artists, and indigenous leaders arrived at Aguascalientes in a caravan to stage a protest of the army's invasion.[15] The Lacandón had become a theatrical reproduction of Mexico's earlier revolution, playing out the romantic ideals of the earlier epoch.

The army may seem to have won the confrontation with the protest group, since they proceeded to bulldoze the Aguascalientes clearing and plant seedlings in what they called a conservation effort to reforest the jungle. But that was only the first of many confrontations that ensued as civil society contested the space taken over by the army, arguing against the right of the army to continue in their barracks. Roger Maldonado, the voice of CONPAZ (Coalition of Non-Governmental Organizations for Peace), announced that the presence of the army in schoolhouses, ecological reserves, and town centers violated international law of war and the national conventions of peace, as well as the conventions of Geneva and the Universal Declaration of Human Rights and Article 129 of the constitution. He pointed to the contradiction that, instead of guarding national sovereignty, the army was becoming a mercenary force acting in the interest of the United States, which had required that the $11 billion loan be repaid in crude oil (Comunicación Popular Alternativo 1997).

A year and four months after the onset of the war, *Proceso* reporters[16] estimated that the government must have spent over 1.697 million new pesos that could have created three hundred thousand new jobs. The estimate, based on the presence of at least ten thousand troops who cost minimally 50 new pesos to maintain each day, and 648 million new pesos a year, leaves out the cost of planes, tanks, arms, and munitions. Adding to this is the expenditure of $214 million in arms from 1988 to 1992 in the first four years of the Salinas administration that led up to the confrontation. Hundreds of Mexican officers trained in the School of the Americas, where ninety-four officers were graduated in 1993 alone, according to a press report released by Global Exchange in September 1995.[17] Carlos Bertoni Unda, Chiapas state representative of the PRD, denounced the expenditure of 50 million new pesos to acquire armaments and prepare a paramilitary police force of more than 1,600 members, noting that "Here in Chiapas a cow has more land than an Indian, and if you complain they put you in prison" (*La Jornada* March 8, 1995).

Human rights organizations denounced the hostilities in the jungle, calling the invasion "a massacre against the civilian population, which suffers hunger and repression caused by the army." The spokesperson for the Interamerican Human Rights group, Heather Sinclair, compared the army's maneuvers to those in Guatemala, El Salvador, and Honduras. Global Exchange said that the strategy was to kill the people by hunger and called for withdrawal of the troops and an end to the White Guards in a document sent to the Mexican Embassy in Washington and to the United Nations.[18]

Assuming that there was logic behind the military invasion of the jungle, the immediate objective seems to have been to prevent the campesinos from planting their fields at a crucial time in the annual cultivation cycle. In the postinvasion period, the long-range objective of the army was to militarize the countryside by creating model villages like those created by the U.S. army in Vietnam and Guatemala. Their relocation of the "pacific" Indians who had left the conflict zone during the early months of the uprising in the villages vacated after the invasion followed the wisdom of counterinsurgency tactics in creating internal dissension. According to reporters who interviewed some of these relocated families, the army assured them they could get better houses.[19] In these control settings, the army could "re-educate the people" with self-defense patrols that could receive exiles and people displaced by the war, as well a serve as landing bases for the swarms of helicopters that coursed the skies over the conflict zone. The army was clearly following the same manual on low-intensity warfare that the Guatemalans had used, creating an internal conflict zone as they had done in the Ixcán.

Beset with "tactical problems" in the rain forest, the military tried to respond to the growing clamor voiced by civil society activists calling for a withdrawal of the army by providing guided tours to the "pacified zones." According to reporters who were allowed in, every attempt was made to impede access to them and to NGOs and groups like Doctors without Frontiers (*Cuarto Poder* February 28, 1995).

In May 1995 I joined a group of observers in one of the contingents of CONPAZ that was housed in Patihuitz, about an hour and a half from the gateway city of Ocosingo, on a rough road that passed through cattle country before entering the cut over edges of the jungle. I had gone to the village as an election observer in August 1994, when it was known as a unified, militantly pro-Zapatista community that had been home to at least one of the Zapatistas who died in the invasion. I watched at a distance the lines of voters as they congregated at the wooden communal hall with tin roof that served for all of the functions for the village of a hundred families. All of the women wore kerchiefs to mask their faces, and they turned abruptly from any cameras pointed in their direction. This was in contrast to the village of San Miguel, closer to Ocosingo, where the townspeople were of mixed allegiance and stared openly at the observers on election day. None of the women and few of the men had voted in any elections prior to the 1994 contest since ballot boxes were never set up in the rain forest. Most of the women were monolingual.

When I returned a year later, I found a community divided, with hundreds of soldiers camped on a hill about a hundred meters from the village. As observers, we were enjoined not to ask questions, but on my rather extended walks to find some privacy for personal functions, often accompanied by a horde of children who had no school to go to and who were desperate for diversion, I would chat with neighbors about the weather or crop prospects. On one occasion I encountered two young men who had seen me in the security lines in San Miguel during the first aborted dialogue of the Zapatistas with the government in April of that year. I commented on the fact that the town seemed relatively free of damage and they replied that their branch of the ARIC had entered into an agreement even before the invasion, accepting the army's proposition that they would not do harm to the people.

Marcos, who had been blamed for the deflation of the peso and the economic crisis in general, was sensitive to the drama played out in Mexico City and even Washington, D.C. In an attempt to diffuse the growing resistance to the $11 billion bailout in a Republican-dominated Congress, Washington turned the monitoring of Mexico's economy over to IMF officials who flew down to Mexico in the first week of March to prepare an austerity program in exchange for the loan. But the economic outlook continued to deteriorate throughout the year as the gross domestic product declined 10.5 percent in the second quarter and 9.6 percent in the third quarter of 1995.

If one of the central objectives of the invasion was to recuperate confidence of investors, it had the opposite effect. With no news forthcoming for three days after the invasion, investments declined 1.90 percent on February 13, and on February 14 they declined another 3.04 percent. By February 15 the peso had fallen to 6.10 to a dollar, and more than 200 million pesos left the country.[20] The contradictions between what President

Zedillo said and what he did made him appear to be a vacillating leader and further weakened confidence among investors.

Zedillo's stated objective in the invasion, that is, to ensure the internal security of the country, was also brought into question. Many Mexicans, including some staunch PRIistas, were opposed to the invasion on the basis that Mexican sovereignty was violated in the debt package linked to the military invasion. These misgivings were augmented when *El Financiero* published the information that military leaders in the offensive were trained in the School of the Americas, and that a major and lieutenant from Defense Intelligence were present as advisers to the operation.[21]

The everyday violations committed by soldiers escalated as they entered into the intimate spaces of the rain forest settlements. Human rights advocates denounced these in international arenas.[22] As the protest against the military presence rose, the Mexican army carried out what they called a program of "social integration" following a tactic used by the Guatemalan army in the Ixcán. They returned twenty-six thousand colonizers who had voluntarily left their homes in the rain forest shortly after the uprising and February 9 invasion, locating them in the homes of those who had been routed by the army in the invasion. This divide-and-conquer strategy turned indigenous people against each other, ensuring the continuation of conflict (*La Jornada* February 28, 1995b; Rojas 1995, 8).

The protests eventually forced the government to send its representatives in the Commission of Agreement and Pacification (*Comisión de Concordia y Pacificación* [COCOPA]) to meet with the mediating team for the Zapatistas, the National Commission of Mediation (*Comisión Nacional de Intermediación* [CONAI]) headed by Bishop Samuel Ruiz. After two abortive meetings in the spring of 1995, the negotiating teams reached an agreement in February 1996 at San Andrés Larrainzar (Nash 1997). But for three more years, the government failed to fulfill even the most minimal objectives of the accord. Instead of advancing peace, the conflict zone extended into the northern region of Chiapas and into highland communities beginning in the second trimester of 1995 and increasing in intensity in the following years.

The undeclared war took on a new and more insidious form, as civilian PRI supporters carried out unpremeditated attacks on neighbors and family members. This was particularly marked in the northern region of the state where the paramilitary group, *Paz y Justicia* (Peace and Justice), had been disrupting village life on the northern frontier of the state in the autonomous pueblos of Sabanilla, Tumbala, Ocosingo, Tila, and Chilom ever since the January 1, 1994, uprising. Taking their name from slogans of civil society protest groups, they developed a model of combat that was copied by other paramilitary groups in the region such as the Chinchulines and the Alianza San Bartolomé (*La Jornada* October 29, 1997). Repeated calls of alarm from the Center for Human Rights failed to gain government attention. Internal conflicts between a faction dominated by the bilingual indigenous schoolteachers and officials of the PRI grew with the contest for government funds in the 1980s. These came to a head in the fall of 1997 when the leader of the opposition to the PRI-dominated town hall disappeared. A newly formed paramilitary group inspired by the Paz y Justicia, calling themselves *Mascaras Rojas* (Red Masks) began torching houses belonging to the opposition group that called themselves *Las Abejas* (The Bees). These harassment and death threats posted by the Mascaras Rojas forced them to seek asylum in Acteal.

On December 22, 1997, the paramilitary group that called themselves Red Masks entered the Las Abejas compound in Acteal and fired on the group, killing forty-five, including nine men, twenty-one women—four of them pregnant—and fifteen children.[23] The heavily armed men ripped open the bellies of the pregnant women and killed the fetuses. Two of the paramilitaries played a game of tossing the fetuses from one to another with their machetes, all the time yelling, *"Que se matan la semilla!"* ("Let them kill the seed!") as they engaged in this extreme violation of women's reproductive being.[24] The attack clearly had genocidal implications.

The story of the massacre spread throughout the world. Eyewitnesses testified that the men, armed with rifles issued only to federal troops, were members of the local PRI party. State police standing nearby did not intervene as the massacre progressed (Comunicación Popular Alternativo Grupo de Trabajo 1997). The federal attorney general resisted investigation of the incident, attributing the attack to political and economic conditions internal to the region (*New York Times* December 27, 1997). None of the paramilitary were detained or disarmed in the first week (*New York Times* January 1, 1998). However, worldwide attention led to the forced resignation of the governor Julio Cesar Ruiz Ferro for his failure to respond to urgent pleas for protection of the population against the armed gangs on January 7, 1998 (*New York Times* January 8, 1998). By mid-January, federal prosecutors accused a state police commander of helping the PRI cacique of Chenalhó, Jacinto Arias Cruz, to arm the paramilitary gunmen with combat rifles and other sophisticated weapons restricted for use only by the army.

The full story of the massacre came out five months later when the PRI government detained a retired federal army general and a Tzotzil-speaking sergeant of the National Security Forces who were accused of training and overseeing the operation (*La Jornada* April 3, 1998). Relatives of the victims rejected the government's offer of U.S.$5,000 offered as indemnity (*New York Times* March 6, 1998).

In focusing on the incidents in which women were the principal targets, I do not want to underestimate the harassment and killing of the male population. In the overall military strategy the attacks on women and children augment the terror experienced by all indigenous people. Such acts are often relegated to paramilitary bands with attempts made to conceal their connections to military strategy. In contrast, army and state security forces are directly involved in attacks on male leaders. On June 10, 1998, government troops attacked a group of campesinos who were meeting in El Bosque, a hamlet of Unión Progreso, killing one and taking seven into custody. Two days later members of the National Commission on Human Rights delivered eight bodies, with clear signs of torture and abuse, to the community. The community considered that the abuse and killing of the men, whose bodies were beaten and disemboweled, were executions committed while they were in custody of government security forces (*La Jornada* June 14, 1998). This time the army could not pass the event off as paramilitary or internecine struggle; instead they chose to inculpate the Commission on Human Rights who had taken on the task of delivering the bodies, apparently to avoid a bloodbath.

The warfare waged in indigenous pueblos that continued throughout the presidency of Zedillo until 2000 was directed at destroying the social reproductive base of the society. It was played out on the two military fronts laid out in the Mexican army's *Manual de Guerra Irregular: Operaciones de Contraguerrilla o Restauración del Orden* (Manual of Irregular War: Counterguerrilla Operations or Restoration of Order, SEDENA [1995], cited in Center for Human Rights "Fray Bartolomé de Las Casas" 1997). These are defined as a military front, whose objective is to respond to strictly military activities in which armed forces ought not to cause excessive pain to the civilian population. The other front is that of military institutions and their civilian auxiliaries, whose objective is that of recruiting civilian support for counterinsurgency measures. Finally they list a public opinion front that requires management of the army's public image and denigration of the enemy. The first two fronts correspond to the Lacandón Rain Forest and the highlands with the army charged with "defending the frontier" (and not coincidently the rich oil deposits discovered there), while the paramilitary discourages the spread of the rebellion in the highlands and into neighboring states.

In perfecting their own model of low-intensity warfare, the Mexican army developed elite forces, special commando operations, and rapid deployment units. Complementing the armed operation is the increase in civilian forces now under the command of the army (Center for Human Rights "Fray Bartolome de Las Casas" 1997, 160 et seq.; *La Jornada* April 3, 1998). These armed civilian groups act outside of the law in the state strategy of control and factionalizing of the opposition in the form of organized civil society and the indigenous communities in rebellion. In contrast to the paramilitary forces that have always operated as the armed force of the ranchers and large landowners (*La Jornada* October 29, 1997, 11–12), the new armed bands are recruited from within communities where they operate. Unlike mercenaries, they are extensions of federal control forces.

We can gain a clearer understanding of the changing constituency of these paramilitary groups still operating in Chiapas from the analysis of Andrés Aubry, an anthropologist and historian based in San Cristóbal, and Angelica Inda, director of the Historical Archives at the Diocese of San Cristóbal. They documented the existence of 246 members of these paramilitary groups in Chenalhó, the municipio in which Acteal is located, in 1997 (Aubry and Inda 1998). Those who participated in these paramilitary groups are almost exclusively young men frustrated by landlessness and unemployment. The long-standing agrarian crisis, coupled with demographic growth, have created a situation in which these young men exist. Some of them are boys of fourteen and fifteen years of age without schooling, and those who are married and have families are forced to wander in search of work. Like their parents, they survive on their wits and by occasionally stealing food and animals from neighboring farms. Because they own no land and have no reliable means of subsistence, they are forced to live outside the law. Their dislocation from community life also means that they have no reason to attend assemblies, and thus have no part in communal decision-making processes (Aubry and Inda 1998, 8–9). These young men collect a "war tax" from compatriots who are supporters of the Zapatistas and/or opposition parties, which gives them personal income. This kind of harassment forced members of the community who supported the opposition party and the Zapatistas, such as Las Abejas, to seek refuge in Acteal. One can imagine that their frustrations in the economic arena contribute to their sexual frustrations since they are unable to raise the betrothal price to obtain a woman in marriage. These frustrations, inflamed by pornographic videos and drugs, can conduce toward the behavior exhibited in Acteal.

With the assistance of these armed civilians, the army attempted to disarticulate organized sectors of the growing opposition to the PRI throughout Zedillo's regime. Presented on the propaganda front as internal conflicts based on religious differences or land problems, they disrupted the economic and social fabric of society. The violence was coordinated with events that might in themselves have alleviated the crisis. The Acteal massacre, for example, occurred just as the coffee harvest was coming in with the promise of higher prices for the crop than in previous years. Paramilitary attacks throughout the spring of 1998 disrupted the cultivation cycle in the growing area of conflict. In the contested lands of Venustiano Carranza, armed civilian patrols attacked the squatters, burning houses and threatening the campesinos. Three years after the massacre, when I visited Acteal in 2001, community leaders told me they were still harassed by paramilitaries and could not return to their homes in the center of San Pedro Chenalhó. They lived as aliens even with the more permissive Party of National Action government, and would wait to see if the new president and governor would fulfill their promises.

Military repression continued after President Vicente Fox took office in 2000, although at a lower pace and with some troops withdrawn. Flashpoints continue in the Lacandón, particularly in twelve areas classified as irregular where the settlers have not been given legal title. The greatest incidence of violence occurred in Montes Azules, a tract of land colonized by indigenous people for some thirty years when the government declared it an ecological conservation area. The army has made three attempts to "surgically remove" the colonizers, who have resisted such attempts and have succeeded in legalizing thirty-nine sites, but 11 sites are still called irregular and subject to arbitrary assaults.

ETHNICITY, CLASS, AND GENDER
IN THE MILITARIZATION OF SOCIETY

The armed forces of any nation reflect a limited segment of the population. They are made up of a predominantly male labor pool of youths from the poorer classes in the lower ranks and an elite officers' corps made up of somewhat better-off men who disregard abuses of civilian populations, what Steven Stern (1995, 48) calls a pattern of domestication of violence that paralleled military discipline.[25] The quintessential expression of the domestication of violence comes with the *descarga*, or unleashing of male violence against females as men impose their power over women in an apparently random or arbitrary fashion, thus keeping them in their place.

The breakdown between the "home front" and the "battlefront," as Cynthia Enloe (1983, 217) tells us, comes when women enter as combatants. This is the novel condition brought about in Central American wars in which women serve in guerrilla armies, no longer dubbed "camp followers" as in the earlier revolution but recognized as foot soldiers bearing arms. In counterinsurgency warfare waged against civilian populations, the soldiers are often pitted against the same ethnic group from which they originate (Enloe 1983).

The incorporation of indigenous populations into the world economy is coincident with the upswing in militarization (Rosh 1988, 683). As the group most committed to subsistence activities, the concerns of small-plot cultivators and women in the domestic economy are most threatened by the militarization of society (Nash 1993; Smith 1990b). As such, they are often the most consistent opponents of the military in counterinsurgency wars. Yet over the long run, their vulnerability as an economic segment in the face of global-market advancement may make them more subject to the advertisements of recruiters. Commentators have observed the youthful population of indigenous villages of Guatemala mimicking militaristic behavior even though they are the chief targets. The distortion of ethnic identification in the face of long-standing militarization has also been observed in the case of Sendero Luminoso in Peru. Psychologically the desire to overcome the sense of impotence may result in the attraction to their enemy's ranks.

Identification with the civilian population they are forced to fight has a class as well as ethnic bias. But whereas their ethnic identity may reinforce their desire to abandon the army when forced to fight, class position has a mixed impact. Lacking the minimal resources to achieve mobility, or even to survive given the high unemployment rates in developing countries, recruits may seize the opportunities advertised by military recruiters, and once enlisted, justify their choice in terms of necessity. The army offers more to its recruits now than twenty years ago. Prior to the massive injection of U.S. military aid extended to Latin America from 1970 to 1990, armies were as poorly clothed and quartered as their groups of origin. Juan Rojas, a miner who served in the Bolivian army before the 1952 revolution (Nash 1992), recalls how he was bused out with new recruits to the Bolivia-Chile border where they were forced to sleep in cattle corrals and fight for threadbare uniforms that rarely fit them. They ate vicuña that they shot with the ancient weapons given to them and garnered what they could from peasants living in the area. Reading the account of Juan, the Chamula Indian whose autobiography was elicited by Ricardo Pozas (1947), we can appreciate a similar impoverishment in the army in which he was mistreated and traumatized in a year of forced service to the nation. He returned to his natal village of San Juan Chamula, deculturated and impoverished.

Women as mothers, wives, sex workers, and vendors have as problematic a relation to the military as men, though it takes distinct expressions. Women risk more open displays of hostility to the army, perhaps with the assumption they will not be as severely punished as men. Bolivian women always marched in the front lines of demonstrations against military repression when they demonstrated in the mining communities. Chilean women went out in the streets to demonstrate against Augusto Pinochet Ugarte's military regime, facing hoses that discharged sewage water on them as they chanted against the government. The women of the Plaza de Mayo in Buenos Aires called attention to the violation of human rights by paramilitaries long before the rest of the society was mobilized.

The army has learned to distance soldiers and their civilian targets by offering higher wages and better conditions to its recruits now compared to twenty years ago. Prior to the massive injection of military aid extended to Latin America from 1970 to 1990, armies were as poorly clothed and quar-

Figure 8.2.   Federal troops stand watch over indigenous residents gathering for the Peace Accords, April 1995, San Andrés Sacamchen. The Agreement has not yet been implemented in Mexico.

tered as their groups of origin. The new generation of soldiers can envision a better life in the army, where they eat more than the civilian population and have superior weapons that give them a fighting chance with the populations they are forced to fight. The living quarters for married couples are superior to what most indigenous people can attain, and they have the security of medical attention and pensions superior to those of many middle-class mestizos. This creates a class division between soldiers and impoverished campesinos that they must confront, ensuring a more committed armed force than in the past when rebels and federal forces were more evenly matched.

Militarization of civil society in Chiapas sharpens gender dichotomies, with women becoming the target of male recruits who take out their frustrations against society on them. Very few women can (or possibly would if they had an opportunity) enter the mobility channels offered by military service. Indian women in particular accept the major responsibility for maintaining ethnic culture intact. This encumbers women's autonomy in wider political and economic circuits at the same time that it releases men from the constrictions of ethnic group identification, permitting them to advance their position in regional and national organizations such as the military. It would undoubtedly create a greater breach with their communities than Juan Perez Jolote encountered sixty years ago when he returned from the Federal army under Venustiana Carranza (Pozas 1947).

Yet indigenous women in the Lacandón have joined the rebels' armed forces. Their experience in settlements cut off from traditional communities resulted in their choosing an alternative destiny that is one of the most challenging aspects of the rebellion. From the early mobilization of the Zapatista movement, women have linked the fight for respect of indigenous culture and of women in the home to the struggle for economic and political rights. They have taken public positions in state and national conventions, claiming "the right to fight together with men in a relation of equality" (Declaration of the State Convention of Chiapas Women, October 3, 1994). As a result of their own attempts to reject the identity of subordination from centuries of colonization and independence, they are most aware of the needs to translate the demands for democracy into everyday behavior. At the 1995 State Convention of Chiapas Women, held only two days after the February 9 invasion, the participants signed a declaration that identified the war with "the most brutal expression of a patriarchal regime, characterized by hierarchy, authoritarianism, discrimination and repression which exists in our country, whose consequences affect the entire Mexican pueblo." The declaration goes on to say, "women, historically discriminated against, have seen how our vulnerability has increased, with the sexual aggression and violations that the army and the white guards have committed against women since they ordered the militarization of Chiapas." That they face this aggression and violation in their own homes puts them in the tragic dilemma of choosing autonomy at the risk of losing family and children. As the group most committed to subsistence activities, the concerns of small-plot cultivators in the domestic economy, particularly women, are most threatened by the militarization of society (Nash 1993; Smith 1990). As such, they are often the most consistent opponents of the military in counterinsurgency wars.

Overcoming centuries of repression as a culture and gender, women have taken public positions in state and national conventions claiming "the right to fight together with men in a relation of equality" (Marcos, citing the declaration of the State Convention of Chiapas Women, October 3, 1994). Noting that women who are directors of the organizations in the State Assembly of the Chiapas Pueblo have been apprehended and jailed and that women in the conflict zone are subject to harassment, they called upon women as a decisive force, "capable of stopping the war and defending the life that we give birth to" and urged President Zedillo to withdraw the troops. The Xi'Nich Committee of Defense of Indigenous Liberty held another state convention in April 1995, which included the Xi'nich, Women for the Dialogue, New Popular Union of Tenochtitlán, the

Witches, Citizens for Democracy, and other organizations, where the women formulated even more specific demands:

- *Economic:* Special funds for projects for Indian women drafted by the community, not the government; just wages; the right to set our own price on products; the right to land for women and men; introduce grinding mills, bread baking, markets for artisan products.
- *Social:* Support women's literacy program; attend to women's health needs, with translators in the hospitals, advice on family planning; prohibit liquor. Women of the Lacandón jungle are challenging the military as they drive by in their armored vehicles at breakneck speed on village streets. Indigenous women organized a peace march on the international day of women in 1995 when they chanted slogans for peace mixed with exhortations against the presence of military. They renewed their demands that the three Tzeltal women raped by twenty soldiers shortly after the New Year's uprising should have their case tried, and two hundred women from the different organizations demonstrated at the door of the chief prosecutor.

Gendered and ethnic identity is manipulated by the state through its military apparatus, but people can and do develop collective identities that enable them to resist such manipulation. Over two hundred soldiers were said to have deserted in the early months after the uprising, many of them drawn from indigenous communities. In Mexico resistance of the people in the rain forest is reinforced by the mobilizations of civil society against the military. This is far greater in Chiapas than in Guatemala, where the indigenous population found few supporters among non-Indians until the late 1980s as the economy moved from an agro-export sector to a financial-industrial elite allied with international monopoly capital that found political expression in more democratic regimes (Aguilera Peralta 1980). Mexico is less dependent on the military than Central American countries, and it has opposed military solutions to civilian problems in the past. Ultimately the ability to further military buildup will depend on international loans. As a parasitical entity, the needs of the military will probably exceed the ability to expand loans in the future. With a growing revolutionary movement and rebellion increasing in Guerrero and Oaxaca, the use of military force does not have unlimited expansive potential.

The structural conditions that define their possibilities for survival enter into the occupied population's calculations as they adapt to the presence of the army in opportunistic ways. Women in the Lacandón Rain Forest are already making money by selling food to the soldiers who do not like SEDENA rations. Cantinas have opened in some of the villages where liquor is sold to soldiers, against the prohibition against alcohol legislated by the Zapatistas. I saw one such café in Patihuitz where women who appeared to be from other parts were consorting with the soldiers as they drank. Their presence has a disruptive effect on the community, women say, and they fear that their daughters will be corrupted. Some women who have married soldiers found themselves turned into prostitutes when their "husbands" brought them to Mexico City and forced them to have relations with other men for money (personal communication, Kathleen Sullivan). For these women who have accommodated to the military peace is feared as they become dependent on the wages of war. The longer the presence of the military, the greater the possibility that attrition of their resistance movements may occur as the needs for survival take precedence over commitment.

But an extended encounter also works to the disadvantage of the army. The kind of war that is fought by counterinsurgents continuously feeds into the resistance movement. The very construction of manhood through military discipline and the power it appears to lend to young recruits is vitiated by the violations against citizens soldiers are forced to commit. In Mexico's counterinsurgent war, the government is pursuing a low body count intensive war of attrition in which the people die of starvation. As this becomes more apparent, the government loses credibility on the "home front" at the same time that it is failing to impress foreign investments to prop up the economy. In this breakdown of the mythical dichotomy between home front and battlefront, as Enloe (1989, 217) points out, the army is undermining its own ideology of protecting national sovereignty and ensuring social tranquility.

CONCLUSION

The results of militarization in Central America during the 1980s after a decade of war, capital flight, and search-and-destroy campaigns in the countryside have had similar repercussions in each of the countries where it took hold. Guatemala's death count exceeds that in other countries of Central America, with two hundred thousand deaths estimated in the thirty-six-year civil war. The FMLN in El Salvador, which suffered over fifty thousand deaths and disappearances, remained undefeated and entered into the peace process following the war. Just as in Guatemala during periods of civilian government, El Salvador's Christian Democratic Party masked the escalation of "low-intensity" warfare as a way of keeping the revolution in check. During the 1980s more Salvadorans were assassinated than in all of the previous dictatorships; the greatest impoverishment of the people in Salvadoran history occurred; and corruption reached its highest point. Electoral democracies that replaced military dictators have not ended the violence.

I visited Central America with a group of CISPES professors to assess the conditions in the universities in 1982. En route we touched down briefly in Guatemala City where we saw soldiers patrolling the streets carrying assault rifles. Most of them were young men, recruited from the countryside, many of them of indigenous origins. They handled their weapons menacingly as they dropped in at convenience stores to buy cigarettes or lounged in the park in front of the governmental palace.

In San Salvador, we found a campus devastated by bombing; the social science building was completely flattened, the library in disarray, and classes were being held in improvised quarters throughout the city. In the countryside, plazas became a bunker each evening as a scarred military contingent in areas we were told were "liberated" tried to defend themselves from an enraged populace that wanted them to leave. Women in the refugee camps we visited spoke of the bombings that destroyed their houses, the seizure of their children, some not even in their teens, to work for the military. I shall never forget the evening we visited a camp with over five hundred orphans cared for by a French medical team. The murmur of their voices, some crying, some shouting, and others laughing as they played with sticks and stones in what had been a village, rose like waves crashing on a beach, as some came running out to see us. As the sea of small bodies crushed to get close to us, I felt like Gulliver in the land of the Lilliputians.

Mexican civil society has not yielded to the military in part because of the constitutional safeguards, backed by a strong civil society, and in part because of the greater autonomy the country enjoys from the United States. The economic dependency has, however, increased with the North American Free Trade Agreement (NAFTA). The active rejection of militarization by civil society has contained the level of brutality exercised by the army and their paramilitary cohorts. The exercise of a free press has enabled human rights activists to disseminate news of violence that becomes transmitted throughout the world, as the Acteal massacre demonstrated.

Domestication of violence in the long-term coresidence of the military with a population held hostage in low-intensity warfare cultivates its own opposition as civilians resist its expansion. In the breakdown of the mythical dichotomy between home front and battlefront, the army undermines its own ideology of protecting national sovereignty and ensuring social tranquility. On the other hand, the long-term coexistence with the army in their midst cultivates opportunistic adaptation to the presence of the military. The militarization of the internal life of communities in continuous contact with the army erodes civilian authorities as officials abandon their functions to military authorities. Cantinas are opening in villages where liquor is sold to soldiers, countering the EZLN prohibition against alcohol. Prostitution is increasing, with truckloads of women arriving in the rain forest, and Zapatista women fear the long-term effect of army barracks in their midst. They know that some women become complicit in militarization as they take advantage of the commercial opportunities offered by the army. But like Berthold Brecht's Mother Courage, these women often defeat their own goals as they respond to the demands of the military.

The most unsettling impact of the militarization of Chiapas is the threat to collective strategies that reinforced Mayan resistance in the five hundred years of colonization and conquest. In the kind of low-intensity counterinsurgent warfare now being waged in the conflict zone, these contradictory tendencies are evolving. The military and paramilitary intervention into community social organization and cultural practices undermines a sense of trust among community members that will have long-term consequences for the reconstitution of a democratic indigenous civil society. The PRI has succeeded in dividing communities within the Lacandón Rain Forest and in highland communities by channeling funds to its supporters and giving arms to local officials to massacre their own people, as in Acteal. Gender antagonism is on the increase with men opposing women's participation in political actions. Women are, as a result, forced to assert their autonomy in the home as well as in civil society.

Yet there is a great deal to hope for in Mexico. Until the uprising, Mexico was less dependent on the military than Central American countries, in part because the PRI gave preference to co-optive approaches over military solutions to civil unrest during the consolidation of the revolution by Lázaro Cárdenas. The mobilization of civil society against the military is greater than in other Central American nations because of the greater autonomy the nation maintained vis-à-vis the United States. This prevailed until recent neoliberal policies eroded nationalist priorities.

The greatest basis for optimism rests in the resistance movement of indigenous women. Their condition of marginality in the hegemonic processes of the 1917 revolution fortified an inalienable sense of autonomy rooted in their culture. Women's participation in the ranks of the Zapatistas from the earliest days of that encounter over a decade ago transformed the guerrilla movement from a bid for power to an attempt to broaden the democratic base for the entire society. In demanding equality within their ranks as well as in the national society, women are broadening and deepening the meaning of democracy in ways that exceed the boundaries defined by eighteenth- and nineteenth-century revolutions that excluded women, blacks, and servile labor from their utopias.

In Guatemala, the major signs of regeneration come from cooperatives of women, many of whom were widowed by the war. The recent passage of the Central American Free Trade Agreement (CAFTA) will further the economic control exercised from beyond the borders of the country. Like Mexico, with the stalled San Andrés Agreement, Guatemala failed to ratify the referendum for indigenous political and social rights in 1999 (Warren 2002b, 149 et seq.). Yet the reassertion of Mayan culture in the schools and wider society grows more evident each year, along with political representation in regional and national congresses. Another positive sign is the waning prestige and influence of the United States in the hemisphere.

NOTES

An earlier version of the paper was presented in 1996 at Smith College when June Nash was the Nielson Professor.

1. Carole Nagengast (1994, 110) points to over fifty such ethnic conflicts that erupted since the fall of the Berlin Wall in 1989. Her exhaustive analysis of the outbreak of ethnic violence throughout the world is an essential handbook for analyzing new forms of multiethnic relations in the process of globalization. She estimates that 95 percent of the casualties of war in the world today are women and children.

2. Michael T. Klare (2001) sums up the trouble spots over "resource wars" in his analysis of the core areas of these conflicts. This paper addresses the peripheral areas where reserves of oil are envisioned as future supply zones, often located in indigenous territories.

3. Beatriz Manz worked in the eye of the storm in the Ixcán village of Santa Maria Tzejá in the northeast area of colonization in the 1970s. She returned to the town to interview survivors of the vicious attacks carried out by the Guatemalan army in Maria Tzejá (1988, 2004). Ricardo Falla served as a Catholic priest in the Ixcán during some of the worst attacks on the settlers (1994). Recent studies in the area assess the physical and social destruction brought about by the wars (AVANCSO 2000; Sanford 2003).

4. Pastors for Peace is an organization formed by Protestant missionaries seasoned by the counterinsurgency wars in Central America to serve as witnesses to the devastation.

5. *Expreso*, February 10, 1995; see also *Mexican Notebook: The Newsletter of the Consulate of Mexico in New York* 4, no. 1 (February 1995): 1–2.

6. Gustavo Lomelin, political commentator for *El Financiero*, wrote in his column "Para su informe," on February 13, 1995, "Pressures within and outside pushed Zedillo to a hard line: the Mexican military, advised by the U.S. and supported by grand finance capital of New York and the Reforma [referring to the Wall Street of Mexico City] pressed him." Dolia Estevez, *El Financiero* reporter in Washington, was quoted as saying that White House intelligence assured them the order of arrest of the Zapatista leader was an ultimatum of the Mexican armed

forces conforming to the line of the Chase Manhattan Bank. Riordan Roett, whose edited book, *The Mexican Peso Crisis: International Perspectives*, has just been published by Westview Press (1995), was implicated in the decision to invade by a memo circulated in Chase Manhattan Bank. The memo, Roett wrote, advised, "While Chiapas, in our opinion, does not represent a fundamental threat to the political stability of Mexico, it is perceived as such by the investing community. The government will have to eliminate the Zapatistas to demonstrate their effective control of the national territory and of political security." Mexicans take the term *eliminate* seriously and suggest that this may have precipitated the invasion. Marcy Kaptur, a Democratic congresswoman who opposed the financial packet, said Wall Street could have prompted the invasion, a rumor nourished by the memo of the Chase Manhattan Bank.

7. Amado Avendano cited in Fredy Martin Perez, "Some 25,000 military search for Marcos," *Expreso*, February 28, 1995.

8. José Gil Olmos, "Documentan observadores nacionales y estranjeros torturas en Chiapas," *La Jornada*, February 28, 1996.

9. José Gil Olmos, "Solo destrucción encontraron los retornados a la Sultana," *La Jornada*, March 13, 1995, 8; Olmos, "Tension y zozobra en comunidades Lacandonas," *La Jornada*, March 13, 1995, 17; Olmos, "Documentan observadores nacionales y estranjeros torturas en Chiapas," *La Jornada*, February 28, 1995; Hermann Billinghausen, "Aguascalientes: Un dialogo en dos actos de la sociedad civil," *La Jornada*, March 31, 1995.

10. José Gil Olmos, "Sometan militares a Santa Elena: Obligan a las indigenas a servirlos," *La Jornada*, February 13, 1995, 20.

11. Miguel Badillo, "El ejército sale de las comunidades, pero cerca ejidos completos," *El Financiero*, March 17, 1995, 45; Carlos Fazio, SUN news agency, "Contra-insurgencia en Chiapas," *Cuarto Poder*, February 28, 1995.

12. Miguel Badillo, "Aislados 600 militares en un rincon de la selva," *El Financiero*, March 26, 1995, 13.

13. Miguel Badillo, "Las post datos de Marcos," *El Financiero*, March 18, 1995; Badillo, "Aislados 600 militares en un rincón de la selva," *El Financiero*, March 26, 1995; Hermann Billinghausen, "Aguascalientes: Un dialogo en dos actos de la sociedad civil," *La Jornada*, March 31, 1995.

14. Amalia Avendano Villafuerte and Miguel Badillo, "Solo 300 metras separan al Ejercito Mexicano y a los rebeldes Zapatistas," *El Financiero*, March 14, 1995, 38.

15. Hermann Billinghausen, "Aguascalientes: Un dialogo en dos actos de la sociedad civil," *La Jornada*, March 31, 1995. In a later article in *La Jornada*, Billinghausen quoted a dancer who told him, "Here we are playing the war of the peace. Here is the thunderbolt. Can you imagine what would happen if we won the war of the war and we remained here?"

16. Julio Cesar Lopez, Pedro Matias, and Guillermo Correa, "Army digging in, violate international laws of war and national conventions of peace," *Proceso* 962, (April 10, 1995): 6.

17. In this same release, it was reported that the Clinton administration authorized $64 million of sophisticated electronic equipment and UH-6 Blackhawk helicopters for the control of narcotraffic. Yet according to the *New York Times* re-

port, cited in the *Global Exchange* release, both Republican and Democratic officials covered up evidence of the trading.

18. Carlos Figueros, "El Ejercito Mexicano aterroriza y asesina civiles en Chiapas," *El Financiero*, March 13, 1995, 42.

19. Figueros, "El Ejercito Mexicano," *El Financiero*, 42.

20. "Informe Especial," *El Financiero*, February 26, 1995, 26–27.

21. "Informe Especial," *El Financiero*, February 26, 1995, 55.

22. Global Exchange press report; *El Financiero*, March 13, 1995, a:17 and b:42, March 17.

23. Global Exchange 1997, *La Jornada*, October 29, 1997, 11–12.

24. Bishop Samuel Ruiz was quoted in *Proceso* as saying that the youths in the paramilitary Red Shirts were given drugs before their attack. Some were as young as fourteen and fifteen, and part of their training included pornographic videos.

25. Reflecting on the Zapatista army in the 1910 revolution, Steven Stern develops his thesis about domestic violence extending the indiscriminant abuse of women by the military into the home. By dividing the "good" women from the "bad," the army served to validate men's right to categorize and exploit the female population in these earlier wars (Stern 1995, 47).

9

At Home with the
Military-Industrial Complex

The launching of a preemptive strike against Iraq has revitalized the
military-industrial complex during the presidency of George W.
Bush. What appears to be a continuing war against terrorism extends
U.S. intervention throughout the world, raising military costs with ever-
spiraling demands for weapons, threatening social programs at home
and in dominated territories. A year after the outbreak of the war in Iraq,
I returned to my fieldwork site in Pittsfield, Massachusetts, where the
General Electric plant was a center for the military-industrial complex
during the Reagan Cold War of the 1980s. An invitation to a conference
on War and the State in 2004 inspired me to visit some of the Pittsfield
Vietnam veterans whom I had interviewed in the 1980s, raising questions
about the impact at home of military intervention in international affairs.
Based on my research in the 1980s, I have argued that the militarization
of society breaks down the social fabric of communities that are host to
the armaments industry, distorting economic priorities and threatening
the very values for which the administration pretends to be fighting. The
growing dependence on the production of military orders distorted economic priorities in the 1980s, leaving Pittsfield a brownfield area when
General Electric closed the plant at the end of the decade. The incipient
critique of imperialist wars by Vietnam veterans was for some silenced
as they became incorporated as patriots more than a decade after their return. Others remain bitter about the recourse to war by those "who push
the buttons" and send young men and women to fight the wars they provoke. Returning to that same field site over twenty years later I saw the

transition from a military-industrial complex that recognized distinct spheres of policy during the Cold War, to a fusion of corporate, Pentagon, and U.S. government command structures that has erased the line between civilian and military life. In waging the war in Iraq, corporate principles governing the globalization of the economy, including privatization of many military operations and outsourcing of the workforce to lower production costs and pursue services such as interrogation of prisoners without congressional oversight, have increased the contradictions that pervade military expenditures and operations. While these new features of war may serve the power elite in their desire to evade redistributive processes and congressional oversight, they are diminishing the patriotic commitment of both the military and civilian sectors. As Washington becomes the control center of an emerging American empire they are losing the hegemonic commitment that once commanded patriotic sacrifices as they promote fear and hatred at home and abroad.

* * *

The military-industrial complex about which President Dwight Eisenhower warned the American people upon leaving office in 1961 is renewing its control over the domestic economy with the emerging American empire. As commander of the Allied Forces in Europe during World War II, Eisenhower saw the intimate relations generated between arms-manufacturing corporations and military command structures. This was an extension of the close relationships between major corporations such as General Electric with the U.S. government that grew in World War I and persisted throughout World War II, the Vietnam and Korean wars, and the Cold War in the 1980s.

Since the attack on the World Trade Center on September 11, 2001, Washington has become the control center of a "war on terrorism" modeled on private corporate capitalism where the divisions between industry and government are erased and national and international rules are ignored. As the new command center called Homeland Security promotes new products to foil "terrorists," the Bush regime promotes militaristic solutions to all foreign relations, justifying the restriction of social welfare programs as necessary sacrifices for national security.

The militarization of society brings home to the United States the violations of human rights that were an export to the Asian perimeter, Central America, and the Middle East in the past half century of intermittent wars. As Catherine Lutz and Donald Nonini argue (2003, 73), the use of violence reinforces the political economy of the state with its own institutional force. The priority given to war as a means of countering terrorism serves to advance the growing imperial power of the United States while threatening domestic polity and society. The "contradictory fusion" as David Harvey (2003, 26) calls it, of a politics based on national territorial identity and the commitment of its population to defend capitalist accumulation worldwide threatens both national and imperial integrity.

I shall argue that the fusion of corporate, Pentagon, and U.S. government command structures used in the Bush strategy of waging war and reconstructing Iraq exacerbates distortions in the domestic political economy, while threatening the American way of life more than any previous war. The privatization of the military-industrial complex in accord with the dominant corporate model exceeds that of the Vietnam and the Cold War of the Reagan and Bush Senior years, further alienating the American citizenry from the political process by the violence committed in their name. Disregard for the safety of American troops who have been put in harm's way on the basis of mendacious claims of an Iraqi threat to national security is now compounded with the corruption of major corporations claiming to serve the troops for superinflated profits. Other contradictions in the shadows of the new military engagement abound.[1] At the same time that George W. Bush claims to be waging war for liberty and democracy in the Middle East, he is depriving immigrants and citizens held as terrorist suspects in other offshore sites of their constitutional rights, and is negating the Geneva Conventions of War regarding captives held in the Iraqi prison Abu Ghraib. Structural violence[2] is increasing as public funds are diverted from health care, education, and public infrastructure to waging war. The privatization of the American economy and polity is creating a permanent underclass that has little opportunity or even hope for realizing the American dream except by joining the military. In accord with global strategies, outsourcing military operations to minimize wage costs and evade congressional scrutiny carries to an extreme the corporate ethos of liberty premised on maximizing profits and competitive advantage.

I shall explore the impact of militarization in the city of Pittsfield, where I studied the buildup of the military-industrial complex in the 1980s, and relate this to current trends in the war on Iraq. Interviews I conducted in 1983 with veterans who fought in World War II and the Korean and the Vietnam wars and return visits in December 2002 to question veterans about the present conflict in Iraq provide a context for analyzing the contradictions in the growing fusion of militarism and the state. The generation forced to fight the Vietnam War questions the validity of military action in Iraq, but differs in the courses they would take to redeem the political process. They have seen a decline in the city's economy when the General Electric Company phased out the

Figure 9.1.   Once the heartland of armaments production during the Cold War of the 1980s, Pittsfield has become a brownfield for chemicals dumped in the community by General Electric.

Power Transformer Division in 1989, finally closing Ordnance Systems by 1990 and withdrawing most other production units by the turn of the millennium. Pittsfield was stigmatized as a brownfield area,[3] contaminated by PCBs that General Electric dumped in the Housatonic River from the 1930s until the 1980s.

With the military orders generated by Bush's war on terrorism, economic growth has turned to military production, but on a far reduced scale than in past wars. General Dynamics Advanced Information Systems, a Pittsfield company that picked up military contracts when GE closed its Ordnance Division, is increasing its workforce from six hundred to eight hundred people to produce programs for submarines that fire Trident ballistic missiles and those launching Tomahawk cruise missiles

(*Berkshire Eagle* July 4, 2004). The Pentagon awarded another contract to a Pittsfield firm, Protech Armored Products, which has grown substantially in the last year to employ 139 workers making protective armor plates used by soldiers in combat. Yet in comparison with thousands who worked in the General Electric Ordnance Division during the 1980s, few opportunities for high-wage employment exist for Pittsfield High School graduates. Some enlisted in greater numbers in the military (*Berkshire Eagle* June 13, 2004) in the early years of the war as the city tied its future to the military-industrial complex, but in the following year the growing antipathy to the war lessened enlistments.

Pittsfield's buildup of ordnance during the 1980s and 1990s illustrates how the application of information technology to defense technology fostered the merging of the domestic and military command structures. The decline of peacetime production in the transformation to high-tech defense industries created distortions in the domestic political economy played out in Pittsfield and other U.S. cities during the Cold War. Lucrative government defense contracts allowed General Electric to farm out civilian production of power transformers to the U.S. South and Canada. Many employees were transferred to Ordnance Systems, producing high-technology military equipment until the U.S. Congress ruled out cost-plus contracts in Reagan's second term. In the 1980s when General Electric in Pittsfield no longer generated super profits, the company closed Ordnance Systems, laying off thousands of workers. By the end of the decade, Pittsfield had become a ghost town, haunted by contaminates dumped in the Housatonic River and host to drug dealers and petty criminals who typically inhabit brownfields.

The fusion of corporate and U.S. government command structures in the Homeland Security department during the current war on terrorism limits the positive spillover in the economy that characterized previous wars. Lucrative contracts for surveillance technology, weapons, army uniforms, etc., are not providing stable jobs covered by union contracts as was the case in past wars. Following the bottom line principles of corporations, production, services, and even intelligence operations often go to offshore companies that are not subject to taxation or regulation. The mounting contradictions resulting from the shadows of the war now threaten domestic stability. Structural violence within the nation, caused by the diversion to the military of public funds for health care, education, and local police and fire services, increasingly alienates a population called upon to fight on foreign soil. Pittsfield teachers, firemen, and police read of the billions of dollars going to pay for services in Baghdad and express their outrage in letters to the local press. The extended tours of duty on foreign land now required of National Guard troops threatens the security of the homeland the government claims to protect.

THE PROCESS OF MILITARIZATION: A CASE STUDY

I chose Pittsfield, Massachusetts, as the site for my study of the impact of a multinational corporation on community in the 1980s because of its hundred-year history of electrical industry. I soon learned the significance of military production on industrial growth. Pittsfield's first industrial production of textiles and weapons began in the War of 1812 with England when mercantile interests on the New England coast and southern cotton plantation owners rejected the revolutionary government's declaration of war. Pittsfield's mills and forges provided uniforms and rifles for U.S. soldiers and sailors. Following the war, and especially after the Tariff Act of 1824, the "infant industries" that helped supply the federal army developed into major textile industries. Tanneries, textiles, and iron forges grew along with the military needs of the nation for uniforms, blankets, and weapons during the Civil War (Nash 1989).

In 1883 the transition from textile production occurred in Pittsfield with the Stanley Electrical Manufacturing Company producing alternating current power transmission. The incorporation of the company with J. P. Morgan financiers in 1891 allowed it to expand capital investment and the workforce a hundredfold. This attracted the attention of the General Electric Company, which bought the firm in 1903 when there were 1,700 employees working in a plant valued at $4 million (Boltwood 1916). The workforce again expanded from 1,700 to 6,000 workers during World War I. The rise in demand for electrical machinery throughout the nation generated more growth in the interwar years.

The emergent corporate philosophy, drawing on the ideology of the social-Darwinian struggle for survival of the fittest, promoted unconstrained competition, which helped coalesce corporate hegemony during the first half century of its growth from the 1880s to 1930s. But the failure to provide even a modicum of security or redistribution of the rising fortunes led to labor unrest. Employees in Pittsfield's GE plant joined workers throughout the nation in 1916 as they carried out strikes for shorter hours, higher wages, and social security benefits. Despite the unity of the movement, workers failed to gain a negotiated union contract.

The Great Depression of 1929 catapulted the leaders of industry and the government into action. Gerard Swope, who was president of General Electric during this period, also served along with chief executive officers of General Motors and the Ford Company as an adviser to the president Franklin Roosevelt, developing the "welfare capital" strategy of secure employment for skilled workers. John D. Rockefeller and Walter Teagle of Standard Oil accepted the Wagner National Labor Relations Board and Social Security Acts that were drafted and legislated during Roosevelt's administration (Nash 1989). In return these big and growing industrial corporations were ensured free trade for the intensified export business (James 2002, 134). The decisions were made not out of the beneficence of leading industrialists but because of the constant pressure from labor organizations that hastened the implementation of social welfare policies for the predominantly male white workforce in well-paid, stable employment.

The New Deal policies instituted by Franklyn Delano Roosevelt rescued working families during the depths of the Great Depression. It was not until World War II, however, that employment opportunities improved and working families were able to look forward to the mobility of their children. The workforce in the Pittsfield GE plant doubled during the war, producing automated panel controls for battleships and airplanes, communication instruments, and other high technology. Patriotism was at a high level, making the no-strike clause in the labor contract, with wages geared to cost-of-living increases, more acceptable.

In the postwar period, demand for consumer products and domestic power generators that had been delayed during the war years kept up production for two decades. Flexible production was a stated aim of the General Electric Corporation from the 1950s (General Electric 1953–1959, vol. 1: 43). Each division was to be judged in terms of its own record of profit and investment, giving power to corporate headquarters to deploy investments, with the accounting department the whip in the operation. The new accounting strategy provided the rationale for relocating low-profit production units like the small appliance division to nonunion towns as large-scale power transformer production and the more lucrative military contracts paying higher wages were awarded to the northern plants during the Korean War. It also provided the rationale for opening up plants in southern "right-to-work" states that later moved offshore.

Following the new corporate principles based on separate accounting for each division, General Electric relocated the Pittsfield Power Transformer Division production to Sun Belt nonunion states after the protracted 1969 strike. Production in General Electric's Pittsfield plant shifted to cost-plus contracts for army ordnance systems during the Cold War of the 1980s. These contracts included antiballistic missiles and the gearshift for the Bradley fighting vehicle. Because government contracts required strict compliance with affirmative action in employment, the Ordnance Department began to employ women and minorities in high-level jobs, often for the first time.

The Ordnance Systems Division for government production of weapons proclaimed their preeminence in the Pittsfield trinity of GE production units in 1979 with the 75th anniversary issue of the *GE Pittsfield News*. On a golden September day I joined fourteen thousand GE workers in a tour of the plant on its annual Family Day. Children could don a battle suit and enter a tot-sized Bradley Fighting Vehicle to experience what their fathers and mothers made while away from home. Toylike replicas of the Trident and Polaris missiles in pastel colors were on display, and visitors were also entertained with videos of the missile systems in action, a never-failing display of Polaris and Nikon antiballistic missiles demolishing "the enemy" in mid-trajectory. Although the GE Pittsfield News (September 15, 1979, Family Day 75th Anniversary Souvenir Issue) addressed the security workers' win through such production, Pittsfield was in fact rated as the number eight target for "the enemy" (read the Soviet Union).

The priorities of the Reagan Cold War of the 1980s are reflected in the employment in the three divisions. Power Transformer that once employed five thousand workers was down to nine hundred employees in 1988, while Ordnance had grown from a few hundred following the Korean War to five thousand. This was virtually a complete reversal of the proportion of those in civilian and war production at the end of the 1960s. Plastics Research and Development never developed according to plans to position Pittsfield as part of a tripartite global enterprise with plants in Bergen Op Zoom and Australia because of the growing threats to petroleum resources needed for this fledgling industry.[4]

Despite the benefits that Pittsfield derived from war production in the 1980s, the billions of dollars in government funds did little to stimulate employment levels nationally. Fewer jobs are created for each billion dollars spent on military investment compared with education or public transportation (DeGrasse 1984), and high bids with cost overruns became the norm (Melman 1983). Accounts of fraud, waste, and corruption by military contractors further distorted the economy throughout the Reagan regime.[5] Linked to the shift to high-tech defense production in the 1980s there was a corresponding change in the workforce from blue collar workers to "steel-collar robots," the famous automated production related to intensive production (SEC K10 Report Monthly Labor Review, September 1982, cited in Nash 1989).

Peace alternatives to defense production were supported nationally by some clothing and textile unions and the public employees unions. Though the local International Union of Electrical Employees (IUE) occasionally hosted delegations of their European counterparts who favored conversion to peace production, the members were well aware that it was only in defense-related production that Pittsfield had recovered from the 1982 recession. The IUE did not support John Kerry's bid for the Senate in October 1984 because of his opposition to the Bradley Fighting Vehicle, the Trident 1, and Trident 2, all made in Pittsfield (Berkshire Eagle November 3, 1984).

Although there was no collective action against military production by the union, individual workers chose to work in the Power Transformer Division rather than take higher paying jobs in Ordnance because they opposed making weapons of destruction. Pittsfield citizens who carried out a silent vigil in Park Square each year on Hiroshima day were primarily women and adolescents, some of whom defied parents who were managers in GE Ordnance Systems. Community activities such as the schools were influenced by the leadership roles undertaken by GE managers. For example, when the Berkshire League of Women Voters was denied the use of the school auditorium for a talk on the proliferation of nuclear weapons, people guessed that it was because four of the five school committee members who voted against it were employed at GE Ordnance Systems.

The military-industrial complex thus achieved a hegemonic agreement in Pittsfield from World War II through the U.S. intervention in the Far East until the Vietnam War. For American workers and their sons, and increasingly daughters, who fought the wars, military service was still considered an episode in which peace remained the objective. Veterans were welcomed home, given scholarships through the GI Bill for college enrollment, and were honored throughout their lives. The army did not lack volunteers, and there was no organized protest against the draft until the Vietnam War.

In the 1980s I found the most consistent sentiments against military solutions to international problems among veterans of Pittsfield (Nash 1989, 233–44). Although I had anticipated this from the Vietnam Veterans of America who were conscripted to fight an unpopular war, I also heard strong ambivalence about resorting to war among veterans of the Korean War and World War II (Nash 1989). Solidarity among veterans was strong and units vied to lead their buddies in Memorial Day and July Fourth parades. In a city where blacks were only 2 percent of the population, the American Legion Post was named after a black man who worked as a handyman so he could do volunteer work with veterans. Leaders of the veterans' organizations who spoke at the gravesites of soldiers who had fallen in battle emphasized their commitment to preserving the peace and avoiding future wars.

The unity of veterans was broken with the Vietnam War. Veterans of Foreign Wars rejected Vietnam veterans when they attempted to gain entry. This affront and the failure on the part of the federal government to recognize service-related medical problems led to mobilization of hundreds of Vietnam veterans in Berkshire County. In the early 1980s, particularly following the hostage crisis when President Reagan welcomed home the Americans held as hostages in Iran, Pittsfield's Vietnam veterans began to organize themselves. Larry Caprari joined a few other Vietnam veterans to start the Pittsfield chapter of the Vietnam Veterans Association in 1982 in an attempt to gain the benefits that World War II and

Korean War veterans had received: college tuition, health benefits for service-related illnesses, and psychological counseling. He told me that upon their return, veterans seeking help for problems related to chemical exposure had to prove that they were in areas sprayed with Agent Orange. The army had for years refused to admit this defoliant caused any damage until the correlation with cancer and genetic breakdown in reproduction became incontrovertible (Nash 1989, 249).

Larry's statement, made back in 1983 when I first talked with veterans' groups, sums up the shock of returning home to find themselves greeted, not as heroes as other veterans had been, but as pariahs.

> I think that what has happened with the Vietnam veterans is that we were under a lot of pressure in a very jungle-like environment. We had people who were not distinguished as enemies. We've seen kids with grenades on their bodies—little kids that you would like to go up to and say "hi" to. The main thing about unconventional warfare, you think of wading through jungles with rice paddies and shells going off and trip wires, and you become very paranoid. Now one day you're in the jungle, and the next day you're in the streets of Pittsfield. (Nash 1989, 249)

Jim Calahan expressed that same sense of alienation in December 2003 when I returned to Pittsfield to talk with Vietnam veterans. I wanted to get a sense of what they felt about the current Iraq war. Jim was waiting in the storefront office of the Vietnam Veterans Association on North Street, along with Larry Caprari and another veteran who helped form the organization. Jim reflected on his mustering out days thirty years before:

> I first tried to join the Veterans of Foreign War. They refused because, they told me, I wasn't a veteran. Honest to God, they said that! Because they considered the Vietnam War was a mistake because we lost the war. And I didn't try again for a long, long time. I think it was 1984 when I joined here. When I just got back from 'Nam, I just forgot all about everything. I forgot anything about being a veteran. It took me a long time before I got over that.

The government was in denial for two decades about desperately needed psychological counseling and exposure to the pesticide Agent Orange. Even when the government finally allowed medical compensations to veterans affected by Agent Orange, there was no punitive action against the chemical companies or the government that had released these toxic substances in the war. Larry told me back in 1983,

> It was a compassionate settlement to the Vietnam Veterans, not a settlement of guilt. It didn't really help. I kind of look at it personally—like Richard Nixon. He never admitted he was guilty, but he resigned from office. And I think the chemical companies did the same thing. . . . The cash settlement, I

think, shows that they feel they were guilty. A lot of Vietnam veterans
wanted to see them go into court because of the press it would get.

The settlement did not satisfy the veterans' claims for justice, even though
the complicity of the military-industrial complex in blaming the veterans
for what was required of them in battle was being aired in public for the
first time. In 1982 Vietnam veterans marched in the Memorial Day parade,
dressed in battle gear in contrast with the dress uniform of the American
Legion and Veterans of Foreign Wars. Congressmen such as Silvio Conti
picked up on the fact that veterans were becoming a political force, but
they limited their support to finding the soldiers missing in action rather
than addressing the structural violence to which they had been subjected
in wartime exposure to Agent Orange. Desperately needed psychological
counseling was not forthcoming from army officials, who were eager to
forget the whole war. The incipient revolt of Vietnam veterans to "get to
the men who press the buttons" in order to influence the government's
decisions against waging future wars was silenced. As August Carbonella
(2003) reflects on his and other Vietnam veterans' experience, the "libera-
tionist and anti-imperialist sentiments and politics of the radical U.S. soldiers were often silenced."

In 1987 while I was finishing my book on the construction of the military-industrial society (Nash 1989), the Pittsfield Ordnance Systems was
the most important division. That year General Electric closed the Power
Transformer Division, joining Westinghouse to produce large transformers in Canada. The reason given was "cost control." Not only did Pittsfield
have a reputation as a militant union town, but also GE could cut costs in
Canada where medical insurance was supplied by the host country. By the
end of the decade, Pittsfield was left with little more than the industrial
wastes that had accumulated in Silver Lake and the Housatonic River.

By the end of the millennium, Pittsfield had become a shadow of its former industrial presence in Berkshire County. It has lost over ten thousand
residents, most of them in the prime productive age group. It has a high
crime rate, with eight murders committed in 2003 alone. The drug trafficking in the Springfield area moved west as drifters took up residence in
low-cost rental units that owners had not been able to sell when they
moved away. The prevalence of single mothers in Pittsfield attempting to
make a living on their own or with welfare has loomed into a national
problem, as a 2003 best seller, *Growing up Fast,* by Joanna Lipper, demonstrates in the narratives of six teenage mothers in Pittsfield. The author attributes the plight of the women to economic decline, and there is abundant evidence for this. Indeed, the rising incidence of crime and drug
abuse in the city and region is a condition often related to unemployment.
But what is happening in Pittsfield is more systemic. It involves the loss

of a collective ethic, a fragmentation of the social fabric that leads to drugs, crime, and a boom-and-bust war economy that causes the breakup of neighborhoods and families. The apolitical stance of many of Pittsfield's citizens stems in part from the sense of injustice that they were the ones to bear the burden of guilt for overseas military misadventures condoned by politicians.

The Pittsfield story is not unusual in the annals of U.S. industrial history. The movement to the South and overseas broke the hegemonic compact related to capital accumulation and accepted by workers in exchange for stable, well-paid jobs. Similar instances can be found in Schenectady when it lost the Singer plant that had stabilized production (Newman 1988), and in the flatlands of upstate New York (Doukas 2003), where Remington, the dominant employer, lost out to overseas competition. The particular distortions related to militarization that we find in Pittsfield are often ignored in the narratives of transformation from a "Fordist regime" ensuring the general welfare of the economy to "flexible production." The Reagan-Bush regimes perfected a formula of military production for a Cold War with deficit spending and cost-plus contracts that could appease American workers' desire for stable, well-paid employment. Demand for armaments seemed infinite, since "the enemy" was unseen and omnipresent given the assumption that the USSR was spreading Communism throughout the world. The Central American revolutions labeled as Communist inspired added a stimulus to deficit spending for pork-barrel requisitions approved by Congress for the "dirty wars" in Salvador and Nicaragua. And with deficit spending, the budget seemed unlimited. General Electric was a willing partner, so long as they were able to get cost-plus contracts for ordnance production.

But when Congress began to exercise control over the burgeoning armaments budget toward the end of Reagan's term, the party was over. Pittsfield and other cities experiencing a decline in armaments production suddenly lost not only the companies that seemed to ensure their future but also the small service companies and institutions that ensured a superior welfare level. Workers realized their worst fears that military production was tied to a boom-and-bust economy, and that its future was jeopardized by the debt incurred in the production process itself.[6]

THE AMERICAN EXPERIENCE IN WARS

Spending in warfare reveals the crucial link between the government and the military-industrial complex. Pittsfield's General Electric workers told me that what got the United States out of the Great Depression was not Roosevelt's welfare policies or the Works Progress (renamed Projects in

1939) Administration—but rather the war economy that promoted factory production even before the United States declared war in 1941. During World War II, 39 percent of the workforce was employed in the defense industry. These workers were released for "peacetime" production of consumer goods until the advent of the Korean and Vietnam wars when defense production rose to 9.8 percent of the labor force. With its present employment of 627,000 civilians, the U.S. military industry is rebuilding to 1980s Cold War levels of 5.7 percent of the labor force, and the defense industry as a whole now employs 3 million, comprising 3.5 percent of the labor force (Hedges 2003, 1–5).

In World War II the U.S. government spent $3 trillion, and from post–World War II to the end of the millennium another trillion was expended on the Korean War, the Vietnam War, and the first Gulf War (Hedges 2003, 1–5). As for the cost of the present war there have been few comprehensive assessments since April 16, 2003, when Defense Comptroller Dov Zakheir briefed the press on the Pentagon's estimates. To that date, the war had cost between $10 billion and $12 billion in military operations plus $9 billion in the first three and one-half weeks of conflict. In July 2003 Secretary of State Donald Rumsfeld testified before the Senate Armed Services that the war cost $3.9 billion a month. A year later the estimated expenditure rose to $5 billion a month and remained at that level long after the declaration of peace in June 2003. By June 2004, when the U.S. Congress approved $25 billion more, the war expenditures surpassed $200 billion (*Berkshire Eagle* June 3, 2004), a figure cited by Democrats during the presidential campaigns in the fall of 2004.

These expenditures on the military promote dependency of the domestic population on the military for jobs and profits generated by the war. This reinforces, as Brecht dramatically affirms in his play, *Mother Courage*, the commitment of noncombatants to the military presence and to the war long after they forget why it is being fought. But the Iraq war exceeds past wars in the degree to which many service-related functions in supply, engineering, and maintenance, allowing multinational firms such as Halliburton, Bechtel, and their subsidiaries such as Kellogg Brown and Fox, to expand their operations with the expectations of huge profits in the Middle East. But these expenditures made outside the country do not stimulate the national economy since they employ foreign workers and suppliers. The army itself is dependent on outsourcing for its troops. Fearing the political impact of compulsory conscription, the universal draft was ended after the Vietnam War, and the army itself has become privatized with volunteers drawn into the service for money and the promise of health care and education. The first Gulf War launched by Bush Senior in 1991 was a preview of the new mode of high-technology warfare with low-military and high-civilian casualties. It allowed the army to test in action the antiballistic missiles and other technology developed during the preceding decade.[7]

Under George W. Bush's leadership, the military-industrial complex is more closely wedded to government than ever, with political functionaries moving from command positions in the corporate hierarchy to serve these same interests as defense specialists and security advisers or from military to civilian posts in Bush's cabinet. Vice President Cheney is one of several former executives who left a lucrative post in private corporations, in his case Halliburton, to join the Bush war team, and Colin Powell changed his hat from that of a retired general to secretary of state. Edward C. Aldridge Jr. exemplifies the revolving door between the Pentagon and corporations (*New York Times* June 29, 2004). He worked under Defense Secretary Rumsfeld until 2003 and now sits on the board at Lockheed Martin, which gets more than $20 billion a year in military contracts, and he also serves on the space advisory commission. The reconstruction of Iraq extends the functions of the national security forces including the army and National Guard to defend the operation of private corporations making extraordinary profits. Although the justification for profits used to be cast as the price for taking risk, in this war U.S. AID provides insurance against takeovers to private investors in a turbulent political domain that private insurance operators refuse to enter.

Defense Secretary Rumsfeld, who served in Bush Senior's administration, has run the war on strict corporate principles. He has given priority to privatization of the contracts regulating army supplies and deployment, and has created a mercenary army recruited on market principles of wages and benefits for soldiers engaged in military action. Like corporations, the army emphasizes technological over human intervention in the deployment of force and prefers outsourcing of ancillary operations. This latter strategy allows multinational firms based in the United States such as Halliburton, Bechtel, and their subsidiaries to expand their operations with contract employees for construction and maintenance work. Those who work in more sensitive employment as security forces and prison interrogators hired by Titan and CACI get as much as $1,500 a day. These strategies, however, have reduced the ability of the army to recruit soldiers into the new volunteer army since the annual base pay of $13,000 is noncompetitive with the privately employed forces. Even with perks amounting to $24,000 and lures of education, travel, and health benefits the army has falling rates of recruitment and is taking the unusual step of direct advertising to high school students to recruit more foot soldiers.

With the onset of the war in Iraq, arms contractors have proliferated. Chalmers Johnson (2003, 56) provides details of the following outsources with DynCorp, which operated in Bosnia: Science Applications International Corporation of San Diego, BDM International of Fairfax, Virginia, Armor Holdings Inc. of Jacksonville, Florida, Cubic Applications Inc. of Lacey, Washington, DFI International of Washington, D.C., and International Charter Inc. of Oregon. These companies employed thousands of engineers and managers earning high salaries. DynCorp provides personal protection for President Hamid Karzai of Afghanistan and was scheduled to take over the training of the Iraqi troops when the Green Berets leave. The sales of these companies, linked in their own trade group called the International Peace Operations Associations, are expected to reach $202 billion by 2010 (Johnson 2003, 56). With the privatization of intelligence, the secretary of defense and the Pentagon can expect less criticism of citizens concerned with human rights abuses, including torture.

The Pentagon now follows the corporate model of "do only what you do best" and leaves the rest to subcontractors.[8] U.S. troops are serviced by private contractors that provide meals, laundry, and other maintenance services. Among the most privileged suppliers are Kellogg Brown and Root (KBR), which has a ten-year, multibillion-dollar contract to provide the military with "logistical support." Peter Singer of the Brookings Institute estimates there is one private contractor for every ten foreign soldiers in Iraq, ten times the private ratios in the Gulf War (*Berkshire Eagle* October 30, 2003). During combat, these privately employed workers have on occasion refused to carry out their duties even though they receive almost two times the compensation of the soldiers. Soldiers complain about the tasteless food and inadequate water—they get only 1.5 liters of water a day—that lowers morale, and may contribute to the high noncombat death rate among U.S. troops. Paul Krugman reports that at least one soldier died of heat exhaustion (*Berkshire Eagle* August 13, 2003). Despite the apparent advantages enjoyed by private enterprises in the war theater, Halliburton was considering putting an end to its war contracts.

In addition to U.S. private merchants providing meals, cleaning services, and the upkeep of troops, Homeland Security is using the services of offshore industries for intelligence work. The *Washington Post* (reprinted in the *Daily Hampshire Gazette* October 18, 2003) reported that Bush has signed a contract with Ben H. Bell in the Bahamas-based Global Information Group to assess large databases of international records. Lexis-Nexis Group has signed up for analysis of passenger records in U.S. air terminals. The procedures of these companies differ from information processing by government agencies since they operate in secrecy overseas and are not regulated by public legal protections and rules. Peter Swire, a law professor at Ohio State University, said in the *Washington Post* interview that "this might meet business interests, but not necessarily the public interest."

In addition to the offshore sourcing in intelligence gathering, the U.S. Army sends military instructors to trouble spots throughout the world to train foreign troops in advanced methods of counterinsurgency. Chalmers Johnson (2003, 55) estimates that each year the United States trains one hundred thousand foreign soldiers in satellites and dependencies throughout the world. This is, he remarks, "a little like a corporation turning to one of its subsidiaries to fulfill its labor requirements." It has the added advantage of maintaining a low profile for high casualty operations since "the death of foreign soldiers does not make news" (Johnson 2003, 56).

I asked Lesley Gill, who has researched the School of the Americas' graduates in Latin America, who constitutes these privatized military cadres operating in the global society, and she responded:

> Because the U.S. military is such an enormous, hydra-headed monster, it is very difficult to get a handle on the myriad ways that foreign militaries are trained and used by the United States. There are over 200 disclosed training centers in the United States and foreign trainees participate in all of them, but most of the training of Latin American security forces is now done by the 7th group of the Special Forces in Latin America via what are called "mobile training teams." The School of the Americas (SOA), which still receives a lot of attention, is really only a very small part of what the military training of Latin Americans is about today. And because of 10 years of pressure from a social movement, the SOA's worst practices have been exported to the jungles of Colombia and elsewhere. Nowadays, the importance of the SOA is less as a torture center than as an elite finishing school for up-and-coming, mid-level officers who come to the SOA to make connections. The US then hopes to have easy access to them once they become the heads. (Personal communication)

Once the SOA received a great deal of publicity, they began to polish their image, so that the kinds of operations they once carried out are now done by myriad smaller private companies privately contracting paramilitaries that are sent out all over the world.

The privatization of the war mimics the corporate model of ethnic and gender manipulation. Recent immigrants felt that they were preferentially selected for front-line combat. Mexican Americans, for example, perceived themselves to outnumber all ethnic groups in the advance troops entering Baghdad.[9] One of the strongest incentives for immigrants to enlist is the promise of citizenship. More than thirty-seven thousand noncitizens serve in the U.S. military, many of them deployed abroad. But many of these soldiers cannot manage to fulfill the bureaucratic obligations to complete the extensive process of application for citizenship, missing deadlines and failing to maintain the paper trail. As Tina Susman,

Newsday correspondent, reported, "The only surefire path to citizenship is getting killed in action" (reprinted in the *Miami Herald, International Edition*, February 1, 2004). Bush promises to remedy the bill, which does not take place until October 2004.

Just as in corporations, the army's implementation of affirmative action opens opportunities for women's advancement, allowing women to run the same risk of dying in battle as men. American women have participated more extensively in combat in Iraq than in any previous war in U.S. history. Women constitute 15 percent of active troops and 17 percent of reserves, which are now being called to the front at a greater rate than ever before (*Berkshire Eagle* December 16, 2003). Bush's team includes a race and color spectrum that is almost like a United Colors of Benetton advertisement, with Colin Powell and Condoleezza Rice proving the pluricultural democracy they preach.

The reconstruction process is attempting to re-create an Iraqi privatized economy modeled on the U.S. economy. Defense Secretary Rumsfeld made this explicit, stating, "Market systems will be favored, not Stalinist command systems" (*New York Times* January 10, 2004). Even before the much-touted democratic constitution for Iraq was written, the Coalition Provisional Authority ended restrictions on foreigners owning property and investing in Iraqi businesses. Nor do the investors have to reinvest profits back into the country. Their plans include selling 150 of the 200 state-owned enterprises, even including the Iraqi national airlines. According to the January 10, 2004, *New York Times* report this may violate international laws governing military occupation. The *Times* goes on to report that the United Nations Security Council states that the occupying forces should follow the Hague Regulations and the Geneva Convention, but adds that the coalition "should play an active role in administration and reconstruction." This contradiction is yet to be settled.

If one of the vaunted values of privatization is to incur efficiencies, the benefits of the corporate model are hard to see in Iraq. By November 2003 mainstream journals featured stories about the corrupt practices of companies operating in Iraq, noting that the largest contractors, Bechtel and Halliburton, acquired their contracts on a no-bid or limited-bid basis, bypassing Iraqi enterprises and dispensing with accountability to Congress (*Newsweek* November 3, 2003). Another free enterprise benefit sorely lacking is the increased flow of oil to the West. Not only has the war failed to increase oil supplies, the United States has had to subsidize 90 percent of oil supplies used in Iraq, a country with the second largest oil reserves in the world.[10] Moreover the ubiquitous charges of corrupt billing procedures indicate billions of dollars in fraud.[11] Since global insurance corporations have rejected the attempts by private corporations to insure themselves against takeovers by nationals in the countries in which they operate, the U.S. Agency for International Aid (US AID) is assuming that function at taxpayers' expense (*New York Times* January 10, 2004).

Yet for the Bush administration, there is one clear advantage in maintaining a high percentage of privatized functions in these foreign military adventures. Secrecy can be assured. When the resistance movement of the Iraqis increased in early April 2004, reporters could not find out what the "maintenance" workers hired by a private company were doing. Their actions are not scrutinized by Congress, and their dead do not add to the casualty lists that led to public outcries. It was not until photographs of Abu Ghraib prisoners being tortured were leaked to a reporter that the violations of human rights, often by private security guards, became public. When European nations became aware the United States was using police chambers in former Soviet satellite states the outcry increased in December 2005.

In their quest to maximize U.S. corporate gains in controlling the future of Iraq, President Bush has barred France, Germany, Russia, and other nations from the $18.6 billion U.S.-financed privatized reconstruction projects. Since these were among the countries that the administration was asking to assist in paying for the reconstruction, it seriously damaged old alliances and alienated new ones. As the editor of the *Berkshire Eagle* (December 13, 2003) opined, "War is hell, business is business."

Business is gaining momentum as the peace process plunders on. Commenting on the mounting disasters, James Galbraith (*U.S. Newsday* November 4, 2003) notes that the Paul Bremer economic plan "looks disastrous: a Morganthau Plan to deindustrialize Iraq masquerading as a Marshall Plan to rebuild it." He added that "the kind of Republican Party policy hacks [that] have been dumped on Iraq, unsupervised . . . are making economic decisions with reckless disregard for local sentiment." The simultaneous weakening of the U.S. economy with prolonged low interest rates, high debt, and low increments of employment even with the third quarter "recuperation" has led to Galbraith's prediction that the U.S. commitment to the reconstruction of Iraq is drastically overextending national resources. Military experts already see a drastic overstretching of U.S. troops.[12] The economic cost of the war in Iraq must be measured not only in the tens of billions of dollars spent there, but also the weakening of currency in relation to foreign exchange because of the rising debt burden. Bush's refusal to raise revenues with tax increases casts a pall on the entire economy now and in the future.

Iraq is proving that the high-technology warfare achieved by a privatized war machine might win a war, but it cannot secure the peace or reconstruct a nation. Like Humpty Dumpty, the breaking of civil society cannot be easily repaired once it has been pushed off the wall. The war continues unabated after President Bush's premature declaration of peace in May 2003 when he appeared in paratrooper's uniform on an aircraft carrier to announce the return of freedom to Iraq. The low point of the "postwar" construction came in late October, when repeated attacks on foreign missions and allied troops exposed the administration's attempts to downplay reports. The deadly attack on the Red Cross headquarters in central Baghdad on October 27, 2003, and the decision of Doctors without Borders to remove their teams a few months later, convinced other countries to stay out of Iraq. Long after Saddam Hussein was flushed out of a spider hole on December 16, 2003, and even after Iraq regained its sovereignty in June 2004, U.S. troops remain to ensure the safe conduct of oil. Mounting death tolls in 2005 topped two thousand U.S. soldiers dead, and well over one hundred thousand Iraqis, and the Bush "peace" process continues to claim the lives of U.S. soldiers and Iraqi civilians.

LOCAL IMPACT OF A GLOBAL WAR

Up until the mid-twentieth century, wars promoted employment and production that fostered industrial growth and prosperity. Industrialists were able to play on patriotism to induce the workforce to work overtime, often with little or no additional compensation, and to recruit volunteer armies during wartime. Although public funds fostered the growth of private capitalist ventures during wartime, public relations experts hired by corporations were able to revamp profits as risk capital justifying super profits made at taxpayers' expense. This hegemonic accord persisted until after World War II when the preemptive wars in Korea and Vietnam raised questions among youths drafted into wars that could no longer be billed as defensive. The billions of dollars pumped into the economy during these aggressions against Communism and the Cold War that followed in the 1980s have left little heritage for subsequent generations. Few new industries were cultivated as had occurred in the nineteenth up to mid-twentieth-century wars when declining numbers of union employees meant that there was little scope for the redistribution of war profits.

In the first two centuries of Pittsfield's history, war provided a stimulus to manufacturing and technological innovation with the General Electric plant providing high wage employment up until the end of the Cold War. The Iraq war growth now drains resources from the wider economy, and wages for production workers remain low, on average less than ten dollars an hour. Pittsfield's war workers now number in the hundreds, not even making a dent in the thousands laid off by General Electric. One of the few signs of economic revitalization came with a $40 million Pentagon contract for body armor to Pittsfield Protech Armored

Products. Senator Edward M. Kennedy, a leading opponent of the war in Iraq, was there to laud the "company that is in the vanguard of leading this nation in terms of this new technology . . . so that our servicemen and women are better protected." He received the dog tags of a Massachusetts soldier killed in Iraq whose parents promoted the equipment in memory of their son (*Berkshire Eagle* June 19, 2004). But the few hundred new jobs "created" by the naval signal systems contract for General Dynamics are not enough to revitalize the military-industrial complex (*Berkshire Eagle* July 25, 2004, D1, D3). Some thriving small businesses are taking the toll of National Guard forced service when the owner is called to duty in Iraq since they cannot hire anyone who could run the business. Few other cities have benefited from the billions of dollars worth of material and services for the war since much of the production is done through outsourcing, and the concomitant losses in goods and services for the peacetime economy are incalculable.

The future for the population of the city and for the nation is jeopardized most of all because of the way the corporations and their allies in government have squandered the patriotism and commitment of the workers and soldiers who served their communities and their nation. This is most apparent in the case of veterans who bore the brunt of the imperialist wars that were fought to control revolutionary uprisings in the Far East and in Central America during the 1960s and 1970s. The contradictions that Vietnam veterans lived as they were censured for doing what was required of them and what conformed to their own sense of patriotic duty caused some to turn against the political process itself. Jim Callahan told me during our interview in December 2003:

> When Desert war started, I was going back in. I actually started to go back in as a combat medic, but then the war ended. I did want to go back in. I felt I didn't save enough lives, I wanted to save more. I'm not saying I believe in our politics. Politics of Vietnam was stupid, wrong. We didn't need to go to war to lose money and to lose lives. Big business made money. General Electric. Anyone who made weapons made money. The poor guy who graduated from high school anytime from '65 to '69 went into the service and he was scared about it. I took care of the guys who cared about it. And they just pushed us out there and didn't care about us. And I don't want politicians; I detest politicians with a passion.

While Jim's commitment to soldiers made him want to return to battle, it was not in support of the war. It was to help save more lives put into harm's way by politicians. Bill, on the other hand, supported the first Gulf War and defended the current battle as a job that had to be done quickly or else abandoned, "I don't have a problem going back there and doing what we're doing. I think it's the right thing to do. There's no more massacres, there's no more torture chambers." He believes in letting them "take back their own government, and get the hell out of there. If we have to go back there again, [we should] make it into a parking lot."

I asked Larry if he felt the same, and he said, looking uncomfortable, "Well I'm a liberal." Later, he added, "Well, I just don't believe in the war, and I don't think it should have been started. That's my own opinion." Bill interjected, saying "We will find the WMDs," but Larry rejoined, "Your definition of mass destruction and mine might be different. Anyway, I wouldn't have started the war, and I wouldn't walk across the street for George Bush."

Vietnam veterans were forced to bear the burden of an unpopular war themselves. Too young to vote or even to order a drink at a bar, they fought a war that made little sense to them and that earned them the epithet of "baby killers." Some, like Jim, have turned against the political process itself, rejecting the politicians who seemed responsible. Others, like Bill, see war as a necessary job that should be carried out as quickly as possible or "pave it over and make a parking lot out of it," as Bill concludes. Larry urges negotiation and diplomacy through the United Nations.

The Vietnam War became a character-defining issue in 2004 for the major presidential candidates during the campaign. John Kerry was nominated by his war buddies but an adroit manipulation in Bush's advertisements turned his heroic record into an unpatriotic criticism of the war upon his return. Some Pittsfield citizens criticized Kerry for voting against the GE missile program in Congress during the 1980s and for the loss of defense contracts. Following Bush's victory on Armistice Day, November 11, 2004, Vietnam veterans were remembered by the mayor as "heroes then and now." The Pittsfield High School band joined veterans' organizations to march up South Street to Memorial Park, where those who sacrificed their lives in that war were honored along with those who died in Iraq.

Given the lack of civilian employment opportunities, Pittsfield High School graduates responded favorably to recruiters urging them to enlist in the armed services "to seek training and new challenges," at least until graduation in June 2004 (*Berkshire Eagle* June 13, 2004). But throughout 2005 recruiters were having trouble meeting their quotas despite pumped-up efforts to draw youngsters into the service by directly contacting those still in high school.

Young Americans who were not yet born when the rejection of the Vietnam War escalated in the 1970s may still be prompted by patriotism to enlist, but with private for-profit companies handling everything but the gunning down of the enemy contradictions arise. Soldiers may be court-martialed for carrying out orders of their superiors at the same time that security guards hired by private corporations such as CACI and Titan that provided the private interrogation teams in Abu Ghraib are unlikely to suffer any punishment. The evasion of public responsibility in the face of the many contradictions posed by privatization in the conduct of war for profit is a denial of the democratic process that threatens not only the national polity, but also the nascent global economy.

The culture of violence spawned by the U.S. military occupation in Iraq has taken on its own dynamic as the temporal and spatial boundaries between peace and war, military and civilian, and government and commerce have become blurred. This contradiction is at the root of Pittsfield veterans' reaction to the Iraq war and its precursor in Vietnam. The violence they are forced to commit against civilians and military prisoners abroad alienates some from the political process itself. These contradictions as of 2004 had little effect in shaping opinions for the election or the aftermath. Yet in the following year, amid the crumbling of confidence in an administration that seemed to be mired in an unending war, Pittsfield's citizens were mobilizing peace protests. Donald Lathrop who was active in the peace demonstrations of the 1980s (Nash 1989, 254) was out in the park with placards calling for an end to the war, and high school graduates in 2005 were rejecting the overtures of military recruiters.

NOTES

Paper presented at the Conference on War and the State, held in Bergen, Norway, in February 2004. I am indebted to participants in the conference, and to Charles Hale and to Lesley Gill for critical comments on earlier versions of the paper that have been incorporated in this version.

1. Carolyn Nordstrom (2004) paints a grim picture of what happens in the shadows cast by the new kind of counterinsurgency and low-intensity warfare ongoing in third world countries. In the preemptive attack on Iraq, the George W. Bush administration brings those conditions back home as it transformed the United States into a third world nation.

2. Susser and Patterson (2001) include in their anthology, *Cultural Diversity in the United States*, numerous case studies of structural violence exemplified in health hazards resulting from poverty, racial discrimination, and gender inequalities that are endemic in the structuring of poverty in capitalist America. I use the term *structural violence* to designate everyday deprivation of human needs for nutrition, shelter, and medical care that affect longevity and welfare, following Lutz and Nonini's (2003) definition.

3. *Brownfield* is the term applied to abandoned industrial sites that have suffered environmental contamination. When Pittsfield applied for EPA superfund cleanup for PCBs dumped by General Electric, they were warned that it would lower real estate values and cripple any future industrialization. They settled for

a few million dollars' cleanup of the river and miles of contaminated waste concealed under GE's parking lot (Nash 1985).

4. During the heady days of cost-plus contracts General Electric financed a Washington, D.C., headquarters with a staff of 120 at a cost of $1.3 million a year for rent alone. These "corporate beachheads," according to Edsall (*Washington Post*, reprinted in the *Berkshire Eagle,* June 8, 1985, cited in Nash 1989, 137), are designed "to mesh a private sector conglomerate with the public sector conglomerate—the U.S. government," with the goal of "manipulating the Washington market."

5. In order to fully appreciate Reagan's presidency, it should not be forgotten that when Reagan's acting career flagged in the 1950s he became a public relations emissary for General Electric. It was in this role that he attracted the attention of the Republican Party after which his political career flourished. Even though the Democratic Party is often felt to be more closely allied with Hollywood, it was the genius of the Republican Party to see that if one wanted a perfect flunky, hire an actor.

6. When Congress cut off defense funding for the increasingly unpopular war fighting revolutionaries in Central America, General Electric began to close down its Ordnance Division.

7. When I watched the Gulf War on television in Mexico City, the footage of antiballistic missiles rising in a perfect arch and always intercepting the enemy missiles, I felt I was back in Pittsfield's Ordnance Systems, watching the videos of Trident and Polaris used to promote sales to the Pentagon and aired on GE's Family Day. No guts were spilled, nor were there any offensive photos of prisoner abuse during that showing. No missile missed a target.

8. Chalmers Johnson details how these operations protect "our" interests, and those of our allies, while expanding armaments sales (2003, 55). The Vinnell Corporation, made up of retired American military officers, has, since 1975, been licensed by the government to train the Saudi National Guard to protect the monarchy. These corporations can be relied upon to train officers in foreign countries using U.S. technology, thus expanding the market for such weapons and providing a corps of sales agents to carry out the Foreign Military Sales Program supervised by the Department of Defense. Jim Krause, Associated Press correspondent, summarizes the many private contractors operating throughout the world in order to free up U.S. troops to fight (*Berkshire Eagle* October 30, 2003). These forms of outsourcing mimic the tactics of corporations in evading the regulations on employment and taxation that once ensured responsibility in U.S. society.

9. The Mexican press *La Reforma* picked up the story of the first soldier killed in the advance on Baghdad, a Mexican who joined so that he could get an education and become a citizen of the United States. His mother was quoted as deploring the high numbers of very young Mexicans along with her son in this first military engagement in Iraq when the army did not yet know whether they would be met by chemical or germ weapons of mass destruction.

10. The *Wall Street Journal* noted that the $8 billion no-bid contract awarded to Halliburton excited some criticism of Bush's vice president Richard Cheney, a former chief executive officer of the firm, leading to a congressional investigation that dismissed all the charges. Despite Halliburton's gains of $2 billion in revenue

and an increase of 12 to 13 cents per share in profit from business in Iraq, they are still mired in asbestos litigation and troubles in their Brazil operations. See Susan Warren and Alexei Barrionuevo, "Despite Iraq, Halliburton Profit Falls Short," *Wall Street Journal*, October 10, 2003.

11. Kellogg Brown and Root, a subsidiary of Halliburton, one of the largest private enterprises operating in Iraq and one in which Vice President Cheney occupied a leading position before becoming vice president, has been caught overcharging the U.S. government for fuel that they imported for the army from Kuwait, although the company disputes the charges, claiming that the company saved taxpayers $164 million (*Berkshire Eagle* December 12, 2003). See also Jackie Spinner, "Halliburton Subsidiary Defends Iraq Work," *Washington Post*, reprinted in the *Berkshire Eagle*, December 18, 2003.

12. Among the many paradoxes in Bush's war is the withdrawal of eight thousand troops from two Hawaii-based brigades of the 25th Infantry Division sent to Iraq and Afghanistan at a time when Bush's aggressive attacks renewed hostilities in North Korea, which claims to have the capacity to make weapons of mass destruction (*Miami Herald International Edition*, January 28, 2004).

References

Adams, Richard N. 1964. *Encuesta sobre la Cultura de los Ladinos en Guatemala*. Segunda Edición. Guatemala City: Seminario de Integración Social Guatemalteca, Centro Editorial "José de Pineda Ibarra." Ministerio de Educación Público.

Aguilera Peralta, Gabriel. 1980. "Terror and Violence as Weapons of Counterinsurgency in Guatemala." *Latin American Perspectives* 25 and 26, Spring.

Aguilera Peralta, Gabriel, and Jorgé Ramon Imery, et al. 1981. *Dialéctica del terror en Guatemala*. Guatemala: Editorial Universitaria Centroamericana.

Aguirre Beltran, Gonzalo. 1970. Los símbolos étnicos de la identidád nacional. *Anuario Indigenista* 30.

Albro, Robert. 2004. "The water is ours, carajo!" Deep Citizenship in Bolivia's Water War. In *Social Movements: A Reader*. Edited by June Nash. 249–71. Malden, Mass.: Blackwell Publishers.

Alecio, Rolando. 1995. "Uncovering the Truth: Political Violence and Indigenous Organizations." In *The New Politics of Survival*. Edited by Minor Sinclair. 25–46. New York: Monthly Review.

Alvarez, Sonia E. 1998. "Latin American Feminisms 'Go Global': Trends of the 1990s and Challenges for a New Millennium." In *Cultures of Politics, Politics of Culture: Re-visioning Latin American Social Movements*. Edited by Sonia Alvarez, Evelina Dagnino, and Arturo Escobar. 293–324. Boulder, Colo.: Westview Press.

Alvarez, Sonia, Evelina Dagnino, and Arturo Escobar, eds. 1998. *Cultures of Politics, Politics of Culture: Re-visioning Latin American Social Movements*. Boulder, Colo.: Westview Press.

Amin, Samir. 1970. "L'acumulación a l'échele mundiale." In *Critique de la théorie du sous-developpement*. Paris: Editions Antropos.

Appadurai, Arjun. 1996. *Modernity at Large: Cultural Dimensions of Globalization*. Minneapolis: University of Minnesota Press.

255

Arac, Jonathan, ed. 1986. *After Foucault: Humanistic Knowledge, Postmodern Challenges.* New Brunswick, N.J.: Rutgers University Press.

Arias Pérez, Jacinto. 1994. "Movimientos indígenas contemporaneos en el estado de Chiapas." In *El arreglo de los pueblos indios: La incansable tarea de reconstitución.* Edited by J. Arias Pérez. 379–99. Tuxtla Gutierrez, Chiapas: SEP, Instituto Chiapaneco de Cultura.

Asad, Talal. 1973. *Anthropology and the Colonial Encounter.* New York: Humanities Press.

Aubry, Andrés, and Angélica Inda. 1998. "Who Are the Paramilitaries in Chiapas? The War Within: Counterinsurgency in Chiapas and Colombia." *NACLA Report on the Americas* 31 (5):8–9.

AVANCSO (Asociación para el Avance de las Ciencias Sociales). 1990. *Politica institucional hacia el desplazado interno en Guatemala.* Cuadernos de Investigación 6.

———. 1994. *The War Within: Counterinsurgency in Chiapas and Colombia.* Guatemala City.

———. 2000. *Por los caminos de la Sobrevivencia campesina.* Las estrategías de producción y reproducción campesina en la zona cafetalera latifundista del Departamento de Sans Marcos. Cuadernos de Investigación 13. Guatemala City.

Babb, Florence. 1989. *Between Field and Cooking Pot: The Political Economy of Market Women in Peru.* Austin: University of Texas Press.

———. 2001. *After Revolution: Mapping Gender and Cultural Politics in Neoliberal Nicaragua.* Austin: University of Texas Press.

Bakunin, Mikhail Alexandrovich. 1972 (first published 1873). "State in Anarchy" (Staat en Anarchie). In *Bakunin on Anarchy. Selected Works by the Activist-Founder of World Activism.* Edited, translated, and introduction by Sam Dolgoff. New York.

Barkin, David. 1987. "The End to Food Self-Sufficiency in Mexico." *Latin American Perspectives* 14, no. 3 (Summer): 271–97.

Bartolomé, Miguel Alberto. 1994. "La repressión de la pluralidad: Los derechos indígenas en Oaxaca." In *Derechos Indígenas en la Actualidad.* 73–99. México, D.F.: UNAM, Instituto de Investigaciones Jurídica.

Bartra, Roger. 1982. "Capitalism and the Peasantry in Mexico." *Latin American Perspectives* 32, no. 9.

Beauvoir, Simone de. 1957. *The Second Sex.* Translated by H. M. Parshley. New York: Alfred A. Knopf.

Bedregal, Ximena. 1995. "Reflexiones desde nuestro feminismo." In *Chiapas: y las mujeres que?* Edited by Rosa Rojas. México, D.F.: Editorial Correa, Instituto de Investiación y Capacitación de la Mujer.

Bennholdt-Thomsen, Veronika. 1981. "Subsistence Production and Extended Reproduction." In *Of Marriage and the Market: Women's Subordination in International Perspectives.* Edited by Kate Young et al. 41–54. London: CSE Books.

Bennholdt-Thomsen, Veronika, Nicholas Faraclas, and Claudia Von Werlhof. 2001. *There is an Alternative: Subsistence and World-wide Resistance to Corporate Globalization.* London: Zed.

Billig, Michael, Susan Condor, Derek Edwards, Mike J. Gene, David Middleton, and Alan Ridley. 1988. *Ideological Dilemmas: A Social Psychology of Everyday Thinking.* London: Sage.

Blanchard, David. 1979. "Beyond Empathy: The Emergence of an Action Anthropology." In *Currents in Anthropology: Essays in Honor of Sol Tax*, 419–44. The Hague: Mouton.

Boltwood, E. 1916. *The History of Pittsfield, Massachusetts from the Year 1876 to the Year 1916*. Pittsfield, Mass.: Pittsfield Eagle Company.

Boot, Max. 2003. "The New American Way of War." *Foreign Affairs* 82, no. 41–58 (July/August).

Bourdieu, Pierre, and Loic J. D. Wacquant. 2002. *An Invitation to Reflexive Sociology*. Chicago: University of Chicago Press.

Bourque, Susan C., and Kay B. Warren. 1989. "Democracy without Peace: Cultural Politics of Terror in Peru." *Latin American Research Review* 24 (1): 7–34.

Bowie, Katherine. 2004. "The State and the Right Wing: The Village Scout Movement in Thailand." In *Social Movements: A Reader*. Edited by June Nash. 46–55. Malden, Mass.: Blackwell Publishers.

Brac de la Perrière, Bénédicte. 1998. "'Etre épousée par un *naq*.' Les implications du mariage avec l'esprit dans le culte de possession birman (Myanmar)." *Anthropologie et Sociétés* 22, no. 2: 169–82.

———. n.d. De l'élaboration de l'identité birmane comme hégémone à la laboration de l'identité birmane comme hégémone à travers le culte birman des 37 seigneurs.

Brown, R. Grant. 1915. "The Taungbyon Festival." *Journal of the Royal Anthropological Institute* 45.

Calder, Bruce J. 2004. "Interwoven Histories: The Catholic Church and the Maya 1940 to the Present." In *Resurgent Voices in Latin America: Indigenous Peoples, Political Mobilization, and Religious Change*. Edited by Edward L. Cleary and Timothy J. Steigenga. 93–124. New Brunswick, N.J.: Rutgers University Press.

Calder, Lendol. 1999. *Financing the American Dreams. A Cultural History of Consumer Credit*. Princeton, N.J.: Princeton University Press.

Carbonella, August. 2003. "Memories of Imperialism: The Figure of the 'Viet Nam' Veteran in the Age of Globalization." *Focaal: European Journal of Anthropology* 41.

Cardoso, Fernando H., and Enriquez Faletto. 1971. *Dependencia y desarrollo en América Latina*. Mexico, D.F.: Siglo XX.

Carmack, Robert M. 1983. "Spanish-Indian Relations in Highland Guatemala 1800–1944." In *Ethnic Relations and Indian Society in the Province of Guatemala*. Edited by M. Macleod. 215–52. Austin: University of Texas Press.

Castaneda, Quetzalcoatl. 1995. "The Program that Chose a Village." *Critique of Anthropology* 15, no. 2: 115–47.

Castells, Manuel. 1997. *The Information Age: Exonomy, Society and Culture. The Power of Identity*, vol. 2. Oxford, UK: Blackwell Press.

CEDOIN (Centro de Documentación e Información). 1986a. *Informe R*. July. La Paz, Bolivia.

———. 1986b. *Informe R*. September. La Paz, Bolivia.

Center for Human Rights "Fray Bartolomé de Las Casas." 1997. *Ni Paz Ni Justicia*. San Cristóbal de Las Casas.

———. 2005. *La política genocida en el conflicto armado en Chiapas: Reconstrucción de hechos, pruebas, delitos y testimonios*. San Cristóbal de Las Casas.

Clifford, James. 1988. *The Predicament of Culture: Twentieth Century Ethnography, Literature, and Art*. Cambridge, Mass.: Harvard University Press.

Clifford, James, and George Marcus, eds. 1986. *Writing Culture*. Berkeley: University of California Press.

Colchester, Marcus. 1994. *Salvaging Nature: Indigenous Peoples, Protected Areas and Biodiversity Conservation*. Geneva: UNRISD/World Rainforest Movement.

Collier, George. 1990. "Seeking Food and Seeking Money: Changing Production Relations in a Highland Mexican Community." *Occasional Papers Series*. Geneva: United Nations Research Institute for Development.

Collier, George, with Elizabeth Lowery Quaratiello. 1994. *Basta! Land and the Zapatista Rebellion in Chiapas*. Oakland, Calif.: The Institute for Food and Development Policy.

Collins, Jane L. 2003. *Threads: Gender, Labor, and Power in the Global Apparel Industry*. Chicago: University of Chicago Press.

Comaroff, Jean, and John L. Comaroff. 2001. *Millennial Capitalism: First Thoughts on a Second Coming*. Durham, N.C.: Duke University Press.

Comunicación Popular Alternativo Grupo de Trabajo. December 12, 1997. Cronología de Una Masacre Denunciada: Acteal, 22 de Diciembre de 1997. San Cristóbal de Las Casas.

Concha Malo, Miguel. 1994. "La Universidad y los Derechos de los Pueblos Indios." In *La Universidad y los Derechos Humanos en América Latina*. 154–60. Mexico, D.F.: Universidad Iberoamerica.

Davis, Shelton H. 1988. "Introduction: Sowing the Seeds of Violence." In *Harvest of Violence*. Edited by Robert M. Carmack. 3–36. Norman: University of Oklahoma Press.

DeGrasse, Robert M., Jr. 1984. *The Military is Shortchanging the Economy*. Washington D.C.: Council on Economic Priorities.

Doane, Molly. 2001. "A Distant Jaguar: The Civil Society Project in Chimalapas." *Critique of Anthropology* 21, no. 4: 361–82.

Doukas, Dimitra. 2003. *Worked Over: The Corporate Sabotage of an American Community*. Ithaca, N.Y., and London: Cornell University Press.

Dowd, Doug. 2002. "Depths Below Depths: The Intensification, Multiplication, and Spread of Capitalism's Destructive Force from Marx's Time to Ours." *Review of Radical Political Economy* 34: 247–66.

Durkheim, Emile. 1915. *Elementary Forms of the Religious Life*. Paris: Alcan.

Durrenberger, E. Paul. 2002. "Structure, Thought, and Nation. Stewards in Chicago Union Locals." *American Anthropologist* 104, no. 1: 93–104.

Earle, Duncan, and Jeanne Simonelli. 2005. *Uprising of Hope: Sharing the Zapatista Journey to Alternative Development*. Lanham, Md.: AltaMira.

Eber, Christine, and Christine Kovic, eds. 2003. *Women of Chiapas: Making History in Times of Struggle and Hope*. New York: Routledge.

Edelman, Marc. 2001. "Social Movements: Changing Paradigms and Forms of Politics." *Annual Review of Anthropology* 30: 285–331.

Edwards, David B. 2002. "Print Islam Media and Religious Revolution in Afghanistan." *Anthropological Quarterly* 68, no. 3: 171–84. Reprinted 2004 in *Social Movements: A Reader*. Edited by June Nash. 89–116. Malden, Mass.: Blackwell Publishers.

Ehrenreich, Barbara, and Arlie Russell Hochschild, eds. 2003. *Global Woman: Maids, Nannies, and Sex Workers in the Global Economy*. New York: Metropolitan.

Engels, Friedrich. 1959. "On the History of Early Christianity." In *Basic Writings on Politics and Philosophy*, ed. Marx and Engels, 168–94. Garden City, NY: Doubleday, Anchor Books.

Enloe, Cynthia H. 1980. *Ethnic Soldiers: State Security in Divided Societies*. Atlanta: University of Georgia.

———. 1983. *Does Khaki Become You? The Militarization of Women's Lives*. London and Boston: South End Press.

———. 1989. *Bananas, Beaches, and Bases: Making Feminist Sense of International Politics*. Berkeley: University of California Press.

Escobar, Arturo. 1995. *Encountering Development: The Making, Strategy, and Unmaking of the Third World*. Princeton: Princeton University Press.

Escobar, Arturo, and Sonia Alvarez. 1992. *Social Movements: Theory and Research*. Boulder, Colo.: Westview Press.

Etienne, Mona, and Eleanor Leacock, eds. 1980. *Women and Colonization*. Brooklyn, N.Y.: Bergin & Garvey.

Falla, Ricardo. 1978. *Quiché Rebelde*. Guatemala City: Editorial Universitaria de Guatemala.

———. 1994. *Massacre in the Jungle: Ixcán, Guatemala 1974–82*. Boulder, Colo.: Westview Press.

Fazio, Carlos. 2001. "Mantener el flujo de bienes para sostener a la industría estadounidence, el ojbectivo." In *Resumen y Gráficos: Declaración de Tapachula, Plan Puebla Panama*. 1–6. San Cristóbal de Las Casas, Chiapas: Presidencia de la República.

Fernández-Kelly, M. Patricia. 1983. *For We Are Sold, I and My People: Women and Industry in Mexico*. Albany: State University of New York Press.

Firth, Raymond. 1959. "Problem and Assumption in the Anthropological Study of Religion." *Journal of the Royal Anthropological Institute* 89: 129–48.

Fischer, Edward F., and R. McKenna Brown, eds. 1996. *Maya Cultural Activism in Guatemala*. Austin: University of Texas Press.

Foster, M. George. 1965. "Peasant Society and the Image of Limited Good." *American Anthropologist* 67, no. 2 (1): 293–315.

Garza Caligaris, Ana Maria, and Rosalva Aida Hernández Castillo. 1998. "Encuentros y enfrentamientos de los Tzotziles Pedranos con el estado mexicano: Una perspectiva histórica antropológica para entender la violación en Chenalhó." In *La otra palabra: Mujeres y violencia en Chiapas antes y después de Acteal*. Edited by Rosalva Aida Hernandez Castillo. San Cristóbal de Las Casas, Chiapas: CIESAS.

Geertz, Clifford. 1973a. "Deep Play: Notes on the Balinese Cockfight." In *The Interpretation of Cultures*. 412–53. New York: Basic Books.

———. 1973b. "Thick Description: Toward an Interpretive Theory of Culture." In *The Interpretation of Culture*. 3–32. New York: Basic Books.

Gelpi, Rosa Maria, and Francois Julien-Labruyere. 2000. *The History of Consumer Credit: Doctrines and Practices*. Hampshire and London: Macmillan Press.

General Electric Company. 1953–59. *Professional Management in General Electric*. Vol. 1: 43. New York: General Electric Co.

General Electric Pittsfield News. September 1979.

Gill, Lesley. n.d. "Creating Citizens, Making Men: The Militarization of Masculinity in Bolivia." *Cultural Anthropology* 12, no. 4: 1–27.

———. n.d. Personal communication.

Gluckman, Max. 1958. *Analysis of a Social Situation in Modern Zululand*. Manchester, UK: Manchester University Press.

———. 1964. *Closed Systems and Open Minds: The Limits of Naiveté in Social Anthropology*. Chicago: Aldine Press.

Goslin, Thomas. 1985. "Bolivia: A Nation in Crisis." *Christian Century* 102, no. 5: 117–18.

Gough, Katherine. 1969. "World revolution and the science of man." In *The Dissenting Academy*. Edited by T. Roszak. 135–58. New York: Pantheon Books.

Gow, David D., and Joanne Rappaport. 2002. "The Indigenous Public Voice: The Multiple Idioms of Modernity in Native Cauca." In *Indigenous Movements, Self-Representation, and the State in Latin America*. Edited by Kay B. Warren and Jean Jackson. 47–80. Austin: University of Texas Press.

Gray, Andrew. 1997. *Indigenous Rights and Development: Self-Determination in an Amazon Community*. Providence: Berghahn Books.

Green, Linda. 1999. *Fear as a Way of Life: Mayan Widows in Rural Guatemala*. New York: Columbia University Press.

Greenhouse, Carol. 2002. "Introduction: Altered States, Altered Lives: Ethnography in Unstable Places." In *Ethnography in Unstable Places*. Edited by C. Greenhouse, E. Mertz, and K. Warren. Durham, N.C.: Duke University Press.

Grimes, Kimberly M., and B. Lynn Milgram. 2000. *Artisans and Cooperatives: Development Alternatives: Trade for the Global Economy*. Tucson, Ariz.: University of Arizona Press.

Guha, Ramachandra. 1997. "The Environmentalism of the Poor." In *Between Resistance and Revolution: Cultural Politics and Social Protest*. Edited by R. G. Fox and O. Starn. 17–39. New Brunswick, N.J.: Rutgers University Press.

Gupta, Ahkil, and James Ferguson. 1997. "Beyond 'Culture,' Space, Identity, and the Politics of Difference." In *Culture, Power, Place: Ethnography at the End of an Era*. 6–23. Durham, N.C.: Duke University Press.

Habermas, Jürgen. 1984. *The Theory of Communicative Action*. Translated by Thomas McCarthey. Boston: Beacon.

Hale, Charles. 1994. *Resistance and Contradiction: Miskitu Indians and the Nicaraguan State*. Stanford, Calif.: Stanford University Press.

Hannerz, Ulf. 1991. "Scenarios for Peripheral Cultures." In *Culture, Globalization and the World System: Current Debates in Art History* 3. Edited by Arthur D. King. 107–128. Minneapolis: University of Minnesota Press.

———. 1996. *Transnational Connections: Culture, People, Place*. London: Routledge.

Hardt, Michael, and Antonio Negri. 2000. *Empire*. Cambridge and London: Harvard University Press.

Hartsock, Nancy. 1987. "Rethinking Modernism: Minority vs. Majority Theories." *Cultural Critique* 7.

Harvey, David. 1989. *The Condition of Postmodernity: An Enquiry into the Origins of Cultural Change*. Cambridge, Mass., and Oxford: Blackwell.

———. 2001. "Cosmopolitanism and the Banality of Geographical Evils." In *Millennial Capitalism and the Culture of Neoliberalism*. Edited by Jean Comaroff and John I. Comaroff. 271–301. Malden, Mass.: Blackwell Publishers.

———. 2003. *The New Imperialism*. Oxford, UK and New York: Oxford University Press.

Hedges, Chris. 2003. *What Every Person Should Know About War*. New York: Free Press.

Henderson, Kathryn. 2005. "Murder Linked to Marlin Mine Workers in Guatemala." www.Cultural.Survival.org. (accessed online March 25, 2005)

Hernandez Castillo, Rosalva Aida. 1995. "Reinventing Tradition: The Women's Law." *Cultural Survival Quarterly* 19, no. 1 (Spring): 24–25.

———. 1998. "Construyendo la Utopia: Esperanzas y desafios de las mujeres Chiapanecas de Frente el Siglo XXI." In *La Otra Palabra: Mujeres y Violencia en Chiapas, Antes y Después de Acteal*. R. A. Hernandez C., coordinadora. 125–42. San Cristóbal de Las Casas, Chiapas. CIESAS. Centro de Investigaciones y Estudios Superior en Antropología Social.

Hersh, Burton. 1992. *The Old Boys, the American Elite, and the Origins of the CIA*. New York: Charles Scribner's & Sons.

Herzfeld, Michael. 1997. *Cultural Intimacy: Social Poetics in the Nation and State*. New York and London: Routledge.

Htin Aung. 1955. "The Lord of the Great Mountain." *Journal of the Burma Research Society* 38: 75–82.

———. 1956. "The Thirty-Seven Lords." *Journal of the Burma Research Society* 39: 81–100.

Human Rights Watch World Report. 2005. New York: Human Rights Watch.

Hymes, Dell, ed. 1974. *Reinventing Anthropology*. New York: Pantheon Press.

IUCN (Intercommission Task Force on Indigenous People). 1997. *Indigenous Peoples and Sustainability: Cases and Action*. Utrecht: International Books.

IWGIA. 1998. *From Principles to Practice: Indigenous Peoples and Biodiversity Conservation in Latin America*. Copenhagen: IWGIA Document No. 87.

Jackson, Jean. 2002. "Contested Discourses of Authority in Colombian National Indigenous Politics." In *Indigenous Movements, Self-Representation and the State in Latin America*. Edited by Kay B. Warren and Jean E. Jackson. 81–122. Austin: University of Texas Press.

James, Harold. 2002. *The End of Globalization: Lessons from the Great Depression*. Cambridge, Mass.: Harvard University Press.

Jameson, Fredric. 1981. *The Political Unconscious: Narrative as Socially Symbolic Act*. Ithaca: Cornell University Press.

Johnson, Chalmers. 2003. "The War Business: Squeezing a profit from the wreckage in Iraq." *Harpers* 307, no. 1842: 538.

Jonas, Susanne. 1991. *The Battle for Guatemala: Rebels, Death Squads, and U.S. Power*. Boulder, Colo.: Westview Press.

———. 2000. "Democratization through Peace: The Difficult Case of Guatemala." *Journal of Interamerican Studies and World Affairs*, special issue. 42, no. 4.

———. 2004. *The Lessons from Guatemala*. Unpublished ms.

Jonas, Susanne, and David Tobis. 1974. *Guatemala*. New York: North American Congress on Latin America.

Kapferer, Bruce. 1997. "Max Gluckman and the Manchester School." First Gluckman Memorial Lecture May 7, 1997: www.comma2000:com/max-gluckman/annual/97.html. (accessed online May 7, 1997)

Kaplan, David, and Benson Saler. 1968. "Foster's 'Image of Limited Good': An Example of Anthropological Explanation." *American Anthropologist* 68, no. 2: 202–5.

Kasmir, Sharryn. 2004. "Activism and Class Identity: The Saturn Auto Factory Case." In *Social Movements: A Reader.* Edited by June Nash. 78–96. Malden, Mass.: Blackwell Publishers.

Kenyatta, Jomo. 1961. *Facing Mt. Kenya: The Tribal Life of the Gikuyu.* London: Mercury Books. First published by Martin Secker and Warburg Ltd., 1937.

Kim, Seung-Kyung. 1997. *Class Struggle or Family Struggle? The Lives of Women Factory Workers in South Korea.* Cambridge: Cambridge University Press.

Kirsch, Max. 2004. "The Politics of Place: Legislation, Civil Society, and the 'Restoration' of the Florida Everglades." In *Social Movements: A Reader.* Edited by June Nash. 203–15. Malden, Mass.: Blackwell Publishers.

Klare, Michael T. 2001. *Resource Wars: The New Landscape of Global Conflict.* New York: Harry Holt.

Kovic, Christine. 1997. "Walking with One Heart: Human Relations and the Catholic Church among the Maya of Highland Chiapas." Ph.D. diss., CUNY Graduate School, Department of Anthropology.

———. 2005. *Mayan Voices for Human Rights.* Austin: University of Texas Press.

Krugman, Paul. 1990. *The Age of Diminished Expectations: U.S. Economic Policy in the 1990s.* Cambridge, Mass.: MIT Press.

Lacan, Jacques. 1977. "The Mirror Stage as Formative of the I." In *Écrit, A Selection,* 1–7. New York: W. W. Norton.

Laclau, Ernesto, and Chantal Mouffe. 1985. *Hegemony and Socialist Strategy: Towards a Radical Democratic Politics.* Translated by Winston Moore and Paul Cammack. London: Verso.

Langham-Carter, R. R. 1933. "Lower Chindwin Nats: (1) Bodawgyi, (2) Amye Yeyin." *Journal of the Burma Research Society* 23.

Larson, Brooke. 1983. "Producción doméstica y trabajo feminine domestico en la formación mercantile colonial." *Historia Boliviana* 3, no. 1: 173–88.

Leach, E. R. 1954. *Political Systems of Highland Burma.* London: Butler & Tanner.

Leacock, Eleanor Burke, and June Nash. 1977. "The Ideology of Sex: Archetypes and Stereotypes." *Annals of the New York Academy of Science* no. 285: 618–45. Reprinted in L. Adler, ed. *Cross Cultural Research at Issue.* New York: Academic Press. 1982.

Lee, Anru. 2004. *In the Name of Harmony and Prosperity: Labor and Gender Politics in Taiwan's Economic Restructuring.* Albany: State University of New York Press.

Lee, Richard. 1979. *The !Kung San: Men, Women and Work in a Foraging Society.* Cambridge: Cambridge University Press

Lehman, F. K. 1972. "Doctrine, Practice and Belief in Therevada Buddhism." *Journal of Asian Buddhism* 32, no. 1: 373–80.

León, Rosario. 1986. *Mujer, campesina, ciudadana: Formas de participación de la mujer campesina.* La Paz: CERES.

Lévi-Strauss, Claude. 1969. *The Elementary Structures of Kinship.* Boston: Bacon Press.

———. 1970. *The Raw and the Cooked.* New York: Harper and Row.

Leyva Solano, Xochitl. 1996. *Lacandonia al Filo del Agua.* México, D.F.: Fondo de Cultura Economica.

Lim, Linda. 1983. "Capitalism, Imperialism, and Patriarchy: The Dilemma of Third-World Women Workers in Multinational Factories." In *Women and Men in the International Division of Labor*. Edited by June Nash and Patricia Fernandez-Kelly. 70–92. Albany: SUNY Press.

Lutz, Catherine. 2000. "Making War at Home in the U.S." *Public Affairs* 104, no. 3.

Lutz, Catherine, and Donald Nonini. 2003. "The Economies of Violence and the Violence of Economies." In *Anthropological Theory Today*. Edited by Henrietta L. Moore. Oxford and Malden Mass.: Blackwell.

Luxemburg, Rosa. 1950. *The Accumulation of Capital*. Translated by Agnes Schwarzschild, with an introduction by Joan Robinson. New York, London: Routledge and Keegan Paul and Monthly Review Press. First published in 1913. Also republished in 1971, Monthly Review Press with introduction by Tarbuck.

MacLeod, Murdo. 1983. "Ethnic Relations and Indian Society in the Province of Guatemala ca. 1620–ca. 1800." In *Ethnic Relations and Indian Society in the Province of Guatemala*. Edited by M. MacLeod. 189–214. Austin: University of Texas Press.

Manning, Robert D. 2000. *Credit Card Nation: The Consequences of America's Addiction to Credit*. New York: Basic Books.

Manz, Beatriz. 1988. "The Transformation of La Esperanza, an Ixcan Village." In *Harvest of Violence*. Edited by Robert M. Carmack. 70–89. Norman: University of Oklahoma Press.

———. 2004. *Paradise in Ashes: A Guatemalan Journey of Courage, Terror, and Hope*. Berkeley: University of California Press.

Marcos, Sylvia. 1994. "Genero y revindicaciones indigenas." *Doble Jornada* 95, no. 5.

Marcus, George E., and Michael M. J. Fischer. 1986. *Anthropology's Cultural Critique: An Experimental Moment in the Human Sciences*. Chicago: University Press.

Marx, Karl. 1973. *The Grunderisse*. New York: Monthly Review Press.

Melman, Seymore. 1983. "Inflation and the Pentagon's Budget." *America* 140 (June 30): 532–34.

Melucci, Alberto, John Keane, and Paul Mur. 1989. *Nomads of the Present: Social Movements and Individual Needs in Contemporary Society*. Philadelphia: Temple University.

Mill, John Stuart. 1848. "Principles of Political Economy." Reprinted and edited by J. M. Robson. In *Collected Works of John Stuart Mill*, vol. 2. Toronto: Toronto University Press, 1966.

Molinari, Diane. 1988. "Motherwork in Nicaragua." PhD diss., Department of Sociology, Lund University, Sweden.

Molyneux, Maxine. 1985. "Mobilization without Emancipation? Women's Interests, the State, and Revolution in Nicaragua." *Feminist Studies* 11, no. 2: 227–54.

Morton, James. 1994. *The Poverty of Nations: The Aid Dilemma at the Heart of Africa*. London: British Academic Press.

Mullings, Leith. 1997. *On Our Own Terms*. New York: Routledge.

Nagengast, Carole. 1994. "Violence, Terror, and the Crisis of the State." *Annual Reviews of Anthropology* 23: 109–36.

Nash, June. 1960. "Protestantism in an Indian Village in the Western Highlands of Guatemala." *Alpha Kappa Delta Quarterly*. Claremont College, California. 49–53.

———. 1966. "Living with Nats: An Analysis of Spirit Animism in Burman Village Social Relations." In *Cultural Report Series* No. 13, Southeast Asia Studies. Edited by Manning Nash et al. 117–136. Yale University.

———. 1970. *In the Eyes of the Ancestors: Belief and Behavior in a Mayan Community*. New Haven, Conn.: Yale University Press. Reprinted 1986, Waveland Press.

———. 1978. "The Aztecs and the Ideology of Male Dominance." *Signs: Journal of Women in Culture and Society* 4, no. 2: 349–62.

———. 1979. *We Eat the Mines and the Mines Eat Us. Exploitation and Dependency in Bolivian Tin Mines*. New York: Columbia University Press.

———. 1981. "Ethnographic Aspects of the World Capitalist System." *Annual Review of Anthropology* 10: 393–423.

———. 1985. "Deindustrialization and the Impact on Labor Control Systems in Competitive and Monopoly Capitalist Enterprises." *Urban Anthropology* 14, nos. 1–3 (Spring): 151–82. Special issue edited by Katherine Newman.

———. 1988. "The Discourse of Medical Science: Corporation and Community in the Construction of Consensus." *Medical Anthropology Quarterly* 2, no. 2: 158–71.

———. 1989. *From Tank Town to High Tech: The Clash of Community and Industrial Cycles*. Albany: SUNY Press.

———. 1990. "Latin American Women in the World Capitalist Crisis." *Gender and Society* 4, no. 3: 338–53.

———. 1992a. "Interpreting Social Movements: Bolivian Resistance to the Economic Conditions Imposed by the International Monetary Fund." *American Ethnologist* 19, no. 2.

———. 1992b. *I Spent My Life in the Mines*. New York: Columbia University Press.

———. 1993. *Crafts in the World Market: Middle American Artisans in Global Exchange*. Albany: State University of New York Press.

———. 1994. "Global Integration and Subsistence Insecurity." *American Anthropologist* 96, no. 2: 1–31.

———. 1997. "'Fiesta of the Word': Radical Democracy in Chiapas, Mexico." *American Anthropologist* 99, no. 2.

———. 1998. "Gender, Ethnicity, and Migration: Teaching Diversity." In *Cultural Diversity in the United States*. Edited by Ida Susser. London and New York: Blackwell Press.

———. 2001a. *Mayan Visions: The Quest for Autonomy in an Age of Globalization*. New York and London: Routledge.

———. 2001b. "Globalization and the Cultivation of Peripheral Vision: Mayas of Chiapas and Guatemala Seek Autonomy within National Boundaries." *Anthropology Today* 17, no. 4: 5–22.

———. 2003a. "Indigenous Development Alternatives." *Urban Anthropology* 32, no. 1: 57–98. Special Issue, edited by Max Kirsch.

———. 2003b. "The 'War of the Peace' in Chiapas: Indigenous Women's Struggle for Peace and Justice." In *What Justice? Whose Justice? Fighting for Justice in Latin America*. Edited by Susan Eva Eckstein and Timothy P. Wickham-Crowley. 285–312. Berkeley: University of California Press.

———. 2004. "Transnational Civil Society." In *A Companion to the Anthropology of Politics*. Edited by David Nugent and Joan Vincent. 437–48. London and Malden, Mass.: Blackwell Publishers.

———. 2006. "Towards Pluricultural States: Indigenous Movements Challenge Neoliberalism in the Third Millennium: A Review Essay of Four Anthologies." *Enlace* 1, no. 1.

Nash, June, ed. 1992. *I Spent My Life in the Mines: The Story of Juan Rojas, Bolivian Tin Miner*. New York: Columbia University Press.

———. 1997. "When Isms Became Wasms: Structural Functionalism, Marxism, Feminism, and Postmodernism." Critique of Anthropology 17: 11–32.

Nash, June, and M. Patricia Fernández-Kelly, eds. 1983. *Women, Men, and the International Division of Labor*. Albany: State University of New York Press.

Nash, June, and Max Kirsch. 1986. "Polychlorinated Biphenyls in the Electrical Machinery Industry: An Ethnological Study of Community Action and Corporate Responsibility." In *Toward a Critical Medical Anthropology. Social Science and Medicine: An International Journal* 23, no. 2: 111–138. Special issue edited by P. J. McEwan.

Nash, June, and Rosario León. 1986. *Testimony against the Myths of the March for Life*. Unpublished ms.

Nash, June, and Helen Safa, eds. 1976. *Sex and Class in Latin America*. New York: Praeger.

Nash, Manning. 1956. *Machine Age Maya*. Chicago: University of Chicago Press.

Newman, Katherine S. 1988. *Falling from Grace: The Meaning of Downward Mobility in American Culture*. New York: Free Press.

Nigh, Ronald, and Nemesio J. Rodriguez. 1995. *Territorios Violados: Indios, Medio Ambiente y Desarrollo en America Latina*. Mexico, D.F.: Dirección General de Publicaciones del Consejo Nacional para la Cultura y las Artes.

Nordstrom, Carolyn. 1995. "Introduction to Women and War." *Cultural Survival Quarterly* 95, no. 1 (Spring): 3.

———. 2004. *Shadows of War: Violence, Power, and International Profiteering in the Twenty-First Century*. Berkeley: University of California Press.

Olivera, Mercedes y Gabriela Vásquez. 2004. "Neoliberalismo, conflicto armado y mujeres en Chiapas." In *De sumisiones, cambios y rebeldías mujeres indigenas de Chiapas*, vol. 1. 92–169. Mercedes Olivera Bustamente coord. Tuxtla Gutiérrez: UNACH.

Olivera, Orlandina de. 1987. "Empleo femenino en México en tiempos de expansión y recesión económica: Tendencias recientes," versión para discussion.

Ortner, Sherry B. 1974. "Is Female to Male as Nature Is to Culture?" In *Woman, Culture, and Society*. Edited by Michelle Zimbalist Rosaldo and Louise Lamphere. 67–88. Stanford, Calif.: Stanford University Press.

Perkins, John. 2004. *Confessions of an Economic Hit Man*. San Francisco: Berrett-Koehler.

Polanyi, Karl. 1957. "The Economy as Instituted Process." In *Trade and Market in the Early Empires*. Edited by Karl Polanyi, Conrad Arensberg, and Harry Pierson. Chicago: Henry Regnery.

Pozas, Ricardo. 1947. "Juan Perez Jolote: Biografía de un Tzotzil, Mexico." *Acta Antropologica* 3, no. 3.

Przybylowicz, Donna, Nancy Hartsock, and Pamela McCallum. 1985. "Introduction: The Construction of Gender and Modes of Social Division." *Cultural Critique* 13 (Fall): 5–14.

Ramos, Alcida. 1998. *Indigenism: Ethnic Politics in Brazil.* Madison: University of Wisconsin Press.

Ramos Sanchez, Pablo. 1986. *Consecuéncias de la politica económica sobre el movimiento popular.* Ms. in files of author.

Reddy, Deepa. 2004. "At Home in the World: Women's Activism in Hyderabad, India." In *Social Movements: A Reader.* Edited by June Nash. 304–26. Malden, Mass.: Blackwell Publishers.

Redfield, Robert. 1941. *The Folk Culture of Yucatan.* Chicago: University of Chicago Press.

Redfield, Robert, and Alfonso Villa Rojas. 1962. *Chan Kom: A Village That Chose Progress.* Chicago: University of Chicago Press.

Roett, Riordan, ed. 1995. *The Mexican Peso Crisis: International Perspectives.* Boulder, Colo.: Westview Press.

Rojas, Juan, and June Nash. 1976. *He Agotado Mi Vida en la Mina.* Buenos Aires: Nueva Vision.

Rojas, Rosa. 1995. *Chiapas: Y las mujeres que? Colección del dicho al hecho.* Tomo II. Mexico, D.F.: Editorial La Correa Feminista; Centro de Investigación y Capacitación de la Mujer.

Rosaldo, Michelle Zimbalist. 1974. "Woman, Culture, and Society: A Theoretical Overview." In *Woman, Culture, and Society.* Edited by Michelle Zimbalist Rosaldo and Louise Lamphere. 17–42. Stanford, Calif.: Stanford University Press.

Roseberry, William. 1982. "Balinese Cockfights and the Seduction of Anthropology." *Social Research* 49, no. 4: 1013–28.

Rosh, Robert M. 1988. "Third World Militarization: Security Webs and the States They Ensnare." *Journal of Conflict Resolution* 32, no. 4: 671–98.

Rostow, Walter W. 1960. *Stages of Economic Growth. A Non-Communist Manifesto.* Cambridge: Cambridge University Press.

Ruiz Garcia, Mons. Samuel. 2000. *Mi Trabajo Pastoral en la Diocesis de San Cristóbal de las Casas: Global Exchange Report Principios Teológicos.* 2nd. Edicion. México, D.F.: Ediciones Paulinas SA de CV.

Rus, Jan. 1986. *Abtel ta Pinka.* INAREMAC. San Cristóbal, Chiapas.

Rus, Jan, Sharon Matiace, and Rosalva Aída Hernandez Castillo, eds. 2003. *El Movimiento Zapatista en Chiapas: La gente indígena y el estado.* Copenhagen and Mexico City: International Work Group on Indigenous Affairs and El Centro de Investigaiones Superiores en Antropología Social.

Safa, Helen. 1996. *The Myth of the Male Breadwinner: Women and Industrialization in the Caribbean.* Boulder, Colo.: Westview.

Said, Edward. 1983. *The World, the Text, and the Critic.* Cambridge, Mass.: Harvard University Press.

Sanford, Victoria. 2003. *Buried Secrets: Truth and Human Rights in Guatemala.* New York: Palgrave Macmillan.

Sangren, Steven. 1988. "Rhetoric and the Authority of Ethnography: 'Postmodernism' and the Social Reproduction of Texts." *Current Anthropology* 29, no. 3: 405–35.

Sanjek, Roger. 1990. "On Ethnographic Validity." In *Fieldnotes: The Makings of Anthropology*. Edited by R. Sanjek. 385–418. Ithaca, N.Y.: Cornell University Press.

Santana Echeagary, Maria Eugenia. 1997. "Mujeres indígenas: una experiencia en la selva de Chiapas." *Anuario del Instituto de Estudios Indígenas* no. 6, UNACH, San Cristóbal de Las Casas, Chis. 193–222.

Sassen, Saskia. 2003. "Global Cities and Survival Circuits." In *Global Women*. Edited by Barbara Ehrenreich and E. R. Hochschild. 254–74. New York: Metropolitan.

Schirmer, Jennifer. 1998. *The Guatemalan Military Project: A Violence Called Democracy*. Philadelphia: University of Pennsylvania Press.

Schremp, Gregory. 1989. "Aristotle's Other Self: On the Boundless Subject of Anthropological Discourse." In *Romantic Motives: Essays on Anthropological Sensibility*, ed. George W. Stocking, Jr. *History of Anthropology* 6: 10–43. Madison: University of Wisconsin.

Schultz, Theodore. 1964. *Transforming Traditional Agriculture*. Chicago: University of Chicago Press.

Scott, J. George. 1900. *Gazetteer of Upper Burma and the Shan States*, 1, part 1.

———. 1911. *Burma: A Handbook of Practical Information*. London: Alexander Moring.

———. 1927. *The Burman: His Life and Notions*. 2nd ed. London: Macmillan.

Scott, James. 1977. *The Moral Economy of a Backward Society*. New Haven, Conn.: Yale University Press.

Sen, Amartya. 1984. "Development: Which Way Now?" In *Resources, Values and Development*. Reprinted and edited by A. Sen. 485–508. Cambridge, Mass.: Harvard University Press, 1994.

Sheppard, Simon. 1998. "Foot Soldiers of the New World Order: The Rise of the Corporate Military." *New Left Review* 228: 128–41.

Silverblatt, Irene. 1987. *Moon, Sun, and Witches: Gender Ideologies and Class in Inca and Colonial Peru*. Princeton, N.J.: Princeton University Press.

Simmel, Georg. 1959. *Sociology of Religion*. New York: Philosophical Library.

Simonian, Ligia. 2004. "Political Organization among Indigenous Women of the Brazilian State of Roraima: Constraints and Prospects." In *Social Movements: A Reader*. Edited by June Nash. Malden, Mass.: Blackwell Publishers.

Sinclair, Minor. 1995. "Faith, Community and Resistance in the Guatemalan Highlands." In *The New Politics of Survival: Grassroots Movements in Central America*. Edited by M. Sinclair. 75–108. New York: Monthly Review Press.

Smith, Carol A. 1988. "Destruction of the Material Bases for Indian Culture: Economic Changes in Totonicapan." In *Harvest of Violence*. Edited by Robert M. Carmack. 206–34. Norman: University of Oklahoma Press.

———, ed. 1990a. *Guatemalan Indians and the State: 1540–1988*. Austin: University of Texas Press.

———. 1990b. "The Militarization of Civil Society in Guatemala: Economic Reorganization as a Continuation of War." *Latin American Perspectives* 17, no. 4: 8–41.

Smith, Dorothy. 1972. "A Peculiar Eclipsing: Women's Exclusion from Man's Culture." Reprinted in *The Everyday World as Problematic: A Feminist Sociology*. 2743. Boston: Northeastern University Press, 1987.

————. 1987. "The Everyday World as Problematic: A Feminist Methodology." In *The Everyday World as Problematic: A Feminist Sociology.* 105–45. Milton Keynes: Open University Press.

————. 1990. *The Conceptual Practices of Power: A Feminist Sociology of Knowledge.* Boston: Northeastern University Press.

Speed, Shannon. n.d. *Dangerous Discourses: Human Rights and Multiculturalism in Mexico.* Unpublished ms. prepared for the University of Washington conference, "Bottom Up: Human Relations from Below." April 2, 2004.

Spiro, Melford E. 1970. *Buddhism and Society: The Great Tradition and its Burmese Vicissitudes.* Berkeley: University of California Press.

Stephen, Lynn. 2004. Gender, Citizenship, and the Politics of Identity." In *Social Movements: A Reader.* Edited by June Nash. 66–77. Malden, Mass.: Blackwell Publishers.

Stern, Steve J. 1995. *The Secret History of Gender: Women, Men, and Power in Late Colonial Mexico.* Chapel Hill: University of North Carolina.

Stevenson, Linda S. 2003. *Confronting Gender Discrimination in the Mexican Workplace: A Social Movement Analysis of Women Taking Action in Transnational Policy Arenas.* Paper presented at the Gender and Globalization Conference, San José, Costa Rica, April 1.

Stiglitz, Joseph. 2000. *Global Economic Prospects and the Developing Countries.* Washington, D.C.: International Bank for Reconstruction and Development. The World Bank.

Strengers, Jeroën. 1985. *La pesada carga de la deuda.* La Paz: CEDOIN.

Susser, Ida. 2004. "From the Cosmopolitan to the Personal: Women's Mobilization to Combat HIV/AIDs." In *Social Movements: A Reader.* Edited by June Nash. 272–284. Malden, Mass.: Blackwell Publishers.

Susser, Ida, and Tom Patterson, eds. 2001. *Cultural Diversity in the United States: A Critical Reader.* Malden, Mass.: Blackwell.

Sylvain, Renée. 2004. "Land, Water, and Truth: San Identity and Global Indigenism." In *Social Movements: A Reader.* Edited by June Nash. 216–33. Malden, Mass.: Blackwell Publishers.

Tambiah, Stanley J. 1970. *Buddhism and the Spirit Cults in North East Thailand.* Cambridge, England: Cambridge University Press.

Tavanti, Marco. 2003. *Las Abejas: Pacifist Resistance and Syncretic Identities in a Globalizing Chiapas.* New York: Routledge.

Tax, Sol. 1937. "The Municipios of the Midwestern Highlands of Guatemala." *American Anthropologist* 39, no 2: 423–44.

————. 1950. *Penny Capitalism.* Washington, D.C.: Smithsonian Institute, Institute of Social Anthropology.

Tedlock, Dennis. 1984. *Popol Vuh: The Mayan Book of the Dawn of Life.* New York: Simon & Schuster.

————. 1993. *Breath on the Mirror: Mythic Voices and Visions of the Living Maya.* San Francisco: Harper.

Temple, R. C. 1906. *The Thirty-Seven Nats.* London: W. Griggs.

Thompson, Eric P. 1963. *The Making of the English Working Class.* New York: Vintage Books, Random House.

Thorne, Barrie. 1983. "Political Activist as Participant Observer: Conflicts of Commitment in a Study of the Draft Resistance Movement of the 1960s. In *Contemporary Field Research: A Collection of Readings*, ed. Robert M. Emerson, 216–34. Boston: Little Brown.

Torres Rivas, Edelberto. 1991. "Presentation by the Prosecutor." In *Guatemala: Tyranny on Trial: Testimony of the Permanent People's Tribunal*. Edited by Susanne Jonas, Ed McCaughan, and Elizabeth Sutherland Martínez. 7–23. San Francisco: Synthesis Publications.

Touraine, Alain. 1971. *The Post-Industrial Society: Tomorrow's Social History: Classes, Conflicts and Culture in the Programmed Society*. New York: Random House.

———. 1988. *Return of the Actor: Social Theory in Postindustrial Society*. Translated by Myrna Godzich. Minneapolis: University of Minnesota Press.

Trouillot, Michel-Rolph. 2001. "The Anthropology of the State in the Age of Globalization: Close Encounters of the Deceptive Kind." *Current Anthropology* 42, no. 1: 125–38.

Turner, Victor. 1974. "Pilgrimages as Social Processes." In *Dramas, Fields, and Metaphors: Symbolic Action in Human Society*. 166–230. Ithaca, N.Y.: Cornell University Press.

Urioste, Miguel. n.d. *Resistencia campesina. Efectos de la politica económica neoliberal del Decreto Supremo. 21060*. La Paz: Centro de Documentación Latina Americana.

Valle Esquivel, Julieta. 1994. "Los derechos de los pueblos indios: el caso del estado Puebla." In *Derechos Indígenas en la Actualidad*. Edited by J. Valle E. 49–72. Mexico, D.F.: UNAM.

Van Cott, Penny Lee. 2002. "Constitutional Reform in the Andes: Redefining Indigenous-State Relations." In *Multiculturalism in Latin America: Indigenous Rights, Diversity, and Democracy*. Edited by Rachel Sieder. 45–73. New York: Palgrave, Macmillan.

Vanderhoff, Nico and Francisco. 2002. *The Adventure of Just Commerce: An Alternative to Globalization*. The Hague, Holland.

Villafuerte Solis, Daniel. 2003. "Chiapas: Las Fronteras del Desarrollo," Liminar, Estudios Sociales y Humanisticos 1, no. 1 (June): 69–9. San Cristóbal de Las Casas: UNACH.

Vinding, Diana. 1998. "Tribal Women in Uttar Pradesh." In *Indigenous Women: The Right to a Vote*. Edited by D. Vinding. Copenhagen: IWGIA.

Vogt, E. Z. and W. Lessa. 1958. *Reader in Comparative Religion*. Evanston, Ill.: Row-Peterson.

Walsh, Susan. 2003. "Development Assistance among Jalq'a Paperos in Potosi, Bolivia: From Trojan Horse toward Strengthened Resilience." PhD diss., Department of Anthropology, University of Manitoba.

Warman, Arturo, Bonfil Batalla, and Nolasco Armas, coordinadores. 1970. *De eso lo que se llaman antropología mexicana*. México, D.F.: Editorial Nuestro Tiempo.

Warren, Kay B. 1985. "Creation Narratives and the Moral Order: Implications of Multiple Models in Highland Guatemala." In *Cosmogony and Ethical Order: New Studies in Comparative Ethics*. Edited by Robin W. Lovin and Frank E. Reynolds. Chicago: University of Chicago Press.

———. 1993a. "Interpreting *la violencia* in Guatemala: Shapes of Kaqchikel Resistence and Silence." In *The Violence Within: Cultural and Political Opposition in Divided Nations.* Edited by K. B. Warren. 25–26. Boulder, Colo.: Westview Press.

———. 1993b. "Death Squads and Wider Complicities: Dilemmas for the Anthropology of Violence." In *The Violence Within: Cultural and Political Opposition in Divided Nations.* Edited by Kay B. Warren. 226–47. Philadelphia: University of Pennsylvania Press.

———. 1998. *Indigenous Movements and Their Critics.* Princeton, N.J.: Princeton University Press.

———. 2002a. "Toward an Anthropology of Fragmented Instabilities and Incomplete Transitions." In *Ethnography in Unstable Places.* Edited by Carol Greenhouse, Elizabeth Mertz, and Kay B. Warren. Durham, N.C.: Duke University Press.

———. 2002b. "Voting against Indigenous Rights in Guatemala: Lessons from the 1999 Referendum." In *Indigenous Movements, Self-Representation, and the State in Latin America.* Edited by Kay B. Warren and Jean E. Jackson. 148–79. Austin: University of Texas Press.

Wasserstrom, Robert. 1983. "Spaniards and Indians in Colonial Chiapas, 1528–1790." In *Spaniards and Indians in Southeast Mesoamerica, Essays in the History of Ethnic Relations.* Edited by M. MacLeod. 92–126. Lincoln: University of Nebraska Press.

Weiner, Annette B. 1976. *Women of Value, Men of Renown.* Austin: University of Texas Press.

Wignaraja, Ponna, ed. 1993. *New Social Movements in the South: Empowering the People.* London: Zed.

Williams, Raymond B. 1986. "The Uses of Cultural Theory." *New Left Review* 158: 18–31.

Wilson, Thomas P. 1983. "Conceptions of Interaction and Forms of Sociological Explanation." *American Sociological Review* 35, no. 4: 697–710.

Wolf, Eric. 1986. "The Vicissitudes of the Closed Corporate Peasant Community." *American Ethnologist* 13, no. 2: 325–29.

Wright, Melissa W. 2001. "The Dialectics of Still Life: Murder, Women, and Maquiladoras." In *Millennial Capitalism and the Culture of Neoliberalism.* Edited by Jean Comaroff and John L. Comaroff. 125–47. Durham, N.C.: Duke University Press.

NEWSPAPERS AND PERIODICALS

Berkshire Eagle

November 3, 1984. A1.

June 8, 1985. Reprint of Thomas B. Edsall report in the *Washington Post.*

August 13, 2003. Paul Krugman column. A7.

October 30, 2003. Jim Krane, Associated Press. "In Iraq, and around the world, U.S. counts on private armies." A1, A4.

December 12, 2003. Elizabeth Bumiller. "Bush Defends Policy on Contract." A1, A4.

December 12, 2003. Matt Kelly, Associated Press. "Halliburton Tied to Overcharging." A3.

December 13, 2003. Elizabeth Bumiller. "Bush defends policy on contract." A1, A4. Reprinted from *New York Times* News Service.

December 13, 2003, editorial, p. 4.

December 15, 2003. Matt Kelley, Associated Press. "Iraq a proving ground as women fight, die." A1, A5.

December 1?, 2003. Martin Crutsinger. "U.S. economy shows burst of strength." A1, A2.

December 1?, 2003. Jonathan Weisman. "Poverty rate rises; household incomes decline." A1, A2.

May 9, 2004. "Privatization Follies." A8.

May 27, 2004. Barry Renfrew, Associated Press. "Al-Qaida growing, fed by Iraq war, think tank warns." A2.

June 3, 2004, A1.

June 13, 2004. John J. Lumpkin, Associated Press. "Troops bound for Iraq, Afghanistan get tours extended." A1, A5.

June 19, 2004. Maura Reynolds. "On eve of trip, Bush likens terror fight to World War II." A1, A4. Reprinted from *Los Angeles Times*.

July 25, 2004. Bill Carey. "Quietly growing: General Dynamics ramps up for New Contracts." D1, D8.

August 8, 2004. Gretchen Morgenson. "Fraud common at Halliburton, employees say." *New York Times* News Service.

December 31, 2004. Robert Barns, Associated Press. "Deadly year in Iraq has grown worse." A2.

January 1, 2005. David Streitfeld, Associated Press. "War and the economy: a double-edged sword." A1, A6.

Cuarto Poder. Tuxtla Gutierrez

February 10, 1995.

February 13, 1995. 27.

February 28, 1995. Carlos Fazio. "Contra Insurgencia en Chiapas." Sun News Agency.

April 20, 2004. "Reforma Agraria niega los desalojos 'quirúrgicos.'" B8, B9.

Daily Hampshire Gazette

October 18, 2004. "Going offshore to assess security threats." B6. Reprinted from the *Washington Post*.

El Financiero

February 21, 1994.

February 13, 1995. Gustavo Lomelin column. "Para su informe." 6.

February 26, 1995. 57.

February 26, 1995. Informe Especial. 26–27.

February 28, 1995. Informe Especial. 28.

March 13, 1995a. Rubin de Leon. "Tensión y zozobra en comunidades Lacandonas." 17.

March 13, 1995b. Lourdes Edith Rudino. "Perjudicará a los trabajadores del campola liberación de predios." 25.

March 13, 1995c. Carlos Figueros. "El ejército mexicano aterroriza y asesina civiles en Chiapas." 42.

March 14, 1995. Amalia Avendano V. and Miguel Badillo. "Solo 300 metros separan el ejercito mexicano y los rebeldes zapatistas." 38.

March 17, 1995. Miguel Badillo. "El ejército sale de las comunidades, pero cerca ejidos completos." 45.

March 18, 1995. Miguel Badillo. "Las post datos de Marcos." 18.

March 22, 1995. 41.

March 26, 1995. Miguel Badillo. "Aislados 600 militares en un rincón de la selva." 13.

May 29, 1995. Carlos Ramirez. "Indicador Politico." Informe Especial.

Expreso

February 23, 1995. Freddy M. Perez. 1, 10.

February 28, 1995. 1, 10.

General Electric Pittsfield News.

September 15, 1979.

Global Exchange

February 12, 1995. Press conference. San Cristóbal de Las Casas.

February 26, 1995. Emergency Response Human Rights Delegation to Chiapas. San Cristóbal de Las Casas: Press Release, quoted in *El Financiero*. 55.

Human Rights Watch

1995. *Human Rights Watch World Report 1995*. New York: Human Rights Watch.

La Jornada

February 12, 1995. 1.

February 13, 1995a. "Solo destrucción encontraron los retornades a La Soltana." 18.

February 13, 1995b. "Sometan militares a Santa Elena: Obligan a las indigenas a salir." 20.

February 28, 1995a. José Gil Olmos. "Documentan observadores nacionales y estranjeros torturas en Chiapas." 12.

February 28, 1995b. Oscar Camacho Guzman. "Vuelvan los primeros grupos de desplazados a las Margaritas."

March 8, 1995. Hermann Bellinghausen. "Despojados, humilados, los pobladores que escaparon de Guadalupe Tepeyac." 13.

March 13, 1995a. José Gil Olmos. "Solo destrucción encontraron los retornados a la Sultana." 8.

March 13, 1995b. José Gil Olmos. "Sometan militares a Santa Elena: obligan a las indígenas a servirlos."

March 13, 1995c. José Gil Olmos. "Tension y zozobra en comunidades Lacandonas." 17.

March 16, 1995. Marcos, cited in Rojas 1995 op. cit.

March 31, 1995. Hermann Bellinghausen. "Aguascalientos: un diálogo en dos a dos de la sociedad civil."

May 13, 1995. 12.

July 8, 1995. Cazes, Daniel, cited in Rojas 1995.

July 12, 1995. Hermann Bellinghausen, cited in Rojas 1995.

February 28, 1996. José Gil Olmos, "Documentan observadores nacionales y estranjeros torturas en Chiapas."

October 29, 1997. Angélica Inda y Andrés Aubry. "Paramilitares." 11–12.

January 1998. Jesus Ramirez Cuevas. "Militarización en Chiapas: Un Soldado por Familia." Masiosare: 25. http://serpiente.dgsca.980.25 /mas-familia.html.

April 3, 1998. Elio Henriquez. "Los puñales, nuevos paramilitares en la zona de Comitán, afirman indígenas."

June 14, 1998. Hermann Bellinghausen. "'Los ejecutaron,' clamor en Unión Progreso." 1–14.

June 17, 1998. "Presiona EU por una solución en Chiapas." 1–8.

March 4, 2003. Carolina Gomez Mena. "Queremos un corredor de empresas campesinas, no de maquiladoras, senala indígena a Lichtinger: Para representante maya el proyecto significa una segunda conquista a la que deben vencer." www.jornada.unam.mx/2003/mar03/030304/044n1soc.php?origenpsoc-jus .html. (accessed online May 8, 2005)

March 8, 2003. Jenaro Villamil. "ONG de Juárez: Más de 4 mil desaparecidas: Tres mujeres más, asesinadas en solo cinco días de febrero."

November 4, 2003. Kenneth Gailbraith. Report on the Iraq War. Reprinted from *U.S. Newsday.*

January 15, 2004. "La Sociedad Civil y el EZLN." 15.

January 19, 2004. "La muerte del sueño Americano." 18.

January 20, 2004. Luis Hernandez Navarro. "Estrechos lazos entre globalización, discriminación y nuevo imperialismo." 27.

March 20, 2004. Hermann Bellinghausen. "Analizan 156 ONG: opciones de resistencia y desarrollo." 10.

March 21, 2004. Hermann Bellinghausen. "Fomentan illicitos para desprestigiar al Zapatismo." 12.

February 6, 2005. AFP. "Anula corte proceso contra 16 militares que asesinaron en 1982 a unos 300 guatemaltecos." 28.

February 13, 2005. AFP. "Rechazan en Guatemala reglamento para pagar indemnizaciones por Guerra." 30.

March 8, 2005. Angelica Enciso L. "Abren a la inversion privada extranjera bosques de Chiapas." 13. "Continúa la salida de especialistas del la Semarnat por 'razones personales.'" 23.
March 20, 2004.

Mexican Notebook, Newsletter of the Consulate of Mexico in New York

February 1, 1995. 1–2.

Miami Herald International

January 25, 2004. Hannah Allam. "Ethnic tensions threaten postwar oil." 6A.
January 28, 2004. Daniel Sneider. "Iraq, Afghanistan stretching U.S. troops." 11A.
February 1, 2004. Tina Susman. "Red tape snares noncitizen soldiers deployed overseas." 5A.

The New York Times

December 25, 1997. Julia Preston. "Killers are believed linked to Ruling Party—Worst Strife in Chiapas in 4 Years." A1, A7.
December 27, 1997. Ian Fisher. "Indians in Mexico Go Home to Where Gunmen Killed." 45.
January 1, 1998. Ramirez. 2.
January 8, 1998. Julia Preston. "Mexican Governor Resigns in Aftermath of Indians' Massacre."
February 27, 1998. Julia Preston. "Mexico Expels French Priest in Latest Move Against Outsiders in Rebel Area."
March 6, 1998. Julia Preston. "Mexico's Overtures to the Zapatistas Bring Tensions in Chiapas to a New Boiling Point." A8.
October 2, 1998. David E. Saner. "As Economies Fail, the IMF Is Rife with Recrimination." A1, A10.
May 24, 1999.
July 13, 2003. 1A, 17A.
September 8, 2003. Section 4: 1, 3.
November 4, 2003. James Galbraith, reprinted from U.S. Newsday.
December 21, 2003. "The Tax-Cut Con." *New York Times Magazine.* 54–62.
January 10, 2004. Daphne Evitar. "Free-Market Iraq? Not so fast." B9: 1, 11.
May 16, 2004. Frank Rich. "Saving Private England: Sequel to a Hit. Arts and Leisure." 1, 8.
June 29, 2004. Leslie Wayne. "Pentagon Brass and Military Contractors' Gold." C1, C5.

Observer

March 9, 2003. Ed Vulliamy. "Murder in Mexico." 34–36.

Presencia

September 10, 1986.

Proceso

April 10, 1995. Julio Cesar Lopez, Pedro Matias, and Guillermo Correa. "Army digging in, violates international laws of war and national conventions of peace." 6.
June 7, 1998. Carlos Monsivais. "La teología solo puede ser de liberación, no de esclavitud ni de violencia, a menos de que sea paramilitar: Obispo Samuel Ruiz." 6–15.

U.S. Newsday

November 4, 2003.

Wall Street Journal

October 10, 2003. Susan Warren and Alexei Barrionuevo. "Despite Iraq, Halliburton Profit Falls Short."

NEWS DOCUMENTARY, TV

June 12, 2002. Romeo Dallaire. "Shake Hands with the Devil: How to master life's negotiations from hell." Interview with Ted Koppel, *Nightline*, ABC.

Index

About the Author

June C. Nash is Distinguished Professor Emerita, the City University of New York. She has carried out research on semisubsistence cultivators in Chiapas, with publication of *In the Eyes of the Ancestors: Belief and Behavior in a Mayan Community*; on Theravada Buddhism and spirit animism in Burma with publication of "Living with Nats"; on the impact of industrial extraction in Bolivia, with publication of *We Eat the Mines and the Mines Eat Us* and *I Spent My Life in the Mines*; and on community and the military-industrial complex in Pittsfield, Massachusetts, with the publication of *From Tank Town to High Tech: The Clash of Community and Industrial Cycles*. She returned to Chiapas in 1989 to see the social movement resulting in the Zapatista uprising, recorded in her recent publication of *Mayan Visions: The Quest for Autonomy in an Age of Globalization*. She has written essays on feminist movements in Latin America and globalization, publishing three anthologies, *Sex and Class in Latin America* and *Women and Change in Latin America*, coedited with Helen Safa, and *Women, Men and the International Division of Labor,* with M. Patricia Fernández-Kelly. She has also published on artisan cooperatives and the fair trade movement, with *Crafts in the World Market, Artisan Production in State Formation*, and *Popular Participation in Change*, with Jorgé Dandler and Nicholas Hopkins. She is currently researching and writing on human rights and militarization.

She has received awards for her book on Bolivian mining communities, the Latin American Studies Association's Kalman Silvert award, and the distinguished Service Award of the American Anthropological Association.